D0974458

NORTHERN GROUP
Visit the mysterious Northern Group, where travellers are few and far between

165°W

10°S

Rakahanga Atoll

Manihiki Atoll

Pukapuka Atoll

NORTHERN GROUP

Nassau

RAROTONGA
Follow jagged trails through taro plantations and tropical rainforest into the island's mountainous interior

Suwarrow Atoll

RAROTONGA
Watch the hips fly and enjoy traditional *umukai* cooking at a Cook Islands dance show

Nika'o   Avatiu
             AVARUA

'Arorangi

Rarotonga   Matavera

                    Te Manga
                    ▲ (653m)

         Te Ko'u   Ngatangi'ia
         ▲ (588m)

*SOUTH
PACIFIC
OCEAN*

15°S

Vaima'anga   Takitumu   Muri
                    Conservation   Beach
                    Area
                         Titikaveka

0   2km

Palmerston Atoll

RAROTONGA
Relax on white-sand beaches between snorkelling excursions in the warm lagoon

AITUTAKI
Cruise the giant lagoon on a traditional Polynesian canoe

Aitutaki
Atoll   Manuae Atoll

                              Mitiaro
Takutea

**SOUTHERN
GROUP**

'Atiu
                    Ma'uke

20°S

0   100   200km
0   60   120mi
(Islands not to Scale)

                    AVARUA
Rarotonga   ☆
                    See Enlargement

MANGAIA
Explore the forest roads by scooter or foot on this giant, deserted wonderland

Mangaia

Rarotonga & the Cook Islands
5th edition – June 2003
First published – December 1986

Published by
Lonely Planet Publications Pty Ltd ABN 36 005 607 983
90 Maribyrnong St, Footscray, Victoria 3011, Australia

Lonely Planet Offices
Australia Locked Bag 1, Footscray, Victoria 3011
USA 150 Linden St, Oakland, CA 94607
UK 72 – 82 Rosebery Ave, Clerkenwell, London EC1R 4RW
France 1 rue du Dahomey, 75011 Paris

Photographs
Many of the images in this guide are available for licensing from
Lonely Planet Images.
W www.lonelyplanetimages.com

Front cover photograph
A brilliant yellow sunset glows in the sky over Aitutaki Lagoon
(Peter Hendrie)

Photograph facing map
Islands of Aitutaki Lagoon (Peter Hendrie)

ISBN 1 74059 083 X

Printed by The Bookmaker International Ltd
Printed in China

**Although the authors
and Lonely Planet try
to make the informa-
tion as accurate as
possible, we accept
no responsibility for
any loss, injury or
inconvenience sus-
tained by anyone
using this book.**

Contents – Text

Contents – Maps

The Authors

Errol Hunt

After growing up in Whakatane, New Zealand (where the *Mataatua* canoe came after leaving Rarotonga), Errol moved to a wee town called Hamilton, where he bluffed his way through a physics degree. That led him across the Tasman, where he bluffed his way through five years as a research scientist at a mining company before joining Lonely Planet. There, he was coordinating author of Lonely Planet's first *South Pacific* and has written for various other Pacific/New Zealand titles, but spends most of his time commissioning other authors for Australia/New Zealand/Pacific guidebooks.

He is still bluffing.

Nancy Keller

Born and raised in northern California, Nancy worked in the alternative press for several years, doing every aspect of newspaper work from editorial and reporting to delivering the papers. She returned to university to earn a master's degree in journalism, finally graduating in 1986. She's been travelling and writing ever since. Nancy has been author or co-author of many other Lonely Planet books, including *Tonga, South Pacific, New Zealand, California & Nevada, Mexico* and *Central America*.

FROM ERROL

Meitaki ma'ata to all the people who helped me with this book. On Rarotonga: Trish Barton and Karla Eggelton (Tourist Authority on Raro), Elliot Smith (Raro), John Abrams (JWA), Gerald McCormack (the natural history king), Josh Mitchell (Ministry of Fisheries), Dianne George, Felicity Te-Akapitera Bollen (and thanks for the karaoke), Ake Lewis (bourbon and *rukau*) and Professor Ron Crocombe (for his *brutal* dissection of my historical text!). On the other islands, thanks to Rey Puapii (Aitutaki), Andrea Eimke ('Atiu), Tuporo Marsters Jr (Ma'uke), Ta (for introducing me to the *tumunu* tradition of Mitiaro) and Mataora Harry (Mangaia).

I couldn't have done it without Kim Shearman's support at home (not to mention assistance in sniffing out the best coffee on Rarotonga) or our daughter Maxine's meticulous taste-testing of Muri Beach sands.

Back at the Planet, thanks to Carolyn Boicos for ace editing, Chris Tsismetzis for making sense of my maps, and Susannah Farfor for her catch-up tour of the Cooks.

This Book

Tony Wheeler wrote the 1st edition of *Rarotonga & the Cook Islands* back in 1986; Nancy Keller updated the 2nd, 3rd and 4th editions. This 5th edition was wholly updated by Errol Hunt.

FROM THE PUBLISHER

This book was produced in Lonely Planet's Melbourne office. Carolyn Boicos coordinated the editing and was assisted by Alan Murphy and Nancy Ianni. Chris Tsismetzis, Leanne Peake and Corie Waddell took care of mapping. Vicki Beale produced the colour wraps and Katie Cason was the layout artist, with assistance from Vicki Beale, Jacqui Saunders and Sally Morgan. The cover was designed by Maria Vallianos, and James Hardy prepared the cover artwork. Quentin Frayne compiled the language chapter and Ilana Sharp reformatted the text. David Burnett ensured there were no technical hiccups and Leonie Mugavin was as helpful as ever in tracking down transport information. Eoin Dunlevy managed the project, with help early on from Ray Thomson. Mary Neighbour and Kim Hutchins commissioned the book, with assistance from Corie. Errol was commissioning editor during production, with assistance from Erin Corrigan.

THANKS
Many thanks to the travellers who used the last edition and wrote to us with helpful hints, advice and interesting anecdotes. Your names appear in the back of this book.

Foreword

ABOUT LONELY PLANET GUIDEBOOKS

The story begins with a classic travel adventure: Tony and Maureen Wheeler's 1972 journey across Europe and Asia to Australia. There was no useful information about the overland trail then, so Tony and Maureen published the first Lonely Planet guidebook to meet a growing need.

From a kitchen table, Lonely Planet has grown to become the largest independent travel publisher in the world, with offices in Melbourne (Australia), Oakland (USA), London (UK) and Paris (France).

Today Lonely Planet guidebooks cover the globe. There is an ever-growing list of books and information in a variety of media. Some things haven't changed. The main aim is still to make it possible for adventurous travellers to get out there – to explore and better understand the world.

At Lonely Planet we believe travellers can make a positive contribution to the countries they visit – if they respect their host communities and spend their money wisely. Since 1986 a percentage of the income from each book has been donated to aid projects and human rights campaigns, and, more recently, to wildlife conservation.

Although inclusion in a guidebook usually implies a recommendation we cannot list every good place. Exclusion does not necessarily imply criticism. In fact there are a number of reasons why we might exclude a place – sometimes it is simply inappropriate to encourage an influx of travellers.

UPDATES & READER FEEDBACK

Things change – prices go up, schedules change, good places go bad and bad places go bankrupt. Nothing stays the same. So, if you find things better or worse, recently opened or long-since closed, please tell us and help make the next edition even more accurate and useful.

Lonely Planet thoroughly updates each guidebook as often as possible – usually every two years, although for some destinations the gap can be longer. Between editions, up-to-date information is available in our free, monthly email bulletin *Comet* (**w** www.lonelyplanet.com/newsletters). You can also check out the *Thorn Tree* bulletin board and *Postcards* section of our website, which carry unverified, but fascinating, reports from travellers.

Tell us about it! We genuinely value your feedback. A well-travelled team at Lonely Planet reads and acknowledges every email and letter we receive and ensures that every morsel of information finds its way to the relevant authors, editors and cartographers.

Everyone who writes to us will find their name listed in the next edition of the appropriate guidebook. The very best contributions will be rewarded with a free guidebook.

We may edit, reproduce and incorporate your comments in Lonely Planet products such as guidebooks, websites and digital products, so let us know if you don't want your comments reproduced or your name acknowledged.

How to contact Lonely Planet:
Online: **e** talk2us@lonelyplanet.com.au, **w** www.lonelyplanet.com
Australia: Locked Bag 1, Footscray, Victoria 3011
UK: 72 – 82 Rosebery Ave, London EC1R 4RW
USA: 150 Linden St, Oakland, CA 94607

Introduction

Tiny and remote, the Cook Islands are a Polynesian paradise in a conveniently handy package. Their attraction is in their stunning beauty, geographical diversity and universal appeal – they offer something for almost everyone.

Rarotonga, the main island, is spectacularly beautiful – mountainous like Tahiti and cloaked in dense jungle. Surrounded by a protective coral reef, it has soft white-sand beaches begging to be lazed on and, to cap it off, they're fringed with rustling coconut palms and clear turquoise waters full of colourful tropical fish. If you can't relax here we'd suggest therapy.

Rarotonga has facilities for most budgets – everything from modern resorts to backpackers' hostels – and there are excellent restaurants and lively entertainment, all on an island with a circumference of only 32km.

But try to drag yourself away from Rarotonga; it should only be your starting point for exploring the Cook Islands. From here you can fly, or jump on a ship, to the other islands of the Southern Group. The first stop for most visitors is Aitutaki – a frequent nominee for any 'Most Beautiful Island in the Pacific' award. It's a combination of high island and atoll and has a huge turquoise lagoon surrounded by tiny, picture-perfect islets. If Rarotonga is the Tahiti of the Cooks, then Aitutaki is the Bora Bora.

Few visitors go further than these two principal islands; a great shame because some of the others are even more fascinating. 'Atiu, Mitiaro, Ma'uke and Mangaia receive few visitors, but each has its own history, culture and attractions, and there are plenty of facilities for visitors. Those who do visit are invariably delighted – as much by the refreshing lack of fellow travellers as by the islands themselves.

These islands are geological wonderlands, with fringing, raised-fossil reefs known as *makatea* – weird and beautiful areas of razor-sharp coral formations riddled with limestone caves. Stalactites and stalagmites may seem a strange thing to find on

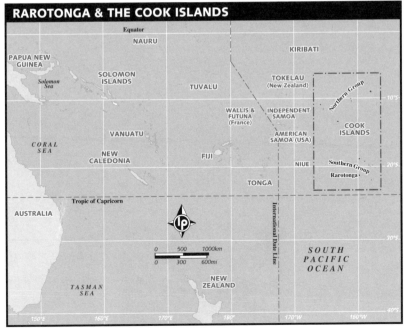

RAROTONGA & THE COOK ISLANDS

tropical islands, but these caves are full of them.

Then there are the remote atolls of the Northern Group, classic South Sea low-lying atolls that you'll need persistence to reach. Though airstrips were built on a few of them during WWII, they went without air connections for many decades due to their isolation, and it's only within the past decade that three of them – Manihiki, Penrhyn and Pukapuka – have been accessible by air.

There's more to the Cooks, though, than the islands themselves. The easy-going people are said to be the friendliest folk in the Pacific, and in a country with barely 14,000 people to its name, you'll soon feel a part of everyday life. Anyone who's spent more than a few weeks in the Cooks tends to find that they run into locals again and again – that guy leading the dance troupe might be the one who helped you push start your scooter the other day, or those kids waving at you from their car might be the ones who showed you how to split a coconut for a cold drink. Even half the politicians you read about in the local newspapers, or hear discussed over a *tumunu* (traditional bush-beer drinking session), are likely to have shared a drink with you at Trader Jack's bar in Avarua.

The other thing you'll notice about Cook Islanders is that they certainly can dance up a storm. They're some of the most spectacular and enthusiastic dancers in Polynesia, and an evening at an 'island night' – perhaps the one thing you really *must* do in the Cooks – is an experience you will long remember.

There are plenty of activities to keep you amused – swimming, snorkelling, diving, deep-sea fishing, canoeing, sailing, windsurfing, cycling, hiking and climbing are all possibilities in this varied island group.

Somehow though, time seems to go slower in the Cooks than in other places, and you may soon find that the most enjoyable thing is slowing down and relaxing into the peaceful way of life (leave the mobile phone at home). It's not long before the day's plan revolves around a bit of snorkelling and a spot of lunch. In between, grab a good book, pick a palm tree (look out for coconuts) and chill out.

Facts about the Cook Islands

HISTORY

Although the Cook Islands only have a written history from the time of European arrival, they have a rich oral history that has been passed on for many generations. Archaeologists have discovered many early marae (religious ceremonial grounds), and traces of settlements many centuries old on several of the islands.

Polynesian Settlement

Cook Islanders are Polynesians: people of the *poly* (many) islands of the eastern South Pacific. They are Maori people, closely related to the New Zealand (NZ) Maori and Tahitian Maohi. The Cook Islands Maori language is very similar to the languages spoken on these islands.

The Pacific was entirely uninhabited until around 40,000 years ago, when people started to move down from Southeast Asia to settle Australia and Melanesia, in the west Pacific. However, it was not until about 3500 years ago that a new people, now known as Lapita, also from Southeast Asia, arrived in Melanesia with the seafaring skills and technology to cross the longer distances to Fiji and the central Pacific. It was there, in Fiji, Samoa and Tonga, that Polynesian culture developed.

It was another 1500 or so years (between 200 BC and AD 200) before voyaging technology developed to the point that Polynesians were able to cross the 2000km to the Society and Marquesas Islands (in the territory now known as French Polynesia). From there, the spiritual heart of Polynesia, voyaging canoes travelled thousands of kilometres in all directions, reaching Rapa Nui (Easter Island), Hawaii, crossing to South America from where they brought back the kumara (sweet potato), and finally southwest to Rarotonga and the Cook Islands, and onwards to Aotearoa (NZ).

The scattering of Polynesians from the Society and Marquesas Islands was a slow process – it was not until about AD 500 that most of the Cook Islands were settled. However, to put this into perspective, the Polynesians at this time were centuries ahead of any other race on Earth – no-one else had sailed the open seas, out of sight of land; the sailing vessels of Europe were still hugging the coastline of the Mediterranean. It was several more centuries before any European culture (eg, the Vikings) was to even come close to the seafaring feats of Polynesia.

Oral history on Rarotonga traces ancestry back about 1400 years. The ancient road known as Ara Metua, still encircling most of Rarotonga, is about 1000 years old. In common with other Polynesian peoples, Cook Islanders' legends say that the ancestors of ancient times originated from the legendary homeland of 'Avaiki.

'Avaiki is as much a concept as a place. Its location is different for each Polynesian race (as is its pronunciation). The first island to bear the name was Savai'i, in Samoa. Polynesian settlers heading east from Samoa to the Society Islands, then on to Hawaii, the Cook Islands and NZ, named

The 'Great Migration'

One of Rarotonga's most notable historical events occurred in the 14th century, when Avana Harbour in Ngatangi'ia was the starting point for canoes heading to Aotearoa (The Land of the Long White Cloud, NZ). The canoes carried the settlers that became the ancestors of the present-day NZ Maori tribes.

You can go to Avana Harbour and see the spot where the canoes departed. Opposite the big white Cook Islands Christian Church (CICC) at Avana Harbour is a circle of seven stones, commemorating the seven most famous canoes that completed the voyage: *Takitumu, Tokomaru, Kurahaupo, Aotea, Tainui, Te Arawa* and *Mataatua*. Some of these canoes originated here on Rarotonga, some travelled first from other islands, but it is said that they all stopped here to receive a blessing before setting out for Aotearoa.

The so-called 'Great Migration' refers to a version of the story in which all the canoes travelled together, in AD 1350. It's a theory that gets little support from archaeological evidence or oral history but it's popular as a nice, tidy version of events. You'll see references to the Great Migration throughout the Cook Islands (and NZ).

successive islands after their homeland, and as dialects changed with the years the name variously became Havaiki, Havai'i, Hawai'i, 'Avaiki and Hawaiki. Strangely, in all Polynesian cultures, the same name refers to the afterworld. Premissionary Cook Islanders believed that when they died they went to 'Avaiki, a land that traditionally lay in the west, in the direction of the setting sun. (Now, of course, they go to heaven.)

Early Cook Islands Society

Rarotonga has always been the most important island of the Cooks, and it's thought that the culture of its early inhabitants was largely replicated on the other islands. Each island was ruled by *ariki* (high chiefs) – Rarotonga had five or six *ariki*, while most others had only three – who each ruled an *ivi* or *ngati* (tribe). Beneath each *ariki* in the social hierarchy were a number of *mataiapo* (chiefs), and below each of them were the *rangatira* (sub-chiefs).

Tribes had a number of marae. The *koutu* was a similar centre, used for secular meetings and political functions. Larger marae and *koutu* served entire districts – the most important of each marae and *koutu* belonged to the *ariki*.

Although in some respects this pattern of relationship was firmly entrenched, in other ways it was quite flexible. Hereditary titles could be created by an *ariki* as a reward for

his faithful supporters, and the line of chieftainship was not always from eldest son to eldest son. Although *ariki* are now often women, in ancient times only men held such titles.

A chief's control over his people was related to his mana (power). Mana came not only from birth but also from achievements and status. It could be gained as well as lost. An *ariki* who became unpopular might've suddenly found that his followers perceived a dramatic decline in his mana, which could have even led to his loss of control.

Control of *tapu* (holy or sacred matters) was a powerful weapon for an *ariki*. For supernatural reasons, certain activities were forbidden, and since a chief could often decide what was or was not forbidden, this gave him considerable power. It was the people's strong belief in an *ariki's* combination of inherent mana and control of *tapu* that made the *ariki* so powerful and allowed them to exert control over their people without necessarily having the physical means to enforce their will.

Another class of people with tremendous power were the *ta'unga*. *Ta'unga* were literally 'experts', and there were *ta'unga* in many fields, including woodcarving, agriculture and navigation. Most powerful of all, even more powerful than the *ariki* in certain ways, was the *ta'unga* in charge of spiritual matters. He was the principal connection between the people and the powerful spirits of gods and ancestors. Another very important *ta'unga* was the one charged with memorising tribal history and genealogy – he was known as the *tumu korero* (speaker). These *ta'unga* were like living libraries in a society where there was no written word.

The roles of *ariki*, *mataiapo*, *rangatira* and *tumu korero* survive to the present day and, as you'll read in the local newspapers, people argue as fervently now as they ever did about who should be holding each title.

European Explorers

A millennium and a half after the Cook Islands were settled, two Spanish explorers became the first Europeans to sight islands in the group: Pukapuka in the north was sighted by Alvaro de Mendaña in 1595. Then, in 1606, Pedro Fernández de Quirós stopped at Rakahanga (also in the Northern Group islands) to take on provisions.

Cannibalism

At one time Cook Islanders certainly practised cannibalism. Early islanders ate pig (on occasion) as well as fish (on all occasions) and cannibalism was not, as it has been in some areas of the world, a protein supplement. In the Cooks, cannibalism was an activity more closely associated with the supernatural acquisition of the mana (power) of one's adversaries. It was also a way of exacting revenge: to eat your defeated opponent was the most terrible indignity you could subject them to.

If you want to learn more about the practice of cannibalism in the Cooks, read *Cannibals & Converts* by Maretu (see Books in the Facts for the Visitor chapter), the only author who has written not only as a historian but also as a participant.

There is no record of further European contact until in 1773 (and again in 1777) the famous English explorer James Cook navigated and mapped much of the group. Surprisingly, Cook never sighted the largest island, Rarotonga, and the only island that he personally set foot on was tiny, uninhabited Palmerston Atoll.

Cook, following a fine English tradition of attaching dull, irrelevant names to wonderful places, dubbed the Southern Group islands the 'Hervey Islands' to honour a British Lord of the Admiralty. Half a century later a Russian cartographer (Admiral Johann von Krusenstern) published the *Atlas de l'Océan Pacifique*, in which he renamed the islands to honour Captain Cook.

The Northern Group islands were called various names by the Europeans, including the Penrhyn Islands and the Manihiki Islands. It was not until 1901, when the islands were annexed by NZ, that the Southern and Northern Groups became known by one name.

Missionaries

Missionaries followed the explorers. Reverend John Williams of the London Missionary Society (LMS) sailed from the Society Islands (modern-day French Polynesia) to Aitutaki in 1821. There he left two Polynesian preachers, and when he returned two years later he found they had made remarkable progress. Indeed, the Cook Islands were converted to Christianity far easier and faster than the Society Islands, from where these missionaries generally came.

Papeiha, a Society Islander, was the most successful of these original missionaries. He was moved to Rarotonga in 1823 and laboured there for the rest of his life. During that period the missionaries totally swept across the islands and established religious control that has held strong to this day. They completely wiped out the original island religion, establishing what was virtually a religious police state. The missionaries also worked hard at keeping other Europeans at arm's length.

The height of the missionaries' power was from 1835 to 1880, when their rigid and fiercely enforced laws were backed up by a system in which money from fines imposed on wrongdoers was split between the police and judges. Naturally this turned police work into an extremely lucrative profession, and in parts of Rarotonga one person in every six was in the police force, ready and willing to turn in their neighbours for a cut in the proceeds. The missionary 'Blue Laws' included strict limitations on what you could do and where you could go on a Sunday. There was even a law requiring any man who walked with an arm around a woman after dark to carry a light in his other hand!

Rarotonga, established as the Cook Islands' headquarters for the LMS, became an important administrative and religious centre for the islands, though the outer islands remained separate and independent political entities. Due to their relative isolation, small populations, lack of economic importance and generally poor harbour facilities, the islands were largely neglected and ignored by traders and whalers.

Disease, Population Decline & Slavers

The missionaries brought more than Christianity to the islands of Polynesia: they inadvertently also brought previously unknown diseases such as dysentery, which killed nearly 1000 people in 1830. The consequence was a drastic and long-lasting population decline on every island. Rarotonga's population, for example, fell to about a third within 30 years. Ironically, Cook Islanders took the onslaught of deadly new diseases as a message from above to abandon their old religion and fall in with the new.

Throughout the 19th century deaths exceeded births in the Cooks as in much of Polynesia. On Rarotonga the population was boosted by Maoris fleeing the outer islands, but the decline in the group's total population did not start to level out until the late 19th century. It was not until early in the 20th century that a real increase in population began.

The trend of migrating from the outer islands to Rarotonga, which commenced in the 19th century, continued. Many islanders left for work on other Pacific islands, particularly Tahiti. This migration has continued to the present day, as islanders move first to Rarotonga and then on to NZ or Australia.

Disease was not the only cause of the drop in population. Brutal Peruvian slave traders, known as blackbirders, took a terrible toll on the islands of the Northern

Group in 1862 and 1863. At first the traders may have genuinely operated as labour recruiters, but they quickly turned to subterfuge and outright kidnapping to round up their human cargo. The Cook Islands was not the only island group visited by the traders, but Penrhyn Atoll was their first port of call and it has been estimated that three-quarters of the population was taken. Rakahanga and Pukapuka also suffered tremendous losses.

Few of the 'recruits' (some did leave freely) ever returned to the islands. Over 90% died in transit to Peru, died in Peru, or died while being repatriated. At the time of repatriation efforts Peru was suffering from a terrible smallpox epidemic and many Polynesians died from this while travelling back or, worse, introduced the disease to their islands.

Protectorate & Annexation

Despite its influence through the missionaries, Britain did not formally take control of the Cook Islands until 1888. In that year the islands were declared a British protectorate. To some degree this extension of British control was due to fears that the French might extend their power from neighbouring Tahiti in the Society Islands.

It is indicative of the hasty manner in which the British finally took over the islands that they failed to make a firm decision on just which islands would be included in the protectorate. However, one by one the islands in the Southern and Northern Groups were brought under British control. The first British Resident (the representative of the British government in a British protectorate) arrived in 1891.

In the late 1890s the question of whether the islands should be associated with Britain or NZ was batted back and forth. Finally, between 1900 and 1901, the Cook Islands was annexed to NZ.

Independence

During WWII the USA built airstrips on Penrhyn and Aitutaki, but essentially the Cooks remained a quiet and forgotten NZ dependency. In the 1960s colonies were becoming increasingly unfashionable and NZ leaped at the chance to off-load its anachronistic, expensive dependency. The path to independence was plotted with considerable

haste, and in 1965 the Cook Islands became internally self-governing (although foreign policy and defence was left to NZ). The continuing problem of the population drain accelerated after independence.

The close links with NZ prevent the Cook Islands from taking a seat in the United Nations, although the islanders derive a number of benefits from the NZ relationship, including NZ citizenship and the right to come and go at will. NZ remains a very important source of income for the Cooks.

Post-Independence Politics

The first leader of independent Cook Islands was Albert Henry, leader of the Cook Islands Party (CIP) and regarded as a prime mover in the push for independence. Sir Albert (he was knighted in 1974) was an Aitutakian – it's said that the people of that island are such keen arguers and debaters that they'll get themselves into trouble simply for the joy of talking their way out of it, and in the 1978 elections Sir Albert got himself into deep, deep trouble.

The problem revolved around the great number of Cook Islanders living overseas, principally in NZ. Both the CIP and the opposition Democratic Party flew hundreds of supporters back to the Cook Islands to vote in the election. Sir Albert and the CIP, however, paid for the tickets out of funds from a NZ Government aid project. Sound slightly illegal? Well it was. The Cook Islands High Court disallowed the CIP's 'flying voters' and effectively handed power to the Democrats. Sir Albert was stripped of his knighthood and died soon after, in 1981. (You can see his slightly unusual grave in the Avarua CICC graveyard.)

The new prime minister was Dr Tom Davis, former chief medical officer to the Cook Islands, author (see Books in the Facts for the Visitor chapter), builder of traditional voyaging canoes, and zero-gravity medicine specialist with NASA. However, Sir Tom (he was knighted in 1980) wasn't prime minister for long, losing in 1983 to Geoffrey Henry, a cousin of Albert Henry. Geoffrey, university educated and another one of those argumentative Aitutakians, was only 43 when he became prime minister. He didn't last long (just a few months) in his first period as leader, but has proved over time to be a formidable politician.

Sir Geoffrey (he was knighted in 1992) spent 10 years as prime minister from 1989 to 1999. His CIP government was overwhelmingly popular during his long reign, although the massive government borrowing and 'jobs for the boys' that propped up that popularity were to prove problematic.

Financial Woes

The heavy spending of Sir Geoffrey's government required equally heavy finance and the government was forced to borrow and borrow…and borrow. Never more so than when it bankrolled a massive Sheraton resort on Rarotonga's south coast. The deal collapsed, leaving the government about NZ$100 million in debt and with an unfinished ghost-resort on the south coast.

The Sheraton was not the only economic problem facing the Cook Islands. In 1994 a controversy concerning the Cook Islands' offshore-banking industry (a tidy little profit earner for many a cash-strapped small Pacific nation) and alleged international tax evasion and money laundering ripened into an international scandal known as the 'winebox affair', with NZ the principal complainant. Although wrongdoing was never proven in court, it certainly made the Cook Islands look bad.

Ultimately, the borrowing and government jobs that had kept the CIP in power proved unsustainable and foreign debt spiralled out of control. With bankruptcy looming, the government was forced to make radical economic adjustments. The severe economic-stabilisation programme, initiated in 1996, eventually resulted in the sacking of about 2000 government employees – 50% of the public service – which in a country of around 20,000 inhabitants was a great proportion of the working population.

A 'transition' project was funded by the NZ government to assist the newly unemployed workers, but with nowhere near enough work available, masses of them left the country in search of jobs elsewhere. (Most went to NZ or Australia, where they had working rights.) Whether these people will ever return to live in their homeland still remains a huge concern for Cook Islanders.

Recent History

The lucrative offshore-banking industry got the Cook Islands into considerable trouble again in the late 1990s, with Organisation for Economic Cooperation and Development (OECD) bodies calling for much stricter controls on who was banking what (offshore-banking facilities are very useful for moving crooked money from A to B). Trade and aid sanctions have been threatened unless the Cooks comply – this issue continues to the present day.

After Sir Geoffrey lost control of the government in 1999, Dr Joe Williams (1999), Dr Terepai Maoate (1999–2002) and finally Dr Robert Woonton (2002–) have held the prime minister's position in rapid succession, at the helm of a number of different coalitions. All three recent prime ministers remain in the Cooks' parliament and in the daily news.

GEOGRAPHY

The Cook Islands has a total land area of just 241 sq km – that's about a quarter of the area of the Australian Capital Territory or of Rhode Island in the USA. However, this measly land mass is scattered over about two million sq km of sea – an area as large as Western Europe. The Cooks are all south of the equator, slightly east of the International Date Line, and sit about midway between American Samoa and Tahiti. Rarotonga is 1260km from Tahiti and 3447km from Auckland, NZ.

The 15 islands are conveniently divided into the Northern and Southern Groups, separated by as much as 1000km of empty sea. The unpopulated islands (Manuae, Takutea and Suwarrow) are not normally visited by anyone – locals or tourists – and the only way to access them is by private yacht.

There are some clear differences between the two groups, apart from their geographical separation. The Southern Group islands are younger, volcanic islands, while the Northern Group islands are older, coral atolls. The southern islands, constituting about 90% of the total land area of the Cook Islands, are generally larger, more heavily populated, economically better off and more closely connected with the outside world.

GEOLOGY

The Southern Group islands are a continuation of the Austral Islands in the south of French Polynesia, lying along the same northwest to southeast fracture in the Earth's crust. Only Rarotonga, the youngest island in the Cooks group, is a straightforward volcanic, mountainous island. Aitutaki has one small mountain (actually more of a large hill) and a surrounding atoll reef. Technically, Aitutaki is called an 'almost atoll'.

Four of the Southern Group islands – 'Atiu, Ma'uke, Mitiaro and Mangaia – are 'raised islands', and have a remarkable topography. They were formed as volcanic islands in the distant past and gradually became encircled by coral reefs. Over time the volcanic cones in their centres sank as the volcano cooled and the Pacific plate moved on. About two million years ago, during another period of volcanic activity, Rarotonga appeared. That same activity caused a buckling of the sea floor in the region nearby, causing the first four islands to be raised above sea level. This exposed their fringing coral reefs, which became jagged, rocky coastal areas known as *makatea*, surrounding the original volcanic island.

All the Northern Group islands are coral atolls – most have an outer reef encircling a lagoon and small islands dotting this reef. Atolls of this type were once volcanic islands with coral growing around the edge. Over time, the volcanic island sank below sea level, while the coral rim, marking the ancient coastline, grew to remain close to the sea's surface. All the Northern Group atolls are very low – waves can wash right over them in cyclones and you have to be very close to see them from a ship.

CLIMATE

The climate of the Cook Islands is very similar to that of Hawaii, although the seasons are reversed: January is the middle of summer, and August the middle of winter.

The Cook Islands has a pleasantly even climate year-round, with no excesses of temperature or humidity, although it can rain quite often. Rarotonga, with its high mountains, is very likely to be wet. Although you'd have to be unlucky to suffer one of the rare week-long rainy periods, be sure to bring rain gear with you at any time of the year. The wettest weather is from December to March, when around 25cm of rain can fall each month. This is also the hottest time of the year, although the seasonal variation is slight, ranging from high/low temperatures of 29/23°C in February to 25/18°C from

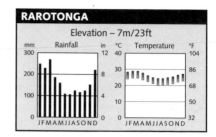

RAROTONGA

Elevation – 7m/23ft

June to September. The weather in the summer months can be quite warm and humid, and the winter nights can sometimes be quite cool, even chilly.

The cyclone season runs from November to March. On average, a mild cyclone will pass by two or three times a decade. Extremely severe cyclones affect the islands on average once every 20 years.

ECOLOGY & ENVIRONMENT

Waste management is a big issue in the Cook Islands. Limited land space doesn't allow the problem to be swept under the carpet (or into landfills, as we like to do in larger countries). Glass, plastic and aluminium are collected for recycling, but there's still a lot of other rubbish left over. Water supplies and management are another big concern, both for agriculture and domestic use. Fertilisers, soil and animal faeces are washed into streams, especially during high rainfall, causing algal blooms in the confined lagoons and contaminating town water supplies. Droughts occur periodically.

On Rarotonga and other islands, deforestation for agriculture has led to erosion and even more soil being washed into streams. Following devastating fires on Mangaia in the early 1990s, which left a large part of the island's hilly interior barren, much of the area was replanted with pine trees. No longer cared for by the forestry service (who mostly found themselves out of a job after the 1996 economic collapse), the trees have lost any financial value, but at least they have successfully prevented erosion.

Native flora and fauna are under siege on many fronts in the Cook Islands. Clearing of land for agriculture and building, use and overuse of chemicals (eg, herbicides, pesticides and fertilisers) and introduced species that harm or compete with native species (eg, mynah birds, cats and rats) are all factors that native species must contend with. Pacific fruit bats (flying foxes) on Rarotonga also have to contend with a few hunters willing to break the law for a tasty bat meal.

Organisations working on conservation in the Cook Islands include the following:

Cook Islands Environment Services (Tuanga Taporoporo; ☎ 21256, fax 22256, e resources@environment.org.ck) This is the arm of government that administers the Rarotonga Environment Act (1995), monitoring development and waste management, and conducting environmental impact assessments

Cook Islands Natural Heritage Project (☎ 20959, fax 24894, e gerald@nature.gov.ck) As well as producing pamphlets, booklets, posters and other informative materials, Natural Heritage undertakes research projects, and is compiling a complete database of Cook Islands fauna and flora

Ministry of Marine Resources (☎/fax 28721, w www.mmr.gov.ck) Near the traffic circle in Avarua, Rarotonga, this is the government ministry that handles marine resources and *ra'ui* (marine reserves)

Takitumu Conservation Area (TCA; ☎ 29906, fax 29906, e kakerori@tca.co.ck) On the Ara Tapu, Avarua, Rarotonga. The office that administers the 380-hectare Takitumu Conservation Area is involved in ecotourism (guided walks), awareness education, the *kakerori* recovery programme and the preservation of native species.

A couple of watchdog organisations keep an eye on the government's environmental performance. They are the **Taporoporoanga Ipukarea Society** *(fax 22189)* and a branch of the **Worldwide Fund for Nature** *(WWF; e mmatepi@wwfcooks.org.ck)*. Their most recent victory was stopping pearl farming in Suwarrow Lagoon. The **Rarotonga Environmental Awareness Program** *(REAP; fax 26759)* is a nongovernmental organisation specialising in waste disposal and recycling.

See Fauna, National Parks and the boxed text 'Traditional Conservation Methods' later in the chapter for some of the initiatives established to protect the Cook Islands' natural heritage.

Global Warming

The greatest environmental threat to the Cooks, eclipsing litter and water treatment, is one over which Cook Islanders have no control at all – global warming. Boosted by ever-increasing levels of carbon dioxide and other gases in the atmosphere, the 'greenhouse effect' is slowly but steadily warming the Pacific along with the rest of the planet. The most dire effects for the Cook Islands will be a die-off of coral, worsening storms and cyclones, and rising sea levels.

The Cooks' coral atolls rarely rise more than 5m (16ft) above sea level. Even conservative predictions state that such atolls, with cultures over a thousand years old, will become uninhabitable within the next hundred years. Large islands such as Rarotonga may not go under entirely, but once rising seas destroy the low-lying, fertile perimeter, fewer people will be able to live there.

FLORA

Although flora varies widely from island to island, the two most noticeable features are the ubiquitous coconut palm and the great variety of flowers.

Rarotonga has a wide range of vegetation in a number of distinct vegetation zones – from valley floors up to cloud-forest; the damp, mountainous, central part of the island is densely covered in a luxuriant jungle of ferns, creepers and towering trees. Look for the book *Rarotonga's Mountain Tracks and Plants* by Gerald McCormack & Judith Künzlé for more about Rarotonga's plant life.

The raised islands of the Southern Group, such as Mangaia and 'Atiu, are particularly interesting for the sharp dividing lines between the fertile central area with volcanic soil, the swampy transition zone between the fossil coral *makatea* and the central region, and the wild vegetation on the *makatea* itself. Although the *makatea* is rocky, it's covered with lush growth and a considerable variety of plants that are supported by pockets of rich soil. Pandanus trees, whose leaves are so important in traditional handicrafts of the islands, grow on the *makatea*. On the atolls of the Northern Group the soil is usually limited and infertile and there is little vegetation apart from coconut palms.

FAUNA

In common with most other eastern Pacific islands, the land fauna of the Cooks is limited.

Mammals

The only land mammals native to the Cook Islands are Pacific fruit bats (flying foxes), which are found only on Mangaia and Rarotonga. The bats were already present on Mangaia when Polynesians arrived, but were introduced from Mangaia to Rarotonga in the 1870s.

Rats and pigs were introduced to the islands by the first Polynesian settlers. Today there are many domestic pigs, which are usually kept by the simple method of tying one leg to a coconut tree. Rarotonga also has many dogs, some cats and goats, and a few horses and cattle. The islands of Aitutaki and Ma'uke have the distinction (you might say the 'privilege') of having no dogs at all.

Birds

The number of native land birds is limited, and on Rarotonga you have to get up into the hills to see them. They have been driven up there by a number of human-related factors, including changes in the natural vegetation, cats, guns and the ubiquitous mynah bird.

The Indian mynah was introduced in 1906 to control coconut stick insects, once a great destroyer of the coconut trees on the island. The birds have since proliferated and contributed to the lack of native birds in the lowlands. Today the mynah is found in great numbers on all the inhabited Southern Group islands except Mitiaro. (The coconut stick insect, on the other hand, is almost unknown. Nice.)

Despite the limited number of native birds, there are some of great interest to birdwatchers, including a surprising number of endemic birds (species found only in the one localised area). Of particular interest are the cave-dwelling *kopeka* ('Atiu swiftlet) on the island of 'Atiu, the *ngotare* (chattering kingfisher) of 'Atiu and Ma'uke and the *tanga'eo* (Mangaian kingfisher). Probably the most colourful endemic bird is the *kukupa* (Cook Islands fruit dove), found in the inland areas of Rarotonga and on 'Atiu.

The country's most spectacular ecological success story has been that of the *kakerori* (Rarotongan flycatcher). Until recently on the verge of extinction, the *kakerori* is now making a comeback due to the efforts of an intensive rat-elimination programme (rats were the bird's major threat). The *kakerori*

population has grown from a terrifyingly low 29 birds in 1989 to over 250 in 2002, and is still increasing. The latest initiative has been to transplant some of the birds to 'Atiu, which, as a rat-free island, offers an alternative home in case of cyclone or other disasters on Rarotonga. You can see the *kakerori* on guided walks within the Takitumu Conservation Area (see Around the Island in the Rarotonga chapter).

The *Guide to Cook Islands Birds* by DT Holyoak is an illustrated field guide. The Cook Islands Natural Heritage Project has published a photographic poster of all the significant birds of the Cook Islands.

Marine Dwellers

Snorkellers in the lagoons inside the reefs and divers outside the reefs will find plenty of colourful tropical fish to keep them enthralled. The coral structures support a variety of fish and other reef life. *Cook Islands Reef Life*, a colourful poster printed in 1992 by the Cook Islands Natural Heritage Project, is helpful for identifying species. Fortunately for swimmers, sharks are not a problem – the islands of the Southern Group generally have such shallow lagoons that sharks and other large fish cannot enter.

Around Rarotonga, on the sandy lagoon bottom of Aitutaki and on other islands, there are great numbers of sea cucumbers, also known as bêches-de-mer or, in Maori, as *rori*. Certain varieties of these strange slug-like creatures are a noted delicacy; see the boxed text 'Matu Rori' in the Rarotonga chapter. On land as well as in the water the Cooks have a great number of crabs – over 200 species at last count – ranging from tiny hermit crabs to large coconut crabs *(unga)*.

Humpback whales, which can reach up to 11m in length, visit Rarotonga and other Cook Islands every year in August and September. Only around 12 to 20 humpbacks come up from Antarctica each year to mate and calf. In season, whale-watching trips are available; see Whale-Watching in the Rarotonga chapter.

NATIONAL PARKS

The Cook Islands has just one national park, Suwarrow Atoll, established in 1978. Suwarrow's status was confirmed in 2001, after public protests forced the government

Traditional Conservation Methods

The Cook Islands had a system of conservation – the *ra'ui* – in place long before most of the rest of the world was familiar with the concept.

A *ra'ui* is called by the traditional leaders (the *ariki*, *mataiapo* and *rangatira*) for the purpose of conserving a particular area or resource. It is designated for a particular place, purpose and period of time.

During a period of *ra'ui*, nothing can be taken from the designated *ra'ui* area. It gives nature a chance to replenish itself without human interference, and it can apply to many situations. Examples might include establishing a time for ground to lie fallow, a *ra'ui* in the lagoon to allow fish and shell-fish to breed, or even on coconut trees, to allow more coconuts to grow.

On Rarotonga, a *ra'ui* for the lagoon at Tikioki (on the south coast) was called by Rarotonga's *ariki*, *mataiapo* and *rangatira* in 1997. Proving that modern *ra'ui* was as successful as ever, the scheme was expanded to six locations around Rarotonga and three around Aitutaki. Other islands also call *ra'ui* as circumstances demand. Contact the **Ministry of Marine Resources** (☎/fax 28721; W *www.mmr.gov.ck*) to find out where *ra'ui* are currently operating.

During *ra'ui*, the designated area of a lagoon is signposted on land and marked by buoys in the water. Swimming and snorkelling are allowed, but nothing can be taken – fishing and gathering of shellfish from the reef is prohibited.

to guarantee that it was 'permanently' safe from the spectre of commercial exploitation.

Apart from Suwarrow National Park, conservation in the Cook Islands has been largely under traditional law, which has been used to conserve resources for centuries. Unsurprisingly, traditional law still works. The traditional landowners of two islands have set up reserves: Manuae Atoll is a marine reserve owned by the people of Aitutaki, and Takutea is a seabird sanctuary owned by 'Atiu. There's also the Takitumu Conservation Area, home of the once-threatened *kakerori* (see the Rarotonga chapter, and Fauna, earlier) and run by the landowners. And then there are the *ra'ui*; see the boxed text on this page.

GOVERNMENT & POLITICS

The Cook Islands is, technically, a 'semi-independent nation, in free association with New Zealand'. It has its own government responsible for all internal affairs, while NZ has responsibilities for international relations (eg, the Cook Islands has no military of its own). When the country first became independent, NZ also had responsibility for relationships with foreign countries. Now, however, the Cook Islands handles foreign affairs itself.

Cook Islanders hold NZ passports, and the country is denied entry to the United Nations (UN) mostly on that basis. Full

independence is unlikely in the near future, as the majority of Cook Islanders value NZ passports more highly than an expensive seat in the UN.

The Cook Islands has a Westminster-derived parliamentary system similar to that of England, Australia and NZ. Like NZ, there's only one house – the House of Parliament – with 25 elected members. Electorates are chosen by geography as well as population, and so vary in size from almost 1000 people (in the larger Rarotongan electorates) to barely 100 on some of the outer islands. One MP represents the Overseas Constituency (the thousands of Cook Islanders who live overseas, primarily in NZ).

As well as an MP, each outer island has a resident-elected/appointed island council presided over by a mayor, and a government-appointed island secretary (who holds the purse strings). On Rarotonga, island councils are replaced by *vaka* (district) councils, one in each of the three traditional *vaka*.

The Koutunui, comprising traditional *mataiapo* (chiefs), and the House of Ariki, comprising *ariki* (high chiefs), are two semi-governmental bodies with advisory powers regarding all matters concerning land and tradition. The country's head of state, England's Queen Elizabeth II, is represented here by a queen's representative (QR) appointed by the government. The QR is largely a 'rubber-stamp' position, the equivalent of the governor general in other Commonwealth countries.

Political parties in the Cook Islands tend to be based more on personality than policy, so it's hopeless to try to explain what they 'stand for'. Politics moves fast in the Cooks (unlike everything else!) so it's hard to say who'll be prime minister when you read this. You're better off reading the papers and talking to the locals. Cook Islanders are naturally political people and *everyone* knows of at least a handful of coups and schemes bubbling away at any given time.

Coalition politics is a fact of life, with the Democratic Alliance Party (DAP) vying for power with the Cook Islands Party (CIP). The smaller New Alliance Party (NAP) and a few independents are often the deciding factors in these coalitions.

DAP is led, at present, by Dr Robert Woonton, who fairly recently toppled his mentor, Dr Terepai Maoate. CIP, which has held power for most of the 37 years since independence, is led by Sir Geoffrey Henry – a consummate politician. NAP is led by blustery ex-policeman Norman George.

ECONOMY

The Cook Islands' economy is far from balanced – exports (about NZ$20 million in 2000) are always far lower than imports (NZ$110 million). The biggest factor in making up the shortfall is foreign aid, particularly from 'big brother' NZ but also from Australia and other countries. Considerable amounts of money are also sent back by Cook Islanders living abroad – remember, there are many more Cook Islanders living in NZ than there are in the Cooks themselves.

Exports have long been almost totally dependent on NZ, both for market and transport; if the Kiwis sneeze, Cook Islanders catch a cold. Although NZ is still the Cooks' most important trading partner, as the pearl industry begins to dominate exports, Australia, Japan and the USA are becoming significant export markets.

Pearls account for 80% to 90% of the Cook Islands' exports. Pearl farming is a relatively new industry in the Cooks, appearing on the economic charts only since 1989, but the country's black pearls have become internationally famous. Pearls are cultivated in the lagoons of Manihiki and Penrhyn. The incredible earning potential of pearls has tempted the government to expand the industry to other atolls, but Cook Islanders, wonderfully political, stroppy buggers that they are, have restrained the government's avarice.

The most important money earner for the Cooks, however, is tourism. Tourism expanded rapidly over the 1990s, and exploded in 2000 and 2001 with a bit of help from the 2000 Fiji coup. The country gets over 70,000 visitors per year; a lot of tourists for a country with a population of only 14,000! With the increased numbers of tourists come jobs, too: from 2000 to 2001 the number of Cook Islanders employed in the tourism industry increased by almost a third.

Other interesting little money earners include offshore banking and the Cooks' status as a tax haven (an industry that gets the country into all sorts of trouble internationally), and the Cook Islands' beautiful and cleverly marketed postage stamps.

For the casual visitor it's hard to get any sort of handle on the economy of the Cooks: it's undeniable that the balance of trade is appalling, and the Cook Islanders live far beyond their means. But on the other hand, everybody is undeniably well fed. There's definitely a lot of food around, even a surplus, with exotic fruits growing in profusion all around the islands. Avocados, pawpaws and coconuts grow in such abundance that they're often used as pig food. The country's cash poor, but no-one's going to starve to death.

There are only three forms of social security in the Cook Islands: the old-age pension, a disability allowance and children's benefit. Unlike NZ, there is no unemployment allowance.

POPULATION & PEOPLE

The population of the Cook Islands is estimated at around 14,000 (having lost up to 3000 people to NZ in the last four years, mostly due to the poor economic situation). The story of the Cook Islands' population is one long tale of continuing movement: from the outer islands to Rarotonga and from there to NZ, and to a lesser extent Australia. (Over 50,000 Cook Islanders live in NZ!)

Over 90% of the Cook Islands' population lives on the Southern Group islands, with over 50% of the country's population on Rarotonga alone.

Strange Names

To most people's ears Cook Islanders have some pretty strange given (first) names. There's no differentiation between male or female names and they're often given to commemorate some event that happened around the time that the name's recipient was born. Big brother just left your island to go off to school on another island? Well, you might end up as 'Schooltrip'. The school was far away in Whangarei, New Zealand? You could be named 'Whangarei'. Big brother won a medal in the Commonwealth Games? You're 'Silver Medal'! But why would somebody be named 'Tipunu' (Teaspoon)? And why 'Sore Leg', or 'Bad Man'?

Over 90% of the population is Polynesian (Maori). There's also a small minority of people of European descent, principally New Zealanders, and some Fijian, Indian and Chinese families.

There are often subtle differences between the islands. The people of Pukapuka in the north, for example, are more closely related to the people of Samoa (a legacy of the settlement by Samoans some 1500 years ago) than to the people of the other islands of the Cooks group.

EDUCATION

The University of the South Pacific (USP), a regional organisation based in Suva, Fiji, has a small extension centre in Avarua. The National Culture Centre also runs many adult-education courses (see Avarua in the Rarotonga chapter). The Environment Service and Natural Heritage Project (see Ecology & Environment earlier) is charged with educating Cook Islanders on matters of environmental awareness.

ARTS
Dance

Dancing in the Cook Islands is colourful, spectacular and extremely popular – both for spectators and participants. Cook Islanders are reputed to be the best dancers in Polynesia (even better than the Tahitians, say the connoisseurs). You'll get plenty of opportunity to see dancing, as there are performances all the time, particularly at the ubiquitous 'island nights', which are usually a combination of meal and dance performance. If you arrive at an island night around 9pm, after the buffet, the entry charges to see the performances are usually only about NZ$5 or NZ$10.

Cook Islands dancing is often wonderfully suggestive and, not surprisingly, this upset the Victorian-era European visitors. You can imagine William Wyatt Gill, the observant early missionary, arching his eyebrows as he reported that:

Respecting the *morality* of their dances, the less said the better; but the 'upaupa' dance, introduced from Tahiti, is obscene indeed.

Things haven't changed much!

The sensual nature of Cook Islands dance is rooted in its history, when dances were performed in honour of Tangaroa, god of fertility and the sea. This also explains the similarity of the dances of the Cook Islanders, Tahitians and Hawaiians, all of whom worshipped Tangaroa.

If you go to the annual dance championships on Rarotonga, during Constitution celebrations in August, the things that judges watch for include the difficulty of the dance, the movements of the hands which must express the music, the facial expressions and the grace with which the dance is done.

Male dances tend to be aggressive and energetic (there's a lot of stomping and grinning going on); female dances are often all languid suggestiveness and gyrating hips.

Island-night performances are a lot of fun. Don't concentrate solely on the dancers – the musicians are wonderful to watch and the audience often gets involved in a big way. Some of the women are quite superb dancers and, despite their weight, can shake a hip as well as any young thing. Take note of how it's done though; a feature of almost every island night is dragging some unsuspecting *papa'a* (foreigners) up on stage to perform! See the boxed text 'Island Nights' under Entertainment in the Rarotonga chapter for a list of places that host island nights.

Another interesting aspect of Cook Islands dancing is the extent to which the traditional dance movements permeate even the modern Western-style dancing. Go to any nightclub and you'll see disco, pop, rock 'n' roll and sometimes even ballroom dancing spiced with hip-swaying, knee-knocking and other classic island movements. Don't be afraid to join in and try it yourself – the locals will love it and you'll have a great time, too!

Traditional Arts & Crafts

In the pre-European period the art of the small Northern Group atolls centred on practical objects – domestic equipment and tools, matting, and inlaid pearl shell on canoes and canoe paddles. In the south, however, a variety of crafts developed, with strong variations between the individual islands.

A number of fine books have been published about the arts and crafts of the Cook Islands; see the Books section in the Facts for the Visitor chapter.

Many arts and crafts are still practised on the islands today. See Shopping in the Facts for the Visitor chapter, and in each individual island chapter, for an idea of the types of arts and crafts that are found on the islands today.

Woodcarving Figures of gods carved from wood were among the most widespread art forms and were particularly common on Rarotonga. These squat figures, described as fisherman's gods or as images of specific gods (such as Tangaroa), were similar to the Tangaroa image which has become symbolic of the Cook Islands today. Staff gods (wooden staffs with repetitive figures carved down their lengths), war clubs and spears were other typical Rarotongan artefacts.

Ceremonial Adzes At first, the *toki* (ceremonial axes) of Mangaia probably had an everyday use, but over time they became purely ceremonial objects and more stylised in their design. In many cases *toki* came to represent a particular god (Tane was popular), just as Rarotonga's human statues represented Tangaroa. Each element of a *toki* was beautifully made – from the stone blade to the carefully carved wooden handle and the intricate sennit binding that lashed the blade to the handle. Some of the best examples of Mangaian *toki* are on exhibit in British museums. The art of making *toki* has not quite died out on Mangaia – there are woodcarvers who still make them in the traditional way.

Canoes *Vaka* (canoes) were carved with great seriousness and ceremony in pre-European times. Construction of voyaging or war canoes was the most ceremonial. Not only did the canoes have to be large and strong enough for long-distance ocean voyages, they had to be made in accordance with the strict rules of *tapu*. *Ta'unga vaka*, experts not only in canoes and woodcarving but also in spiritual matters, had to guide every step of the process. A suitable tree had to be found, chosen and cut, with proper supplication to the god of the forest. Once cut, the carving had to proceed in a certain manner, all the way to the launching of the canoe, which once again had to be done in accordance with all the proper spiritual and physical laws and requisites.

None of those pre-European canoes survive today, but you can often see modern reconstructions at Avana Harbour on Rarotonga. These modern *vaka*, sailing from island to island using traditional navigation methods, have done much to fine-tune ancient Polynesian settlement theories. On a smaller scale, Mitiaro's everyday fishing canoes are some of the most beautiful canoes made today.

Buildings Traditionally, houses and other buildings were made of natural materials that decayed rapidly, so no ancient buildings survive and very few buildings of traditional construction remain on any of the Southern Group islands. Woodcarving was only rarely used in houses, although some important buildings, including some of the first locally built mission churches, had carved and decorated wooden posts. Artistic

Island Houses

The houses you see around the islands today are almost all European style, with fibro walls and tin roofs. Very few of the old *kikau* houses with their pandanus-thatched roofs remain (you'll see more on Mitiaro than elsewhere). That may sound like a shame if you're looking for a nice photo, but Cook Islanders have decided over the years that the picturesque aspect of *kikau* houses pales in comparison to their inability to withstand a strong gale and the health hazards they pose.

sennit lashing was, however, found on many buildings: since nails were not available, the wooden framework of a building was tied together with carefully bound sennit rope.

Tivaevae Colourful and intricately sewn, these appliqué works are traditionally made as burial shrouds, but are also used as bedspreads, and smaller ones for cushion covers. You'll occasionally see them for sale (see Shopping in the Facts for the Visitor chapter), but like most Cooks Islands arts and crafts they're mostly made for personal use.

See the Atiu Fibre Arts Studio in the 'Atiu, Ma'uke & Mitiaro chapter for more information.

SOCIETY & CONDUCT
Traditional Culture
See Early Cook Islands Society under History, earlier in this chapter, for a quick introduction to Maori cultural hierarchies.

Visitors to the Cooks often get a superficial impression of the place and are disappointed, upon seeing close-cut lawns, Western-style clothing and modern houses, that there is so little sign of Polynesian culture. Yet right underneath this thin Western veneer, layer upon layer of the old Maori culture survives. It's in the land system – how it's inherited, how it's managed, how it's leased but never sold. It's in the way people transact business. It's in the concept of time. Tradition survives intact in hospitality, in dance, music and celebration, in the preparation of food, the wearing of flowers, the language, the overwhelming attention to 'politics' that pervades all aspects of Cook Islanders' lives, and in many other day-to-day ways of doing things.

Every Cook Island Maori is part of a family clan, and each family clan is connected in some distinct way to the ancient system of chiefs that has survived for centuries in an unbroken line. Rarotonga's six main tribes are still based on the original land divisions from when the Maori first arrived on the island many centuries ago.

Even today, when an *ariki* is installed, the ceremony takes place on an ancient family marae. The new *ariki* and all the attendants are dressed in the traditional ceremonial leaves, and the ancient symbols of office – a spear; woven shoes; a headdress made from feathers, shells and tapa; a woven fan;

Land Ownership

The Cook Islands' land-ownership policy has a great influence on the islands' economy and social patterns. A law prohibiting anybody from selling or buying land makes it impossible for outsiders to own land in the Cooks. Land ownership is purely hereditary and land can only be leased, not sold, to an outside party. The maximum term of a lease is 60 years.

Because land is passed from generation to generation, people start to acquire curiously divided chunks of property. A family can end up with a house by the coast, a citrus plantation somewhere else, a taro patch somewhere else again and the odd group of papaya trees dotted here and there. It can be a full-time job commuting from one farmlet to another. Thank goodness for motor scooters!

a huge mother-of-pearl shell necklace and other emblems – are presented. You'll see these things in museums, but for Cook Islanders they are not just museum pieces.

For a few pointers on how to interact with Cook Islands Maori culture, see the Social Graces section in the Facts for the Visitor chapter.

RELIGION
Only very few people today know much about the pre-European religion of the Cook Islands, with its sophisticated system of 12 heavens and 70-odd 'gods', each ruling a particular facet of reality. See the special section 'Cook Islands Myths & Legends' for a whirlwind tour of premissionary religion, or, better yet, share a cup of tea with a *tumu korero* (a tribe's 'speaker') and ask him about the old days.

Many early missionaries held pagan beliefs in such utter contempt that they made virtually no effort to study, record or understand the traditional religion. They did, however, make great efforts to wipe it out and destroy any heathen images they came across. Fortunately, some fine pieces of religious art were whisked away from the islands to European museums (unfortunately, most of them are still there while Cook Island museums have to make do with photos or reconstructions).

The Cook Islands today is overwhelmingly Christian – in fact, people from Christian cultures who haven't been to church for years (weddings and funerals aside) suddenly find themselves going back to church just for fun! The major local denomination is the Cook Islands Christian Church (CICC). Founded by the first LMS missionaries who came to the islands in the early 1820s, it's a blend of Church of England, Baptist, Methodist and whatever else was going on at the time – Roman Catholicism definitely excepted. Today the CICC attracts about 70% of the faithful. The remaining 30% is split between Roman Catholics, Seventh-Day Adventists, the Church of the Latter-day Saints (resplendent as ever in white shirts and ties) and Jehovah's Witnesses.

The CICC still has an overwhelming influence on local living habits and is an integral part of village life and local politics. Each family in a congregation contributes a monthly sum to the church fund, which goes towards church costs. The church minister is appointed for a five-year period, after which he moves to another church. He gets a small weekly stipend, supplemented by a weekly village collection.

Village responsibility for the CICC minister works both ways. The minister is responsible for far more than just his church: if the village teenagers are playing up or hanging around the local bars, the blame is likely to be laid at his door!

Visitors are more than welcome to attend a Sunday church service and it's a fantastic experience. The service is held mostly in Maori, although if there are any *papa'a* present there will be a token welcome in English and parts of the service may be translated into English as well. The islanders all dress in their Sunday best and the women all wear strikingly similar wide-brimmed hats. When you go, show respect by observing a few simple rules of dress: no shorts for men or women and no bare shoulders. CICC services throughout the islands are held at 10am on Sunday, with other services held on Sunday evening and early on several mornings throughout the week.

The missionaries won the war in the Cooks; traditional Polynesian religion is dead and buried, and poor old Tangaroa has been reduced to selling bottle openers and novelty fridge magnets (see Shopping in the Facts for the Visitor chapter).

Echoes of the ancient religion are evoked, however, in many traditional ceremonies. The investiture of a new *ariki*, who will almost invariably be a Christian, involves ancient chants to Tangaroa and other pagan deities. Similarly, you'll see many graves of the ancestors beside modern houses.

For many Cook Islanders, the spirits of the ancestors are an ever-present reality. The spirits are not feared as ghosts are in some other cultures. It is simply a fact of life that they live here along with everyone else. How these beliefs sit alongside Christianity is a wonder – Cook Islanders seem to be so confident in their Christianity that they are not threatened by the existence of so many ancient, 'pagan' traditions.

LANGUAGE

The language of the Cook Islands is Cook Islands Maori (also called 'Rarotongan'), but English is spoken as a second language by virtually everyone; you'll have no trouble at all getting by with English.

Among themselves, however, the people speak their own language. If you'd like to learn some yourself, pick up a copy of *Kai Korero: A Cook Islands Maori Language Coursebook*, which is available on Rarotonga with an accompanying audio tape. If you'll be here for some time and are serious about learning the language, the Cook Islands Library & Museum Society in Avarua has a number of books for learning the language, and the University of the South Pacific (USP) centre in Avarua offers classes.

Cook Islands Maori was traditionally a spoken language, not a written one. The language, in its Rarotongan form, was first written down by missionaries in the 1830s. Later they produced a Rarotongan version of the Bible, which is still used today.

Although each island has its own distinctive speech, people from all the Cook Islands can understand one another. Cook Islands Maori is also closely related to the Maori language of NZ and to other eastern Polynesian languages, including Hawaiian, Marquesan and Tahitian.

See the Language chapter for common Cook Islands Maori words and phrases, and a guide to pronunciation.

COOK ISLANDS MYTHS & LEGENDS

Getting It Right

There are always several different versions of any particular legend, and in some cases the differences can be quite important. Leaving out details when retelling a legend can get you in a lot of trouble, as can recounting the 'wrong' version. As far as the storyteller is concerned, legends that cast your own people in a bad light are best quickly forgotten!

There's a reason these stories are taken so seriously – some of the more recent legends, those that are about 'real' people rather than figures of legend, can establish which families, tribes or islands can claim ownership of particular land. Such legends, by being disrespectful to revered ancestors, can also insult whole families, tribes or islands.

On the island of Ma'uke, when updating this book, I had parked my scooter on the side of the road to check something in the previous Lonely Planet edition, when a man yelled at me from a nearby shop, 'That book is full of lies'. Careful inquiry found that LP had used an 'Atiuan version (as opposed to the Ma'ukean version) of a legend about an ancient battle between the two islands. My informant considered the error a personal affront and became more worked up as we spoke. It was several days before I owned up to working for the company.

Errol Hunt

Pre-Christian religion was remarkably consistent between islands scattered over the entire, vast Polynesian area. Gods such as Vatea, Tangaroa, Rongomatane and Tane, and demigods such as Maui and Rata, were known to Polynesians everywhere from Hawaii to Easter Island to Aotearoa (New Zealand).

It was the prodigious navigation and voyaging feats of the Polynesians in their long *vaka* (outrigger canoes) that made such homogeneity of religion possible, although in many cases the driving force behind *vaka* sailing off to settle new lands was religious dissent.

Gods

Tangaroa was known as the 'creator' deity across much of the Pacific. Known variously as Ta'aroa, Tangaloa and Kanaloa, he was worshipped as the father of the gods. Tangaroa's children were so-called 'departmental' gods, responsible for fields such as the forests (Tane) and agriculture (Rongo).

In the Cook Islands (and Aotearoa), however, Tangaroa was not the father of the gods, but one of the kids. He was, though, the most important of the departmental gods, even more important than his father, Vatea (also known as Te Tumu) and mother, Papa (The Earth). Tangaroa was the god of the seas (no lightweight job in a culture where the sea was so important) and fertility.

Only on Mangaia, southeast of Rarotonga, did Tangaroa lose his position as pre-eminent god. On Mangaia, they say, when Tangaroa's parents discussed their children's inheritance, Vatea wanted to give all the food to his first-born, Tangaroa, but his wife Papa suggested giving Tangaroa only the 'chiefly' food, meaning only the food that was red.

GRANT DIXON

Vatea agreed that this was a fine salute to his favoured son, but the red food turned out to form only a very small heap; Rongo's share, on the other hand, was so plentiful that his huge pile of food kept falling over! Papa was happy, because although she was forbidden to eat with her first-born by the complex rules of *tapu* (the laws that define what is sacred and what is not), she *was* permitted to share Rongo's huge stash. Tangaroa, unsurprisingly, was not happy – storming off to sea, he left Rongo to rule Mangaia. Ever after, when human sacrifices were made to appease Rongo, a piece was always thrown aside for the hungry Papa.

Carvings of Tangaroa were very popular in the Cook Islands in pre-Christian times and are the most common carving you'll see on the islands today. There's no doubting, when you see the carvings, that Tangaroa was the god of fertility.

Demigods & Heroes

Myths and legends can serve many purposes, such as preserving historical facts, explaining natural phenomena or just entertaining the troops. The oldest legends are the most widespread, such as that of the god Tangaroa. If Tangaroa ever existed, he must have lived millennia ago, before Pacific islanders became so scattered. In comparison, the most recent, 'local' stories are those about heroes such as Tangi'ia (see later), who almost certainly existed (since many people on Rarotonga can trace ancestry back to him and his fellow travellers). Between gods such as Tangaroa and heroes such as Tangi'ia, there is a continuum of 'demigods'. Of these, Maui Potiki is the most famous.

Maui Potiki The only legendary Polynesian figure who rivals Tangaroa for his widespread fame is the trickster Maui. A cross between Prometheus and Brer Rabbit, Maui achieved his great feats (such as slowing the sun, bringing fire to people, and creating the first coconut) in a very Polynesian way – not through the use of force, but by cleverness and trickery.

Maui's most famous achievement, remembered in legends all over the Pacific, was to fish an entire island out of the sea. The Tongans say the island was Tongatapu, the New Zealand Maoris say it was the North Island of their country, but in the Cook Islands they say it was the twin islands of Manihiki and Rakahanga.

Long ago, three brothers, all named Maui, held a fishing competition near an underwater coral outcrop. The first two caught only everyday fish, but Maui Potiki (Maui the Last Born) had arranged things beforehand with a woman, Hine i te Papa, who dwelt on the sea bed. She hooked Maui Potiki's fish-hook into the coral outcrop and Maui was able to pull it up above the surface to form a large island.

Top: Statue of Tangaroa, near Aitutaki Lagoon

Maui Potiki, ecstatic, jumped onto his catch and taunted his brothers about his fishing prowess.

Now if you know anything about Polynesian legends, you'll know that something *always* goes wrong…

A Rarotongan named Huku had already discovered the underwater coral outcrop, and returned at once to demand 'his' island. Maui was a trickster, not a fighter; he sprang into the air to escape, unfortunately breaking the island into two pieces as he leaped. Huku was left in possession of the two islands, which he named Rakahanga and Manihiki.

Maui is the archetypal Polynesian hero. Besting one's enemies (or brothers) through the use of cunning and – let's face it – downright *cheating*, seems to appeal to something in the Polynesian storyteller. Maui was a clown as well as a hero – a prankster so irritating that his brothers forbade him to go fishing with them, so that he had to disguise himself as an insect to sneak aboard their boat. No Hollywood-style hero, Maui is fondly remembered as being particularly ugly.

'Ina & the Shark On one side of the Cook Islands three-dollar note is an illustration of a beautiful woman riding a shark, and holding a coconut up in the air. The woman is 'Ina, who lived on Rarotonga and loved a man from Mangaia, and *that* coconut got her into a lot of trouble.

Desiring to visit her lover but with no canoe to get her there, 'Ina asked Mango, the shark, to take her to Mangaia. Mango agreed and the two set off, with 'Ina clutching a stash of coconuts for sustenance on the long journey. After a while she became hungry and, lacking a stick to open one of the coconuts, smashed it, instead, on the head of the shark. Mango was *not* impressed; he flipped 'Ina into the sea and promptly ate her. According to the legend, that's why all sharks today carry that large dent in their foreheads.

Mangaians, adding the rustic 'sting' that the Maori so love in their stories, say that the shark had further reason for making a meal of its ungrateful hitchhiker: before the incident with the coconut, 'Ina had relieved herself while sitting on the shark's back (which is why, they explain, shark flesh sometimes tastes of piss).

Tangi'ia & Karika The story of Tangi'ia and Karika is Rarotonga's most famous legend. Tangi'ia was a Tahitian who quarrelled with his brother, Tutapu, an *ariki* (chief) of Tahiti. Tangi'ia took his people and fled in a large voyaging canoe across the ocean, visiting many nearby eastern Polynesian islands. At sea, Tangi'ia met another voyaging canoe, this one under the command of Karika, a Samoan. The two crews fought at first, but when a man was killed they were shocked, stopping the fight at once and declaring peace.

Still at sea, Tangi'ia asked Karika for directions to the renowned island of Tumu Te Varovaro (the ancient name for Rarotonga). However, Karika had plans for that island himself, so gave Tangi'ia inaccurate instructions, sending him deep into the south. When Tangi'ia found cold seas and no land, he realised he had been cheated and turned back, finding Karika already settled on the island that Tangi'ia (according to this particular legend) named to commemorate having erroneously sailed so far down *(raro)* to the south *(tonga)*.

Putting their differences behind them, the two chiefs joined forces to defeat the incumbent population of Rarotonga, and then allied again to fight Tutapu, who had pursued his brother at the head of a Tahitian war fleet. After defeating Tutapu, the two chiefs divided Rarotonga between them, sailing off in opposite directions around the island, and meeting again on the other side to establish their two tribes' boundaries. Today, Rarotonga's Pa and Tinomana *ariki* titles descend from Tangi'ia's people, while the Makea *ariki* descend from Karika.

Facts for the Visitor

HIGHLIGHTS
Some of your most enjoyable times will probably be just relaxing and enjoying the simple pleasures of life; like watching the sunset, lazing on the beach, lolling in a lagoon, bicycling along the back roads or talking with someone you've just met. For some reason it seems easier to relax in the Cooks than in many other places.

Many of the highlights of the Cook Islands are listed in the Activities section. Everything mentioned here is covered in more detail in the individual island chapters.

Physical Beauty
The top highlight of the Cook Islands would have to be the physical beauty of the islands. Soft white-sand beaches, swaying coconut palms, turquoise lagoons replete with colourful tropical fish, their lush vegetation and flowers, and the velvety-warm air – what more could anyone ask for?

The lush, craggy mountains of Rarotonga and the large turquoise lagoon of Aitutaki are unforgettable beauties and definite highlights of the Cooks. But every other island also has its own characteristics and beauty: the weird, jagged *makatea* (raised, fossilised coral reefs) and caves of several Southern Group islands; the red earth and grey cliffs of Mangaia; the rich agriculture practised on all the islands; and the coral reefs.

Music & Dance
The Cook Islands is famous for its dancing. Be sure to attend at least one dance performance; they're held several nights a week at 'island nights' on Rarotonga and Aitutaki, accompanied by lavish buffets of traditional Cook Islands food.

Cook Islands music is magnificent, too, with a variety of styles, including string-band music, drumming on wooden slit drums, rousing church singing and action songs.

Cultural Events
Many types of cultural events are held on the islands. There are public events, such as Gospel Day, the 10-day Constitution Day celebrations, the Island Dance Festival week, Tiare Festival week and many sporting competitions, which everyone is welcome to attend – don't miss them if they happen while you're here. There are also a number of more family-based traditions, like hair-cutting ceremonies, investiture ceremonies, weddings and funerals and so on. It's a rare privilege to be invited to these kinds of events.

Food
Be sure to try some traditional Cook Islands food while you're here – preferably prepared in an *umu* (traditional Maori underground oven). Sample some fresh tropical fruits and tasty seafood, try *ika mata* (raw fish in coconut sauce), taro, *rukau* (taro leaves) and *kuru* (breadfruit), drink coconut water fresh from the coconut, or a tropical fruit juice like passionfruit or mango.

Island nights on Rarotonga and Aitutaki usually feature lavish buffets of traditional island foods. Or you can participate in an *umukai* (a traditional Cook Islands Maori underground oven feast), assisting in the preparation and learning how it's done. It's a memorable experience.

SUGGESTED ITINERARIES
If you only have a week to spend in the Cooks, you'll probably get no further than the two principal islands: Rarotonga and Aitutaki. It's worth visiting both, as they are both wonderful islands and quite different from one another.

You can easily visit both Rarotonga and Aitutaki in a one- or two-week holiday. From Rarotonga there are several flights (and day tours) to Aitutaki every day except Sunday.

If you have a little more time it's worth visiting other islands of the Southern Group – 'Atiu, Ma'uke, Mitiaro and/or Mangaia. These islands are completely different from Rarotonga or Aitutaki, and all have plenty of interesting features and activities.

Visiting the Northern Group islands requires more time. They're right off the beaten track, and while few visitors ever go there, those that do come back enchanted.

PLANNING
When to Go
Anytime is a good time to visit the Cook Islands. Seasonal variations are slight (see

the Climate section in the Facts about the Cook Islands chapter).

What Kind of Trip

The Cook Islands can be visited as a destination on its own, as a stopover when crossing the Pacific, or as part of a Circle Pacific or round-the-world trip (see the Getting There & Away chapter). From some places, the Cooks are a pleasant and affordable spot for a package-tour lasting a week or two – and you can always stay on somewhere else after the package period is up.

Some people travel to the Cooks to pursue special interests such as diving, snorkelling, hiking, caving, dancing and handicrafts. Others come on a variety of research or aid projects.

You can have a fine trip to the Cooks if you visit Rarotonga alone, or a combination of Rarotonga and Aitutaki, the two islands most visited by tourists. Or you can get right off the tourist highway and visit the other islands of the Southern Group, or even, if you're hardy, the Northern Group islands, which most tourists (and, in fact, most Cook Islanders) never see.

Maps

The (now defunct) New Zealand Department of Lands & Survey produced excellent 1:25,000 topographical maps of each of the Cook Islands in the 1980s and 1990s, showing physical features, roads, villages, walking tracks, lagoons, reefs etc. These maps are still available at many places on Rarotonga. The Cook Islands Tourist Authority office in Avarua hands out a few free tourist publications containing good maps. See the Rarotonga chapter for details on where to find maps.

What to Bring

The Cook Islands' even and moderate climate makes clothing choice a breeze. You rarely need anything warmer than a short-sleeve shirt or T-shirt. However, bring along at least one jumper (sweater) or jacket for cooler days and nights, especially between June and September, or for riding motorbikes. Bring rain gear for any time of year.

You'll need an old pair of running shoes (sneakers) for walking in areas where there's loose coral and/or stonefish. You'll also need those runners, or a pair of sturdy shoes or hiking boots, if you intend to go walking or climbing on Rarotonga, or across the razor-sharp *makatea* of 'Atiu, Ma'uke, Mitiaro or Mangaia.

A torch (flashlight) will come in handy, especially if you visit those outer islands where the power goes off at midnight. There are also caves to explore, for which a torch is essential.

The Cook Islands are wonderful for snorkelling and diving. You can bring your own equipment with you or rent or buy it on Rarotonga.

The Cook Islands is a major supplier of clothes to NZ, so there's a pretty good choice of clothes locally, although prices tend to be high.

Most Western consumable commodities are readily available but, again, somewhat expensive. It's almost always cheaper to bring extras (a spare tube of toothpaste or another roll of film) rather than buy it locally.

TOURIST OFFICES
Local Tourist Offices

In the centre of Avarua is the **Cook Islands Tourist Authority** (☎ 29435, fax 21435; **w** www.cook-islands.com; open 8am-4pm Mon-Fri). You can contact it for printed information and free maps before you arrive, and stop in when you're here.

On the outer islands there are tourism officers only on Ma'uke, Mangaia and Aitutaki. On other islands you can find out what's going on from the people running the place you're staying at, or via the island secretary (listed under Information in the individual island chapters).

Tourist Offices Abroad

Overseas offices or representatives of the Cook Islands Tourist Authority include the following:

Australia (☎ 02-9955 0446, fax 9955 0447, **e** mereana-cookislands@bigpond.com) PO Box H95, Hurlstone Park, NSW 2193
Canada & USA (☎ 01-604-301 1190, fax 687 3454, **e** cookislands@earthlink.net) 280 Nelson St, Suite 202, Vancouver V6B2E2
Germany, Austria, Switzerland, UK, Benelux & Scandinavia (☎ 49-30 4225 6027, fax 30 4225 6289, **e** cooksrep@t-online.de) Petersburg-strasse 94, 10247 Berlin

New Zealand (☎ 09-366 1106, fax 309 1876,
e albert-tourism@cookislands.co.nz) Level 1,
127 Symonds St, Parnell, Auckland

VISAS & DOCUMENTS
Passport
Every international visitor to the Cook
Islands (Kiwis included) must be in possession of a passport valid for the duration of
their stay.

Visas & Visitors Permits
No pre-arranged visa is required to visit the
Cooks, as long as you're here on holiday. A
visitors permit, good for 31 days, is granted
on arrival for all nationalities. The only
things you need do are present a valid passport, an onward or return airline ticket, and
honour the loosely policed 'prior booking'
arrangement (see Accommodation later in
this chapter).

Visa Extensions If you want to stay
longer than the initial 31 days, you should
have no problems so long as you can show
you've got adequate finances and still have
your vital onward or return air ticket.
Extensions cost NZ$70/120 for up to three/
six months.

Visitors permits can be extended on
Rarotonga at the **Ministry of Foreign Affairs
& Immigration office** (☎ 29347, fax 21247;
e tutai@immigration.gov.ck; PO Box 105,
Avarua, Rarotonga), on the top floor of the
government building (the big three-storey
white building behind the Banana Court in
Avarua). Come in a week before your current visitors permit expires.

If you want to stay more than six months,
you must apply in advance from outside the
country to the Ministry of Foreign Affairs &
Immigration. If you are intending to visit
the outer islands you'd be wise to extend
your permit beforehand, as there are often
delays.

Travel Insurance
However you're travelling, it's worth taking
out travel insurance. You may not want to
insure that grotty old army-surplus back-
pack, but everyone should be covered for
the worst possible case: an accident, for
example, that will require hospital treatment
and a flight home. It's a good idea to make
a copy of your policy in case the original

gets lost. The insurance may seem expensive, but if you can't afford it, you certainly
won't be able to afford to deal with a
medical emergency overseas.

Medical care is very basic in the Cook
Islands. Even the locals don't depend solely
on the medical care available here; the national health system provides for them to fly
to New Zealand (NZ) for medical treatment
when necessary. As a foreigner, however,
you're not covered by this same protection
unless you have personal insurance.

Driving Licence
The only document you'll need in the Cook
Islands, aside from your valid passport, is a
Cook Islands driving licence if you want to
drive. See the Car & Motorcycle section
under Getting Around in the Rarotonga
chapter for details on how to get a local
licence.

Copies
Make photocopies of all your important
documents – eg, passport data pages, airline
tickets, travel insurance policy, credit cards
and travellers cheque serial numbers. Keep
at least one copy in a separate place in your
luggage, and leave a copy with someone
back home for safekeeping.

CONSULATES
Cook Islands Consulates
The Cook Islands has consulates or high
commissions in various countries, including
the following:

Australia (☎ 02-9907 6567, fax 9949 6664)
Sir Ian Graham Turbott, 8/8 Lauderdale Ave,
Fairlight, NSW 2094
New Zealand
Auckland: (☎ 09-366 1100, fax 309 1876)
Iaveta Short, 1st floor, 127 Symonds St, PO
Box 37-391, Auckland
Wellington: (☎ 04-472 5126, fax 472 5121)
56 Mulgrave St, PO Box 12-242, Thorndon,
Wellington
Norway (☎ 02-430 910, fax 22-444 611)
Hallbjorn Hareide, Bydgoy Alle 64, 0265
Oslo 2
USA
California: (☎ 805-987 0620, fax 383 2084,
e mets@gte.net) Metua Ngarupe, 1000 San
Clemente Way, Camarillo 93010
Hawaii: (☎ 808-842 8999, fax 842 3520)
Robert Worthington, Kamehameha Schools,
c/o 144 Ke Ala Ola Rd, Honolulu 96817

Consulates in the Cook Islands
Foreign consulates and high commissions in the Cook Islands are all on Rarotonga. They include the following:

France (☎ 22009, 24009, fax 22031) Marie Melvin, c/o Island Craft Ltd, PO Box 28, Avarua
Germany (☎ 23306, 23304, fax 23305) Dr Wolfgang Losacker, beside the Banana Court building, PO Box 125, Avarua
New Zealand (☎ 22201, 55201, fax 21241, [e] nzhcraro@oyster.net.ck) New Zealand High Commission, upstairs over the Philatelic Bureau, beside the post office; PO Box 21, Avarua
UK (☎ 22000, 26662, fax 28662) Neil McKegg, Muri Beach

CUSTOMS
You can bring in, duty free, 2L of spirits or wine or 4.5L of beer, plus 200 cigarettes or 50 cigars or 250g of tobacco. As the Cooks are isolated islands, free of many diseases that trouble continental countries, fairly strict agricultural quarantines also apply: bringing in plants or plant products, and animals or animal products is restricted or prohibited, and camping or sporting equipment may have to be fumigated. Firearms and other weapons are prohibited. Don't import drugs unless you want to see the inside of the Rarotongan Prison.

MONEY
All prices in this book are quoted in New Zealand dollars (NZ$), which are used throughout the Cook Islands.

Currency
New Zealand coins and notes are used in the Cooks. There is some Cook Islands money in circulation, and it's identical in value to NZ's. The only Cook Islands note is the $3 note – a novelty collector's item (if you don't find one by accident, ask for one in your change when you pay your departure tax at Westpac). There's also a complete set of Cook Islands coins – 5c, 10c, 20c, 50c, $1, $2 and $5. The old, huge $1 Tangaroa coin is now a collector's item (they're available at the Philatelic Bureau on Rarotonga), having been replaced by a smaller, wavy-edged $1 coin, still bearing Tangaroa's image. The $2 coin is an oddity – it's triangular! The $5 coin is larger than the rest and made of brass.

Cook Islands money, whether coins or notes, cannot be changed anywhere else in the world, so be sure to either spend it or exchange it before you leave the country. It will only be good for a souvenir when you arrive somewhere else.

Exchange Rates
The exchange rates for NZ dollars (identical for Cook Islands money) are as follows.

country	unit		NZ dollar
Australia	A$1	=	NZ$1.08
Canada	C$1	=	NZ$1.23
euro zone	€1	=	NZ$1.95
Fiji	F$1	=	NZ$0.94
Japan	¥100	=	NZ$1.53
UK	UK£1	=	NZ$2.88
USA	US$1	=	NZ$1.81

Exchanging Money
There are not many places you can change money – just the Westpac and ANZ Banks in Avarua and at some hotels. You're better off changing all your money on Rarotonga rather than hoping to be able to change money on the outer islands, although you might get away with it. Westpac has a branch at the Rarotonga international airport, open for all arriving and departing international flights.

You get about 4% more for travellers cheques than for cash. Some of the outer-island bank agents will change NZ-dollar travellers cheques but not US dollars.

ATMs ANZ Bank has the Cook Islands' only three ATMs, all on Rarotonga: downtown Avarua, at the airport and at Wigmores on the south coast. ANZ is linked to the international Cirrus/Maestro systems so most travellers can access their home bank account (for a healthy fee).

Credit Cards Visa, MasterCard and Bankcard are readily accepted at most places on Rarotonga. Westpac and ANZ banks in Avarua give cash advances on all three cards; outer-island branches may or may not honour these cards. American Express and Diners Club are accepted at more-expensive hotels and restaurants.

Outer-island bank agents will usually give cash advances on Visa, MasterCard and Bankcard, but it can be a slow process.

Make sure you're going to be around for a few days or the cash might arrive after you leave.

Costs

Thumbing through the pages of this book will give you an idea of the costs for everything from accommodation and dining out to hiring a motorcycle, riding the bus or going diving.

The Cook Islands is more expensive than Fiji, but prices are nowhere near the horrendous levels of Tahiti and French Polynesia.

The Cook Islands is heavily dependent on imports (primarily from NZ) and there's a healthy slug on top of NZ prices to cover the shipping costs (shipping is a major element in the high prices of most Pacific islands).

A plus about the Cook Islands' strong links to NZ is that for a number of years the NZ dollar has not been the world's strongest currency. So if the NZ dollar sinks, relative to your home currency, prices in the Cook Islands translate to that much less. (And for Kiwis: at least if you visit the Cooks your NZ dollar won't shrink any further!)

Camping out is not allowed, but cheaper accommodation can help to cut costs. Most importantly: all the low-cost accommodation offers opportunities for preparing your own food, which is substantially cheaper than eating out. See the Food section later in this chapter for details.

Many visitors to the Cooks come on all-inclusive package holidays. Check out the packages available from travel agents; sometimes you can get accommodation-and-air-fare packages for about the same price as air fare only, or even less! Don't feel bound by the package terms: there's usually nothing stopping you from taking five days in relatively luxurious accommodation as part of your package and then moving into a hostel for another couple of weeks.

Tipping & Bargaining

Tipping and bargaining are not customary in the Cook Islands. In fact, some people say that you'll offend Cook Islanders by tipping them, but that's not really true – they'll just think you're a mug. Haggling over prices *is* considered rude by almost everyone. The price marked on items for sale is the price the merchant expects to receive.

Taxes

A 12.5% value-added tax (VAT) is figured into the quoted price of just about everything. If a price is quoted to you 'plus tax' or 'plus VAT', you must add 12.5% to see what you'll actually pay. If you're staying at a resort that includes VAT in its restaurant prices, and charging meals to your room, make sure you don't get VAT added again when you pay the bill.

POST & COMMUNICATIONS
Post

Postage stamps are a major source of revenue for the Cook Islands. Some beautiful stamps are produced, and limiting the supply and availability has managed to make many of them valuable collector's items. The Philatelic Bureau office, next to the post office in Avarua, offers a wide selection of stamps, coins and bills. As an ideal souvenir, you can send some attractively stamped postcards home from the Cooks.

You can receive mail care of poste restante at the post office, where it is held for 30 days. To collect mail at the post office in Avarua it should be addressed to you, c/o Poste Restante, Avarua, Rarotonga, Cook Islands. Poste-restante services are also available on the other islands.

Telephone

All the populated islands (except Nassau) are connected to the country's modern telephone systems; each island has a Telecom office offering international and interisland telephone and fax services. On Rarotonga, there's a **Telecom office** (☎ 123; open 24hr) in Avarua; hours are more limited on other islands.

The country code for the Cook Islands is ☎ 682. There are no local area codes.

The Cook Islands Telephone Directory has information about making international telephone calls. To direct dial from the Cook Islands to another country, dial ☎ 00, then the country code (listed in the Telephone Directory), area code and number. International collect calls can be made free from any telephone (dial ☎ 015) – the person at the other end will be charged an extra NZ$12. Other international calls can be made from private phones, public phones (using pre-paid 'Kiaorana' cards) or from Telecom offices.

Local calls cost NZ$0.15 for 10 minutes on the same island (but don't be surprised if your Kiaorana-card account is charged at a much higher rate), and NZ$1 per minute to other islands. International directory is ☎ 017; the local directory operator is ☎ 010, and you can search Telecom Cook Islands' websites (Ⓦ www.whitepages.co.ck and Ⓦ www.yellowpages.co.ck).

Telecom also has mobile phone (analogue only) and pager systems – useful if you're in the Cooks on business, or want to look like you are.

Many Cook Islanders don't seem particularly comfortable on the telephone. Someone who might come across as grumpy and uncooperative over the phone can turn out, in person, to be delightfully helpful.

Email & Internet Access
Public email and Internet connections are available on Rarotonga only (see that island's chapter). If you'll be staying longer in the Cooks and have your own computer, ask Telecom how you can get hooked up.

Many businesses on Rarotonga and Aitutaki have email addresses – search Oyster's email directory (under the Directories menu at Ⓦ www.oyster.net.ck) if you're looking for someone in particular.

DIGITAL RESOURCES
The Internet is a rich resource for travellers. You can research your trip, hunt down bargain air fares, book hotels, check on weather conditions or chat with locals about the best places to visit (or avoid!).

There's no better place to start your online explorations than the Lonely Planet website (Ⓦ www.lonelyplanet.com). Here you'll find summaries on travelling to most places on Earth, postcards from other travellers and the Thorn Tree bulletin board, where you can ask questions before you go or dispense advice when you get back. The subwwway section links you to the most useful travel resources elsewhere on the Internet.

Many Rarotongan and Aitutakian businesses now have websites or email addresses. (The government's decision to use two-character commercial suffixes – .co instead of .com – was, in retrospect, rather unfortunate.)

The following websites might be useful:

Cook Islands Herald (Ⓦ www.ciherald.co.ck) The website of this newspaper is great for keeping abreast of current events in the Cook Islands

Cook Islands News (Ⓦ www.cinews.co.ck) This newspaper's website is also a good source of topical information

Cook Islands Tourist Authority (Ⓦ www.cook -islands.com) The main Cook Islands information office, with details of domestic flights and other information

Kia Orana (Ⓦ www.kiaorana.com) Myths, legends and images of each of the Cook Islands

Pacific Island Report News (Ⓦ pidp.ewc.hawaii .edu/PIReport/) Reports about all the countries of the Pacific are archived at this site and can be easily searched for. An excellent resource if you're after background information on past events.

Telecom Cook Islands (Ⓦ www.oyster.net.ck) Searchable telephone directories: white pages and yellow pages (with company websites), plus an email directory

The Cook Islands website (Ⓦ www.ck) A great summary of Cook Islands information, including contact details for most of the accommodation in the country

Weather Online (Ⓦ www.weatheronline.co.uk /Pacific.htm) Predicted and recorded weather for Rarotonga, Ma'uke, Mangaia and Penrhyn

Several of the travel agents on Rarotonga (see Information in that island's chapter) have websites that carry good general information about the Cook Islands.

BOOKS
There have been a surprising number of books written about the Cooks. Unfortunately some of the most interesting are out of print and you will have to search libraries or second-hand bookshops if you want to find them. There are also many interesting books about the Cook Islands being written today.

Many of the following books are readily available in the Cook Islands, but they may be difficult to find in other countries. All the bookshops in the Cook Islands are in Avarua; see the Rarotonga chapter. You can borrow books from the Cook Islands Library & Museum Society – including its extensive Pacific Collection – and from the National Library, both in Avarua, by signing up for a temporary borrower's card. See the Rarotonga chapter for more information.

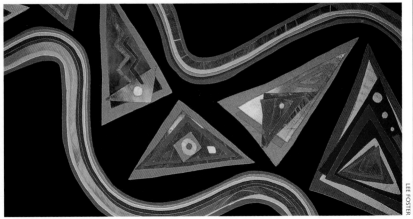

Detail of appliqué work, 'Atiu

Frangipani flower

Water lily

Pareu (sarongs) for sale, Punanga Nui Market, Avarua

Traditional Cook Islands dancers

Lonely Planet

If you're travelling further afield in the Pacific, check out the many other Lonely Planet books on Pacific nations. *South Pacific* covers (almost) every nation, territory and tiny speck of land in the region. For more detail there are individual guides, such as *Fiji*, *Hawaii*, *Micronesia*, *New Zealand*, *Papua New Guinea*, *Samoan Islands*, *Solomon Islands*, *Tahiti & French Polynesia*, *Tonga* and *Vanuatu*.

Guidebooks

Cook Islands Companion by Elliot Smith is an amusing, resident's-view guide to the Cook Islands. The 'hard' travel information is a little out of date now, but the background information and impressions are still valid.

Travel

Across the South Pacific by Iain Finlay & Trish Shepherd is an account of a trans-Pacific jaunt by a family of four. The section on the Cook Islands is particularly interesting.

How to Get Lost & Found in the Cook Islands by John & Bobbye McDermott is another in the Air New Zealand–funded series by a Hawaiian ex-adman, with a concentration on the Cooks' many colourful characters.

Exploring Tropical Isles & Seas by Frederic Martini makes interesting reading if you want to know more about what types of islands there are, how they are formed and what lives in the sea around them.

History

Alphons MJ Kloosterman's *Discoverers of the Cook Islands & the Names they Gave* offers a brief history of each island, the early legends relating to that island and a record of its European contact. It makes interesting reading and there's an exhaustive listing of early European visitors' descriptions of the islands.

History of Rarotonga, up to 1853 by Taira Rere is a short, locally written history of Rarotonga. *The Gospel Comes to Rarotonga*, by the same author, is a concise account of the arrival of Christianity in the Cook Islands, with interesting thumbnail sketches of the various important participants in this chapter of the islands' history.

Years of the Pooh-Bah: A Cook Islands History by Dick Scott is a newer and more readable book. Illustrated with plenty of historical photos, it tells the history of the Cooks with an emphasis on how they have been administered by Britain and NZ.

They Came for Sandalwood by Marjorie Crocombe is the story of Philip Goodenough and the *Cumberland* on Rarotonga, written for children.

Missionaries' Accounts

The Reverend William Gill turned up on Rarotonga in 1839 and lived in the Cook Islands for the next 30 years. His book *Gems of the Coral Islands* is perceptive although heavily slanted towards the missionary view of life.

The Cooks had a second William Gill: William *Wyatt* Gill (no relation to the other William Gill) lived on the island of Mangaia for 20 years, from 1852, and wrote several important studies. His book *From Darkness to Light in Polynesia* is widely available in the Cooks.

Mission Life in the Islands of the Pacific by Aaron Buzacott is a recently reissued missionary account. It traces the life and work of Buzacott, who arrived on Rarotonga in 1828 and laboured as one of the island's foremost missionaries until his death in 1864.

As well as these reports on the Cook Islands by foreign-born missionaries, there are a couple of interesting books telling the story from an islander's point of view. One author, Maretu, was born in the Ngatangi'ia area of Rarotonga sometime around 1802. He was a young man when the missionaries first arrived in 1823. Maretu later became a missionary himself and worked on several other islands in the Cooks. In 1871 he sat down to write, in Rarotongan Maori, an account of the extraordinary events he had witnessed during his lifetime. Translated into English and extensively annotated, his illuminating work has been published as *Cannibals & Converts*.

Residents' Accounts

A number of Cook Islands residents have gone into print with their tales of life in the South Pacific.

Mangaia & the Mission by Te Rangi Hiroa (Sir Peter Buck) is an interesting ethnological study that Buck wrote about his time as the Resident Agent of Mangaia from 1929 to 1930.

Robert Dean Frisbie's books *A Lone Trader on a South Sea Atoll*, *The Book of Puka-Puka* and *The Island of Desire* are classics of South Pacific life. Frisbie was born in the USA and ran a store on Pukapuka. Frisbie's eldest daughter, Johnny, also wrote of the Cook Islands in *Miss Ulysses from Puka-Puka* and *The Frisbies of the South Seas*.

One of the best-known residents would have to be Tom Neale, who wrote of his life as the hermit of Suwarrow in *An Island to Oneself*. See the Suwarrow Atoll section of the Northern Group chapter for more details.

Julian Dashwood (called Rakau, or 'Tree' in Maori) was a long-time islands character who wrote two books about the Cooks. *I Know an Island* was published in the 1930s and he followed that in the 1960s with a second book, published as *Today is Forever* in the USA and as *Island Paradise* in England.

A more recent book, *From Kauri Trees to Sunlit Seas: Shoestring Shipping in the South Pacific* by Don Silk, Rarotonga's recently retired harbourmaster, tells of the author's life and adventures in the Pacific over nearly four decades.

Politics & Politicians

Cook Islands Politics: the Inside Story is an anthology of articles by 22 writers from the late 1970s. Representing many points of view, it tells the story of the toppling of Prime Minister Sir Albert Henry from power – the historical background, the intrigues, the corruption and the bribery.

Sir Thomas Davis (known as 'Sir Tom' or 'Papa Tom' in the Cooks), who succeeded Albert Henry as prime minister of the Cook Islands in 1978, has written a number of books. *Island Boy – An Autobiography* tells the story of his life up to 1992. Another autobiographical book, *Doctor to the Islands* by Tom & Lydia Davis, is an earlier work about his years as an island doctor. Sir Tom also wrote *Vaka* (see Legends).

Legends

Once you're in the Cooks you'll see numerous paperback books about the traditional legends of the various islands. Many of these have been published by the University of the South Pacific's Institute of Pacific Studies. *Cook Islands Legends* and *The Ghost at Tokatarava & Other Stories from the Cook Islands* are both written by notable Cook Islands author Jon Jonassen. *Te Ata O Ikurangi – The Shadow of Ikurangi* by JJ MacCauley is another collection of legends. *Atiu Nui Maruarua* presents bilingual stories and legends from the island of 'Atiu.

Vaka: Saga of a Polynesian Canoe by Sir Thomas Davis is a historical novel based on the story of the *Takitumu* canoe (one of the canoes of the 'great migration' to NZ in the 14th century) over a span of 12 generations. It's a novel, not a history book, but it makes fascinating reading.

The late Manihikian author and poet Kauraka Kauraka published a number of books of legends, stories and poetry. *Oral Tradition in Manihiki* is a fascinating scholarly analysis of the Maui myth (Maui being an important figure in the legends of many parts of the Pacific; see the special section 'Cook Islands Myths & Legends'), Manihiki culture and the relation between the two. Kauraka's books of Cook Islands legends, principally from his home island of Manihiki, include *Legends from the Atolls* and *Tales of Manihiki*. All his books are bilingual, with the text published side by side in English and Manihikian Maori.

Arts & Crafts

Cook Islands Art by Dale Idiens is illustrated with black-and-white photos of all kinds of arts and crafts from around the Cook Islands, explaining how they are or were used and their cultural significance.

Tivaevae: Portraits of Cook Islands Quilting by Lynnsay Rongokea introduces 18 Cook Islands women from five islands, with colour photos of the women, their environment and the colourful *tivaevae* (appliqué works) they sew.

Cook Islands Drums by Jon Jonassen gives information about Cook Islands drums and drumming, including rhythms, cultural significance and diagrams of how to make the various drums.

The culinary art of the Cook Islands is celebrated in the *Cook Islands Cook Book* by Taiora Matenga-Smith, a collection of Cook Islands recipes side by side in English and Maori. If you ever wanted to learn how to make *ika mata* (raw fish in coconut sauce), here's your chance.

Photographs

Visions of the Pacific by David Arnell & Lisette Wolk is a coffee-table book of truly exceptional colour photographs showing all the different Pacific island peoples and voyaging canoes that gathered on Rarotonga for the 6th Festival of Pacific Arts (Maire Nui festival) in October 1992.

A new book, simply entitled *The Cook Islands*, by Ewan Smith and Graeme Lay features magnificent aerial photographs as well as close-up glimpses of Cook Islands life.

South Seas Cook Islands by Dr Wolfgang Losacker, physician and honorary German consul on Rarotonga, is another coffee-table book of colour photos of all the Cook Islands and their peoples.

Nature, Plants & Birds

Rarotonga's Mountain Tracks & Plants by Gerald McCormack & Judith Künzlé is a guide to the mountain tracks of Rarotonga and the plants you'll see when you walk them, as well as a general guide to the island's flora. Also look for *Rarotonga's Cross-Island Walk* by the same authors.

Guide to Cook Islands Birds by DT Holyoak has colour photos and text to help you identify a number of local birds. *Kakerori: Rarotonga's Endangered Flycatcher* by Gerald McCormack & Judith Künzlé is a small, illustrated book on the efforts to save one of Rarotonga's rare birds.

Language & Dictionaries

Kai Korero: A Cook Islands Maori Language Coursebook by Tai Carpentier & Clive Beaumont gives a good general introduction to the language of the Cook Islands. The *Cook Islands Maori Dictionary* by Jasper Buse with Raututi Taringa is available in paperback on Rarotonga and is extremely helpful.

A visit to the Cook Islands Library & Museum Society in Avarua will turn up a number of other resources for tackling the language.

NEWSPAPERS & MAGAZINES

The *Cook Islands News* (**w** www.cinews.co.ck) is published every day except Sunday and provides coverage of local events and a brief summary of international events. Another newspaper, the weekly *Cook Islands Herald* (**w** www.ciherald.co.ck) is published on Wednesday.

The two newspapers make sure they devote at least a few pages each week to petty sniping at each other.

The daily *New Zealand Herald* is sold on Rarotonga the day after it's published. A small selection of foreign magazines is also available, principally at the **Bounty Bookshop** in Avarua.

RADIO & TV

Rarotonga has two radio stations. **Radio Cook Islands** (**w** www.radio.co.ck) broadcasts at 630kHz AM from 6am to 11pm (until midnight Friday and Saturday). Apart from local programmes (in Maori and English) it also broadcasts Radio New Zealand's and Radio Australia's overseas world-news service; Radio Cook Islands reaches all of the Southern Group islands and some of the northern islands. Rarotonga's second station, **KC-FM** broadcasts at 103.8MHz during similar hours; it can be received only in the northern part of Rarotonga.

Outer-island radio stations also operate, mostly on a volunteer/part-time basis.

Cook Islands Television broadcasts on Rarotonga only. As well as local content, in Maori and English, there are international news services from CNN and NZ.

There are a large number of video shops around. On Rarotonga you can rent video tapes, a video machine and even a colour TV to go with it (check the yellow pages in the Telephone Directory). Not a bad option for a rainy Rarotongan afternoon.

VIDEO SYSTEMS

If you want to record or buy video tapes to view back home, you won't get a picture unless the image registration system is the same. The PAL system is used in the Cook Islands, the same one used in NZ, Australia and most of Europe. Tourist videos (eg, dance competitions) in the Cook Islands are usually available in NTSC (used in North America) and sometimes in SECAM format (used in France).

PHOTOGRAPHY & VIDEO

You can buy colour print and colour slide (transparency) film, and video tapes at

Cocophoto, in the CITC Pharmacy in Avarua. Prices are considerably higher than those you'd pay back home, so it's a good idea to bring your film with you. You'll need to bring your own film if you visit the other islands, because it's only reliably available on Rarotonga.

Cocophoto has a good selection of film and it also sells cameras and does photo processing. Colour print and slide film costs around NZ$16/24 for 24-/36-exposure film. One-hour colour print processing costs NZ$16/21 per roll of 24/36 prints. Cocophoto doesn't do black-and-white or slide processing; if you need these services, you'll have to send your film out of the country to get it done.

There is no film or film processing available on the outer islands – they have to send their film to Rarotonga.

Cook Islanders are generally quite happy to be photographed, but the usual rule applies – it's polite to ask first.

It's worth bringing some high-speed film with you. If you're taking photos in the densely forested mountain country of Rarotonga, or in the *makatea* of 'Atiu or Ma'uke, it can be surprisingly dark. Bring a flash and small tripod if you plan to take photos in the caves on any of the outer islands.

TIME
The Cook Islands are east of the International Date Line – tomorrow starts later here than almost anywhere else. When it's noon in the Cooks (making no allowances for daylight saving), it's 10pm the same day in England; 5pm the same day in New York, USA; 2pm the same day in Los Angeles, USA; noon (same time) in Tahiti and Hawaii; 10am the next day in Fiji and New Zealand; and 8am the next day in Sydney, Australia.

Remember, however, that in common with many places in the Pacific, the Cook Islands also has 'island time', which means 'sometime, no hurry, *mañana*, no worries'.

ELECTRICITY
Electricity is 240V AC, 50Hz as in Australia and NZ, and the same three-blade plugs are used. On Rarotonga, Aitutaki and 'Atiu, power is available 24 hours a day. On other islands the availability is more limited, eg,

from 5am to midnight. The outer islands also have great fluctuations of current, so unless you have a voltage regulator, don't plug in sensitive appliances such as computers. (Take note: even a surge protector cannot protect the appliance against fluctuating low voltage.)

On all the islands, power comes from generators burning diesel fuel shipped in at great expense from NZ. Electricity is, therefore, horrendously expensive – you'll notice the price difference if you stay anywhere with air-conditioning. Incidentally, if other countries paid as much for *their* electricity, perhaps the future for the Cooks' low-lying northern atolls wouldn't be so grim; see Global Warming under Ecology & Environment in the Facts about the Cook Islands chapter.

WEIGHTS & MEASURES
The Cook Islands uses the metric system. If *you* don't, see the table at the back of this book for help with conversion from imperial to metric.

LAUNDRY
Most accommodation makes some provision for guests' laundry needs. On Rarotonga the **Snowbird laundry** (☎ 21952) is in Avarua, and there's another **branch** (☎ 20952) in 'Arorangi.

TOILETS
Toilets in the Cooks are the same as in most Western countries. You won't see many public toilets on the streets, but if you're out in public and nature calls, you can always duck into a restaurant or pub and ask permission to use the facilities.

HEALTH
The Cook Islands is generally a healthy place for locals and visitors alike. Food and water are generally good, fresh and clean, and there are few endemic diseases. The most common health problem visitors suffer is sunburn, blocked ears (from snorkelling), infected coral cuts, and upset stomachs from unfamiliar food. Motorcyclists can add to that list: muffler burns (the Rarotongan tattoo) and skinned knees (Honda rash).

Despite the Cooks' lack of health hazards, it never hurts to know some basic travel health rules. Travel health depends on your predeparture preparations, your daily health care while travelling and how you handle any medical problem that does develop.

Predeparture Planning

Immunisations No vaccinations are required for travel in the Cook Islands, but discuss your requirements with your doctor. Vaccinations you might consider for this trip include hepatitis A and B, diphtheria and tetanus, and polio. Seek medical advice at least six weeks before travel.

Health Insurance Make sure that you have adequate health insurance. See Travel Insurance under Visas & Documents earlier for details.

Travel Health Guides If you are concerned about your health, or you're planning to be away for a long period of time, consider Lonely Planet's *Healthy Travel Australia, NZ & the Pacific*, which contains all the information you could possibly desire about health issues in the Pacific.

There are also a number of excellent travel health sites on the Internet. For links, see the subwwway section on the Lonely Planet website (**w** www.lonelyplanet.com).

Water

Tap water is fairly safe to drink on Rarotonga and on most of the other islands. Do ask about it, though. In Aitutaki, for example, there are some places where you should take your drinking water from a rainwater tank beside the house or hotel, rather than from the tap. Even on Rarotonga the tap water is not chlorinated, and while most people have no complaints, some visitors (and indeed some locals) seem to be sensitive to it.

If you suffer any upsets (diarrhoea, for example), try boiling the water before drinking it – or buy bottled water (expensive on the outer islands). Remember that if you are sensitive to the water, ice is just as suspect.

On rare occasions tap water can become cloudy. If you are suspicious of water for any reason, boil it for about five minutes before drinking.

Make sure you drink enough – don't rely on feeling thirsty to indicate when you should drink. Not needing to urinate, or very dark yellow urine, is a danger sign.

Excessive sweating can lead to loss of salt and muscle cramping.

Medical Treatment

Basic medical care is available in the Cook Islands – every island has either a hospital or medical clinic. Patients on the outer islands are often sent to the hospital on Rarotonga for care. As well as a hospital, Rarotonga has an outpatient clinic and several private doctors. For serious conditions, however, Cook Islanders go to NZ for treatment, but it's expensive; see Travel Insurance, earlier in this chapter.

Environmental Hazards

Ciguatera Present throughout the tropics, ciguatera is a form of food poisoning that comes from eating fish that carry a poison known as ciguatoxin. Fish living in reef-enclosed lagoons pick up the poison by feeding on a particular seaweed (or by feeding on fish that have already picked up the toxin). There are no outward signs that a fish is infected (although there's a wealth of folklore to give you hints, such as flies not landing on an infected fish).

Symptoms of ciguatera poisoning include vomiting, diarrhoea, nausea, dizziness, joint aches and pains, fever and chills, and tingling around the mouth, hands and feet. One of the most 'interesting' effects is a reversal of your sense of temperature (hot water feels cold and vice versa – you can't drink so you have to go on an intravenous drip). Seek medical attention if you experience any of these symptoms after eating fish.

In the Cooks, ciguatera is most common on Rarotonga. Don't let paranoia about ciguatera keep you from enjoying the Cook Islands' delicious seafood. Ciguatera poisoning is almost never life threatening, and a ciguatera outbreak is always common knowledge. If you're concerned, seek local advice before eating reef fish. Deep-sea fish, such as tuna – yum – are safe. Ask the friendly staff at the **Ministry of Marine Resources** (*☎/fax 28721;* **w** *www.mmr.gov.ck*), near the traffic circle in Avarua.

Heat Exhaustion Dehydration and salt deficiency can cause heat exhaustion. Take time to acclimatise to high temperatures, drink sufficient liquids and do not do anything too physically demanding.

Salt deficiency is characterised by fatigue, lethargy, headaches, giddiness and muscle cramps; salt tablets may help, but adding extra salt to your food is better.

Heat Stroke This serious, occasionally fatal, condition can occur if the body's heat-regulating mechanism breaks down and the body temperature rises to dangerous levels. Long, continuous periods of exposure to high temperatures, and insufficient fluids can leave you vulnerable to heat stroke.

The symptoms are feeling unwell, not sweating very much (or at all) and a high temperature (39°C to 41°C, or 102°F to 106°F). Where sweating has ceased, the skin becomes flushed and red. Severe, throbbing headaches and lack of coordination will also occur, and the sufferer may become confused or aggressive. Hospitalisation is essential, but in the interim get victims out of the sun, remove their clothing, cover them with a wet sheet or towel and then fan them continually. Give fluids if they are conscious.

Sunburn In the tropics you can get sunburnt surprisingly quickly, even through cloud. At the risk of sounding like your mother, use sunscreen and a hat, and barrier cream for your nose and lips. Protect your eyes with good-quality sunglasses, particularly if you will be near water or sand. And always wear clean underwear.

Infectious Diseases

Diarrhoea Simple things like a change of water, food or climate can all cause a mild bout of diarrhoea, but a few rushed toilet trips with no other symptoms is not indicative of a major problem.

Dehydration is the main danger with diarrhoea, particularly in children or the elderly. Fluid replacement (at least equal to the volume being lost) is the most important thing to remember. Weak black tea with a little sugar, soda water, or soft drinks allowed to go flat and diluted 50% with clean water are all good. With severe diarrhoea a rehydrating solution is preferable (ask at a pharmacy).

Giardiasis This is another type of diarrhoea, caused by a parasite sometimes present in contaminated water. The symptoms are stomach cramps, nausea, a bloated stomach, watery, foul-smelling diarrhoea and frequent gas. Giardiasis can appear several weeks after you have been exposed to the parasite. The symptoms may disappear for a few days and then return; this can go on for several weeks. Treatment is easy and effective – talk to a pharmacist.

Intestinal Worms These parasites are most common in rural, tropical areas. Worms may be ingested in food such as undercooked meat or may enter through your skin. Infestations may not show up for some time, and although they are generally not serious, if left untreated some can cause severe health problems later. If you're still not feeling right after returning home, consider having a stool test to check for worms.

Insect-Borne diseases

Dengue Fever There is no preventative drug available for this mosquito-spread disease, which is very rare, but not unknown, in the Cooks. (If there is a dengue outbreak, the newspapers will report it.) A sudden onset of fever, headaches and severe joint and muscle pains are the first signs before a rash develops. See Insects under Cuts, Bites & Stings for how to avoid mosquito bites.

Filariasis This is a mosquito-transmitted parasitic infection found in many parts of the Pacific. Travellers aren't at risk – infection requires repeated exposure to the parasite over many years – but if you're wondering why some Cook Islanders have swollen ankles and legs, it's probably filariasis.

Malaria There's no malaria in the Cook Islands.

Cuts, Bites & Stings

Coral Cuts from coral are notoriously slow to heal, and if they are not adequately cleaned, small pieces of coral can become embedded in the wound. Avoid coral cuts by wearing reef shoes in areas where there might be some coral, and clean any cut thoroughly with an antiseptic. Severe pain, throbbing, redness, fever or generally feeling unwell suggest infection and the need for antibiotics promptly, as coral cuts may result in serious infections.

Insects Mosquitoes can be a real nuisance in the Cooks at certain times of year, particularly during the rainy season from around mid-December to mid-April. Use repellent (those containing the compound DEET are the most effective). Mosquito coils are available everywhere in the Cook Islands; lighting one will keep your room free of mosquitoes for about six hours. Screens on windows or mosquito nets over beds are also helpful.

Bee, wasp, centipede and other insect stings are usually painful rather than dangerous. Large centipedes can give a painful or irritating bite, but they're no more dangerous to your health than a bee or wasp sting.

Calamine lotion or Stingose spray will relieve insect bites and stings. Ice packs or antihistamine cream will reduce the pain and swelling. Or you can reduce the itch by using a local remedy: pick a frangipani leaf and rub the white liquid oozing from the stem onto the bite. Aloe vera may also help.

Jellyfish & Other Sea Creatures Jellyfish are not a big problem in the Cook Islands because most swimming is done in protected lagoons inside the coral reefs. However, on rare occasions when there have been particularly high or rough seas, jellyfish have been washed into the lagoons.

The locals will always know if there are jellyfish around, so you'll probably be warned and won't have to worry about stings. If you are stung, don't panic – stings from most jellyfish are simply painful rather than dangerous. Dousing in vinegar will neutralise the venom and deactivate any stingers that have not 'fired'. Calamine lotion, antihistamines and analgesics may also reduce the reaction and relieve the pain. The most effective folk remedy for jellyfish stings, used all over the world, is to apply fresh urine to the stings as soon as possible.

On rare occasions someone will see a poisonous stonefish in a lagoon, although the fish, which really do resemble stones, can be difficult to spot. The sting is *very* painful and can be dangerous – go to a hospital for treatment with the appropriate antivenin.

More commonly encountered inside a lagoon is stinging coral – bright, sulphur-yellow coral with a smooth surface. Don't touch this coral; its sting is quite painful (although not dangerous). Applying vinegar or fresh urine will neutralise the sting.

The sting from certain cone shells found in the Pacific can be dangerous or even fatal. The best advice is not to pick up any shells – think of the cone shell as a slightly overzealous environment protection officer!

SOCIAL GRACES
Friendliness and respect for others are highly valued in Cook Islands culture; a soft, friendly demeanour will smooth your way here in every interaction with others. Always be politely respectful of everyone, including old people and children. Being rude to people will definitely get you nowhere, even more so than in most other countries. When you interact with others, offer a greeting and a smile before anything else. If you're genuinely in a hurry it can be frustrating, but, trust us, you'll get there faster if you take a bit of time at the beginning.

Be modest and respectful in dress. Women should see the Women Travellers section for tips on dress, including what to wear when you visit a Cook Islands Christian Church (CICC).

Don't stress yourself *too* much about behaving correctly in the Cook Islands. Cook Islanders, particularly on Rarotonga, are sophisticated, modern people. Tiptoeing around them like they're made of glass will only bring on howls of laughter and encourage them to have you on. (Although Cook Islanders rarely need any encouragement to pull your leg!)

WOMEN TRAVELLERS
It's tempting to say that the Cooks present no special problems for women travellers, and leave it at that. Most of the time, and in most situations, women travellers will never have a problem in the Cooks. As a visitor to the islands, you will usually be treated with courtesy and kindness.

Nevertheless, you should not suspend all good sense. Be cautious about going alone to deserted places, such as tramping in the mountains, or swimming alone in a lagoon late at night. As in other parts of the world, your best protection is to be accompanied – go with a friend, or get a group of travellers together at the place you're staying.

On Rarotonga there's a women's counselling centre, **Punanga Tauturu** *(☎ 21133)*, which you can contact 24 hours.

What to Wear

Like everywhere, your travelling experiences will go a lot smoother if you observe the local customs of dress and don't offend people by your appearance. This is easy to do in the Cooks by observing a few basic courtesies.

In the Cooks, swimming wear is for swimming; it's fine at the beach or by the pool but elsewhere you should cover up. Don't swim or sunbathe topless or in the nude; you will cause grave offence to locals. Shorts and sleeveless blouses are fine to wear anywhere, but 'short shorts' up to your bum will cause many eyebrows to be raised in disapproval. Wearing a *pareu* (sarong) is fine.

If you visit the outer islands, remember that the standards of dress are more conservative than on Rarotonga and Aitutaki, which have been visited by plenty of foreign tourists.

If you go to church, it's best to wear sleeves, so your shoulders and upper arms are covered. Don't wear a *pareu* or shorts to church; a skirt or dress is best, preferably with the hemline at or below the knee. It's customary for women to wear hats in the CICC, but don't worry about it if you don't have one – locals understand that visitors to the islands are not usually travelling with hats! Flowers can be worn any other time, but not to church.

GAY & LESBIAN TRAVELLERS

Homosexuality is an accepted fact of life in the Cook Islands, as in most of Polynesia. There's no need for gays or lesbians to hide their sexuality, and there's no need to fear 'gay bashing'. Public displays of sexual affection are frowned upon, though, whether gay or straight, so behave yourself while in public. There are no particular 'gay bars' or places for gay people to gather; you can meet gay people anywhere.

DISABLED TRAVELLERS

Special facilities for the disabled are few and far between in the Cook Islands – only the Rarotongan Beach Resort on Rarotonga is fully accessible. All of its rooms and public areas are wheelchair accessible, and a couple of rooms are specially equipped with facilities for the disabled. Rarotonga's airport has few facilities for wheelchairs.

SENIOR TRAVELLERS

Many senior travellers visit the Cooks – the warm climate, relaxed pace of life and the easy-going friendliness of the Cook Islanders are all ideal for seniors. Older people are respected and venerated in the Cooks, and seniors are treated well here.

Many local seniors are very spry – it's not unusual for people in their 70s and 80s to have lifestyles just as active as their children and grandchildren. The 'Golden Oldies' have rugby and cricket tournaments every year, and also occasional events such as song-and-dance competitions. If you stop by to watch a Golden Oldies cricket game you'll probably be invited to join in!

TRAVEL WITH CHILDREN

Children are loved in the Cook Islands and travelling with them presents no special problems. Some hotels allow children to stay free of charge, others have a reduced children's rate, and a few do not accept children at all. Ask about the policy when you make your bookings.

There are plenty of things to do that will keep children happy in the Cooks. Soft, sandy beaches on calm lagoons couldn't be safer for children to swim in (though, of course, they must still be supervised), and if your kids like snorkelling they'll be enthralled. (Be sure they understand not to touch the coral.)

There are plenty of other activities that children will like, such as walking, cycling, horse riding and canoeing. An island-night performance is always fun for the kids, as is the Cook Islands Cultural Village. Children dance in some of the island-night dance troupes, and they do very well!

There are no baby-sitting organisations in the Cook Islands. The more expensive places to stay offer baby-sitting, usually with one of the staff. You might be able to arrange something via the staff even at the cheaper accommodation places, or you could try ringing one of the resorts.

Disposable nappies (diapers) are expensive, so you might want to bring some along (if you decide to stick with cloth nappies while on holiday, we salute you, but it'll be hard work – make sure the place you're staying at has a cheap laundry). Be certain that your health and travel insurance also covers your child. Dairy-based/dairy-free baby formula is available on Rarotonga; only dairy-based formula is available on outer islands. Processed baby food is available on Rarotonga, Aitutaki and Mangaia.

Car baby seats are available on Rarotonga at Avis, Budget or Rarotonga Rentals. (Strapping bub to your back with a piece of cloth when you're riding a motorbike, although common practise on Rarotonga, is not recommended.) See Travellers With Special Needs in the Getting There & Away chapter for more information.

Lonely Planet's *Travel With Children*, by Cathy Lanigan, is a helpful book for travel with children anywhere in the world.

DANGERS & ANNOYANCES

The Cook Islands is safer than most places in the world, but a certain amount of common sense is still called for. In general, you will find the Cooks to be just as idyllic as the tourist brochures lead you to expect and the people to be some of the friendliest you will ever meet. As anywhere, crime does exist, but it's practically unheard of for anyone to be attacked or robbed. With normal, minimal caution you should have no problems.

Theft

For some reason, when people come on holiday to the tropics, they leave their sense of security at home. As anywhere else in the world, if you leave wallets lying on car seats or hotel-room doors unlocked, you're at risk of losing your possessions. Even theft of clothes from clotheslines at night can be a problem. It's not a bad idea to check your valuables with your hotel management, to prevent theft from your room when you're not there. (If you *do* get something stolen, think twice before you automatically blame the locals; some of the travellers staying in the Cooks are at the end of round-the-world trips and your cash might see them home.)

Swimming

In the sheltered lagoons, swimming could hardly be safer, but be very wary of *ava*

(passages and breaks in the surrounding reefs). Currents are especially strong here; the lagoon waters sweep swiftly out to the open sea and often straight downwards due to the very steep drop-offs just off the reef. Rarotonga has several such passages, notably at Avana Harbour, Avaavaroa, Papua and Rutaki, and they exist on other islands as well.

Check the Rarotonga map for the position of reef passages before you go swimming. Several unnecessary deaths have occurred when people have been swept away in these passages. You should only venture outside the reef if you are fully aware of the tidal flow and currents, and then only with great care.

Check the Health section earlier in this chapter for advice on other things you should watch out for when swimming.

Insects & Other Creatures

At certain times of the year, mosquitoes can be a real nuisance. Other insects that bite or sting include bees, wasps and small red ants. The insect people fear the most is the large centipede. Though it looks very frightening – they can reach about 15cm (six inches) long – their sting is no more dangerous than a bee or wasp sting. See the Health section earlier in this chapter for more on insects and other creatures found in the Cook Islands, their stings and what to do if you do get stung.

Not really a danger, but definitely an annoyance, are the large cockroaches that live in the Cooks, as in the tropics all over the world. They won't hurt you, but you can buy insect spray at grocery shops. It's said that if the cockroaches are flying, it means it will rain the next day.

BUSINESS HOURS

The usual business week is 8am to 4pm Monday to Friday, and shops are also open on Saturday morning until noon. Small local grocery stores keep longer hours, often from around 6am or 7am until around 8pm or 9pm. The Westpac and ANZ banks in Avarua are open from 9am to 3pm Monday to Friday and 9am to 11am on Saturday.

Nearly everything is closed on Sunday – bars close at midnight on Saturday and even the local airline doesn't fly on Sunday. The only exceptions, again, are the small local grocery stores, some of which open for a couple of hours very early Sunday morning and for a few hours again in the evening. A couple of shops are operated by Seventh-Day Adventists, who celebrate the Sabbath on Saturday rather than Sunday, so they're closed on Saturday and open on Sunday. It's very handy to find out which are the Seventh-Day Adventist stores! Many restaurants are closed on Sunday, except for hotel and resort restaurants, which are open seven days a week. On Rarotonga, several of the larger hotels serve up special Sunday meals – brunches in late morning, barbecues in late afternoon.

Opening hours in the Cook Islands are notoriously variable, so we've taken the liberty of not listing all of them in this guidebook.

PUBLIC HOLIDAYS

The Cook Islands' public holidays, when shops and banks are closed, are:

New Year's Day 1 January
Good Friday & Easter Monday March/April
Anzac Day 25 April
Queen's Birthday First Monday in June
Gospel Day (Rarotonga only) 26 July
Constitution Day 4 August
Gospel Day (Cook Islands) 26 October
Flag Raising Day 27 October
Christmas Day 25 December
Boxing Day 26 December

SPECIAL EVENTS

In addition to the annual holidays, many other island-wide events occur. 'Any excuse for a good time' seems to be the motto, and the locals exuberantly turn out to support all manner of marches, runs, walks, sports competitions, music/dance/art/cultural events, youth rallies, religious revivals, raffle drawings, international mobilisations for one cause or another – you name it! Don't be shy about attending any function – visitors are always welcome.

Sports-wise, Rarotonga has a couple of big canoe- and sailboat-racing competitions, many golf tournaments (plus one on Aitutaki), a sevens rugby tournament, lawn bowls tournament and running races all year long. Check the Tourist Authority website (w www.cook-islands.com) and local newspapers for dates.

The following are some of the more interesting and important festivals and events.

February
Cultural Festival Week Second week of February – a week of festivities featuring *tivaevae*-quilt competitions, and arts and crafts displays

April
Island Dance Festival Week Third week of April – dance displays and competitions, including the important individual male and female Dancer of the Year competition

July
Song Quest Held over several weeks beginning in July – this event culminates in a big finale during the final two weeks, where performers from all of the Cook Islands come to Rarotonga to compete for stardom
Gospel Day Takes place on 26 July on Rarotonga, elsewhere on 26 October – celebrates the arrival of the gospel to the Cook Islands, in 1823, with *nuku* (religious plays); every major church participates with Biblical dramatisations involving music, processions and colourful costumes

August
Constitution Celebration Around 4 August – this 10-day festival, also called Maire Maeva Nui, celebrates the 1965 declaration of independence with sporting activities, dances, musical performances, historical and cultural displays, and many other events; this is the country's major festival of the year

November
All Souls Day (Turama) 1 November – the Catholic community decorates graves with flowers and candles
Tiare (Floral) Festival Week Final week of November – celebrated with floral float parades, a Miss Tiare pageant, a Mama Muumuu pageant, flower display and arrangement competitions, and all the public businesses on Rarotonga decorate their premises with flowers

December
New Year's Eve 31 December – the new year is welcomed with dancing and other entertainment

ACTIVITIES

The Cook Islands is relaxed, slow and easy-going. But there are plenty of activities to keep you busy if you're so inclined. All the activities mentioned here are covered in more detail in the individual island chapters.

Swimming

Of course with all the water around, water sports are the most obvious activity in the Cooks, and swimming is the first water sport on most people's minds. The two most visited islands, Rarotonga and Aitutaki, are great for swimming. Other islands of the Southern Group have no enclosed lagoon, so the swimming possibilities are fewer, but even these islands have somewhere or other to swim – sometimes in caves! The various island chapters point out the best places to swim on each island.

Diving & Snorkelling

Rarotonga and Aitutaki both have excellent possibilities for snorkelling in the lagoons inside the reef, and for diving outside the reef.

There are many features that make diving on Rarotonga and Aitutaki particularly attractive, especially the high 30m to 60m (100ft to 200ft) visibility and the variety of things to be seen down below. Diving and instruction prices in the Cooks are quite reasonable.

Diving operators on both islands offer daily diving trips, and if you aren't already a certified diver you can take a four-day course and receive PADI certification, which will permit you to dive anywhere in the world.

Snorkelling is enjoyable on both islands. Snorkelling gear is sold on Rarotonga and is available for hire on Rarotonga and Aitutaki. Both islands have lagoon-cruise operators to take you to some of the best snorkelling spots. See the Rarotonga and Aitutaki chapters for more information.

There aren't as many possibilities for snorkelling on the other islands of the Southern Group; their lagoons are narrow or nonexistent. If you venture to the islands of the Northern Group, be sure to bring your snorkelling gear. Those islands have large lagoons with clear water, abundant fish and exotic shells. And, other than snorkelling, there's not much else to do to pass the time!

Other Water Sports

The sheltered lagoons of Rarotonga and Aitutaki are also great for other water sports. On Rarotonga, head to Muri Beach, where sailing boats, windsurfers, kayaks and other equipment is available for hire.

Sailing races are held at Muri Beach every Saturday, starting at 1pm. Aitutaki has less paraphernalia for hire, but the lagoon there is a truly magnificent spot for a leisurely kayak trip.

Yet More Sports

Tennis is a popular sport on several islands. Rarotonga has the most facilities that visitors can use (see that island's chapter), 'Atiu has a remarkable number of tennis courts and Mangaia also has courts.

Rarotonga also has plenty of opportunities for organised running races, golf (there's also a smaller golf course on Aitutaki), lawn bowls, horse riding, aerobics and body building. Check out the Rarotonga chapter, ask at the Tourist Authority office in Avarua or check the yellow pages in the Telephone Directory.

Whale-Watching Cruises

In season (from July to October) whale-watching trips operate from several islands. Most of the boats that take visitors on fishing trips outside the reef will divert to check out whales if they are nearby. See individual island chapters for details.

Lagoon Cruises

Aitutaki must be one of the best places in the world for lagoon cruises. The lagoon is large, warm, brilliantly turquoise, and full of brightly coloured tropical fish and a variety of living corals. The main island is surrounded by a number of *motu* (smaller islands) and cruises to these islands, which operate every day except Sunday, include swimming, snorkelling, a barbecued-fish lunch and stopping at some of the lagoon's best snorkelling spots. Don't miss taking a lagoon cruise if you go to Aitutaki.

Rarotonga's lagoon is smaller, so you don't really need a boat to get around on the lagoon. Glass-bottom boats operate from Muri Beach and cruise to some of the best places to see coral and tropical fish. The cruises provide snorkelling gear, and conclude with barbecue lunches.

Deep-Sea Fishing

Commercial deep-sea fishing boats, equipped with everything you need, operate from Rarotonga and Aitutaki, and will take you along for a price (you may or may not get to keep any fish). If you visit some of the outer islands, where tourism is not as organised, you might get some of the locals to take you fishing the local way, in outrigger canoes.

Hiking & Walking

All the islands have innumerable possibilities for tramping and exploring. Rarotonga, with its craggy interior mountains, lush valleys and beautiful white-sand beaches, has something for everyone, from challenging mountain treks to easy strolls through valleys and along beaches and streams. For more information, see the Hiking section in the Rarotonga chapter.

Rarotonga is the only mountainous island in the Cooks; the other islands offer less-strenuous walking possibilities. Mangaia, 'Atiu, Ma'uke and Mitiaro all have caves to visit, a good reason to take off through the *makatea* to reach them. Aitutaki, with its single, small 'mountain', Maungapu, and limitless beaches and trails, is also great for walking and exploring.

Cycling

Cycling is a popular activity on Rarotonga and Aitutaki. Bicycles can be rented on both these islands, as well as on 'Atiu (sometimes), Ma'uke and Mitiaro. The distances are short, roads are pretty flat, and a bicycle enables you not only to get around but also to get right off the beaten track, and to see the islands at an island pace.

If you're a really keen mountain biker, and are heading to the outer islands, take your own bike.

Caving

'Atiu, Ma'uke, Mitiaro and Mangaia all have interesting caves to explore. If you're really keen, take your own, bright, torch – most guides will have one you can borrow but some do not. It's a real shame (not to mention quite disconcerting) to be inside an enormous subterranean cavern with only a flickering penlight for illumination. See the relevant island chapters for details about caves you can visit.

On 'Atiu and Mangaia you must be careful to gain permission from appropriate landowners before entering caves. You'll find, too, that not all the people know about all of the caves. As one keen caver we met told us:

Some people know about some caves, others know about others. To visit all the caves on an island, you'll probably have to do a lot of asking around, and get several people to take you to caves that they know. We met a fellow on Ma'uke who took us to a cave that even most locals don't know about.

Visiting Marae

History and archaeology buffs will enjoy visiting the historic marae on many of the islands. Rarotonga and Aitutaki have some particularly impressive marae. Traditional religious meeting places associated with particular chiefs, high priests or clans, the marae are still very significant in some aspects of culture on Rarotonga and on many other islands. Although the carved wooden figures on the marae were destroyed, burned or taken away by the zealous British missionaries, the stones of many of the ancient marae are still there.

Some marae are in better shape than others. Vegetation grows fast in the tropics, and often a marae that has been industriously cleared will be a tangled jungle a few years later. This can be a little frustrating for the visitor who has tramped through equally tangled jungle to see the marae. If the neglected state of these ancient sites annoys you, you could always help out – ask for permission and the loan of a machete and you'll have something to do for a couple of weeks!

COURSES

There are several scuba-diving courses available on Rarotonga (see Things to See & Do in that island's chapter).

If you're in the Cook Islands for long enough, contact the University of the South Pacific regarding Maori language courses (see the Avarua section in the Rarotonga chapter).

WORK

Tourists are prohibited from working in the Cook Islands. If you get caught working on a visitors (tourist) permit, you'll be in big trouble.

You will see a number of *papa'a* (foreigners) working, though, especially on Rarotonga. Most of these are permanent residents of the Cook Islands – many are married to Cook Islanders – and often they have skills to perform jobs which could not be filled by locals and thus were granted special work permits. Other *papa'a* are here on various volunteer programmes – the following organisations sometimes have volunteer programmes in the Cooks (except for the United Nations, you must be a resident of the country in which the organisation is based).

Australian Volunteers International (☎ 03-9279 1788, W www.ozvol.org.au) Melbourne, Australia

United Nations Volunteers (☎ 0228-815 2000, W www.unv.org) Bonn, Germany

US Peace Corps (☎ 800-424 8580, W www .peacecorps.gov) Washington DC, USA

Volunteer Service Abroad (☎ 04-472 5759, W www.vsa.org.nz) Wellington, NZ

Voluntary Service Overseas (☎ 020-8780 7200, W www.vso.org.uk) London, United Kingdom

Because of the steadily decreasing population and booming tourist industry, some exceptions are made for foreigners willing to work in hospitality. You must obtain a work permit from the **Ministry of Foreign Affairs & Immigration** (☎ 29347, fax 21247; e tutai@immigration.gov.ck; PO Box 105, Avarua, Rarotonga) in the big white three-storey government building behind the Banana Court in Avarua. Contact the ministry to find out the current requirements.

Work permits are not easy to obtain. You may have to come up with an employment sponsor in the Cooks, who must convince the government that the job could not be done by a local. You're not likely to be paid much more than NZ$5 per hour, and without the free rent and vegies that the locals have access to, many working *papa'a* find it hard to make ends meet.

ACCOMMODATION

Although there is no visa requirement for short-term visitors to the Cooks, there is one stipulation for all visitors: you are supposed to have booked accommodation before you arrive.

Recently, enforcement of this rule has become a little more relaxed. Many of the places to stay have someone at the airport to meet every flight, and nowadays if you have not booked a place to stay, you may be ushered to an area where you can get information about your options and be introduced to the representative of the hotel you pick. Nevertheless, the prior-booking rule is still officially on the books, and you will do best to have a booking – or at least say you have – when you arrive.

The prior-booking rule isn't quite as totalitarian as it sounds. Firstly, they don't say how long you have to book for – you could book for the first night only. Secondly, there's nothing to stop you changing your mind as soon as you see the place you've booked into and go looking elsewhere. And thirdly, nobody really checks – you could easily walk out of the airport saying you'd booked into Hotel A or Z, when you'd done nothing of the sort.

The rule is there to stop people sleeping on beaches or camping out. It's also done to try to make sure that every visitor has a place to stay. Many hotels on Rarotonga are routinely booked up for months in advance; if you simply arrive and expect to find a room at these places, you'll probably be sadly disappointed. If you don't book, you might end up staying somewhere distinctly less luxurious – or more luxurious and more expensive – than you hoped.

The Cook Islands Tourist Authority administers an accreditation scheme that accommodation (and other) businesses can voluntarily decide to join if they meet certain criteria. Any place not showing the accreditation sticker (a big blue 'tick' mark) is likely to be a little shabbier (and a little cheaper).

People staying long-term often rent houses locally. You can get quite a reasonable place, fully furnished with everything you need, including linen and kitchenware, for around NZ$400 a week.

Rarotonga is far and away the Cook Islands' major attraction and it has by far the most places to stay. Aitutaki has an increasing number of places to stay, and there's organised accommodation on all the other Southern Group islands that have air services.

In the Northern Group, only Manihiki and Penrhyn have guesthouses. On other islands where accommodation is very limited you may have to stay with local people. Since visitors to these islands are few and far between, arrangements are likely to be very informal. In such a case, make certain that you do not take advantage of Polynesian hospitality – be sure to pay your way. Bringing along an ample supply of food, not only for yourself but also to share, is always appreciated.

On Rarotonga there are two huge resorts, a number of smaller resorts, some hostel-style accommodation and pretty much everything else is motel-style, similar to NZ motels. Nearly every place has some sort of kitchen or cooking facilities, although only a few are distinctly 'Pacific' in nature – thatched roofs will usually cost you dearly.

'Share' room prices, listed under many of the places to stay, describe rooms of two or more beds where you share with someone you don't know.

FOOD

Rarotonga has a number of good restaurants, and Aitutaki has a few. But elsewhere in the islands the choice of places to eat is much more limited. Fortunately, most accommodation places have kitchen facilities so you can fix your own food and save some money along the way. The catch here is that a lot of food is imported and is consequently expensive. Look for local produce and minimise how many packaged goods you buy. That's not always possible though, and you may find yourself opening a lot of cans (bring a good can opener). Turnover can be pretty slow in some outer-island grocery stores, so check those use-by dates; some cans have been on the shelf since Tangi'ia was a boy.

There are plenty of locally grown fruits and vegetables. Look for them in local shops, big supermarkets, at the Punanga Nui Market, and even on the side of the road. Locally grown fruits and vegetables can be very reasonably priced, but in the supermarkets you often find the vegetables have come straight from NZ and cost several times the NZ or Australian prices. Bread and doughnuts are baked locally on most of the islands and are reasonably priced.

Another way to economise on food is to bring some supplies with you. All food imports must be declared on arrival, and although fresh produce is prohibited, you'll have no problem with packaged goods.

Remember that just as food costs on Rarotonga are higher than in NZ, Australia or North America, costs are also higher again on the outer islands than on Rarotonga. If you are going to the outer islands you would be wise to take some food supplies with you. If you're going to a place with no formal accommodation it's only polite to supply as much food as you eat and some more besides.

Local Food

You won't find too much local food on the restaurant menus, but at island-night buffets or at barbecues you'll often find interesting local dishes. An *umukai* is a traditional feast cooked in an underground oven; food is *kai*.

Some dishes you might come across include:

Eke Octopus
Ika mata Raw fish, marinated in lemon or lime juice, mixed with coconut cream and other ingredients. Delicious on a hot day!
Kumara Sweet potato
Kuru (breadfruit) Spherical fruit which grows on trees to grapefruit size or larger. It is more like a vegetable than a fruit and can be cooked in various ways (eg, cut into french fries).
Poke Pawpaw or banana pudding, mixed with coconut sauce and arrowroot starch to give it a gummy texture
Puaka Suckling pig
Rukau Taro leaves (which look and taste much like spinach) cooked and mixed with coconut sauce and onion
Taro All-purpose tuber vegetable; the roots are prepared rather like potato

DRINKS
Nonalcoholic Drinks

The truly local drink is coconut water, and for some reason Cook Islands coconuts are especially tasty. The *nu* (young coconuts), green and still hanging on the tree, are the drinking nuts. The older, yellow nuts fall from the trees and are used for their meat.

Try the Cook Islands' two brands of coffee, grown and processed on 'Atiu. Both are sold in bags at various places around Rarotonga, and served in some restaurants. If you visit 'Atiu, you can take a tour of one of the coffee plantations and factories.

Alcoholic Drinks

Cooks Lager, Rarotonga's own beer, is quite good, as well as being the cheapest beer in the Cooks. Free tours are given of the Rarotongan Brewery in Avarua, followed by a free beer.

A wide variety of NZ beers are also available, Steinlager being the favourite. There are also several Australian beers and a wide variety of other countries' produce. They cost around NZ$2 to NZ$3 a can in bars and are cheaper from shops, where a large bottle of Steinlager costs around NZ$4. The cheaper bars will sell a large Steinlager for NZ$5 – a dangerously low price. Alcoholism and drink driving are as much a problem in the Cook Islands as in any other nonteetotal country.

If you go to 'Atiu, check out a *tumunu*, or bush beer-drinking session (see the boxed text 'Tumunu – Bush-Beer Drinking Sessions' in the 'Atiu, Ma'uke & Mitiaro chapter), related to the ancient Polynesian *kava*-drinking ceremonies you might see in Fiji or Samoa. 'Atiu is the best place in the Cooks to experience this custom – other islands' *tumunu* sessions tend to be merely a group of people gathering around for home brew – no less fun to join in, but nothing unique.

Liqueurs made from local products (coconut, pineapple, banana, mango and 'Atiu coffee) are made on Rarotonga and sold at The Perfume Factory, on the back road in Avarua, and at Perfumes of Rarotonga, with outlets in Avarua and Matavera. They are strong (40% alcohol) and taste good either straight or mixed with juice or coffee.

ENTERTAINMENT

Cook Islands dancing is some of the best in the Pacific and there are plenty of chances to see it at the 'island nights' held around Rarotonga and Aitutaki. Island nights start off with a buffet dinner of local foods, followed by a floor show of dance, music and song. The grand finale is when the performers come out into the audience, choose unsuspecting partners and take them up on stage to have a go. It's good fun and definitely worth doing at least once during your stay. The Cook Islands Cultural Village on Rarotonga is another good place to see Cook Islands dancing.

You can also go out dancing. Cook Islanders love to dance and Friday night is the popular night. Rarotonga and Aitutaki both have venues, and even 'Atiu, Ma'uke and Mangaia manage to have a dance on Friday and Saturday nights. Hips sway and shake, and knees quiver like they never do back home! It's good fun.

The Empire Theatre in Avarua is the only cinema in the Cook Islands (see the Rarotonga chapter for details).

SPECTATOR SPORTS

Cook Islanders are enthusiastic sportsfolk and there are plenty of chances to see a variety of sports – everything from sedate lawn bowls to rousing rugby or cricket games, to sailing races.

The two major sports in the Cooks are rugby, which is played with all-out passion from May to August, and cricket, played over the summer months, particularly from January to April. Each village has a team vying against the others in tournaments, and it's all great fun. Even the seniors compete in 'Golden Oldies' rugby and cricket tournaments! Though the tournaments are played by organised teams, there's always a chance of coming upon a casual game – don't be shy to ask if you want to play.

Netball is as popular among women as rugby is for the men, and inter-village rivalry is equally fierce. Soccer is becoming increasingly popular, especially among younger Cook Islanders.

Anytime there's any kind of game on, everyone is welcome to go and watch. See the local newspapers for announcements of upcoming games.

SHOPPING

There are many things that you can buy as souvenirs of the Cooks, ranging from unique, high-quality handicrafts to some fantastically kitsch, cheap tourist products. Several islands in the Cooks have their own handicraft specialities. Most of them can be bought on Rarotonga, but if you take a trip to the outer islands you may find things you haven't seen on Rarotonga, and they'll probably cost less.

Tangaroa Figures

Tangaroa is the squat, ugly but well-endowed figure represented on the Cook Islands' $1 coin. Polynesia's traditional god of the sea and fertility, Tangaroa is a beloved figure for Cook Islanders and has become the symbol of the Cooks. It's been a long-term rehabilitation though, because the early missionaries, in their zeal to wipe out all traces of heathenism, did a thorough job of destroying traditional gods wherever they found them. Tangaroa, along with the rest of the old gods, was banned.

When the Cook Islanders did start carving Tangaroa figures again, they were often emasculated, but now they're fully endowed once again. When the Tangaroa $1 coin was first minted, there was some consternation in England that Queen Elizabeth's portrait would be associated with such a lewd chap. They got over it.

You can get Tangaroa figures ranging from key-rings a couple of centimetres high up to huge figures standing 1m or more, and just about requiring a crane to move them. A figure about 25cm high will cost around NZ$40. You'll also find Tangaroa liquor bottles, Tangaroa fridge magnets and – if you search hard – even Tangaroa figures with spring-loaded, pop-up penises!

It's a sign of how completely Christian Cook Islands culture is that no-one worries much about the presence of this pagan figure. Unfortunately for old Tangaroa, he just isn't perceived as a threat these days. Few people fret, either, that this once-sacred figure has been appropriated to sell bottle openers and to fuel cheap laughs.

Other Wooden & Stone Products

Pate (carved wooden slit drums) are a Polynesian speciality; you can find them in most of the crafts shops. Ukuleles, made of wood and coconut shells, are another good souvenir.

Toki (traditional Mangaian ceremonial stone adzes with intricately carved wooden handles or stands and sennit binding) are still made on Mangaia. You can take a look at them in the museums on Rarotonga, and visit the craftspeople on Mangaia to buy one, or you might find them for sale on Rarotonga. Stone taro pounders are also still made and used on Mangaia.

Rito Hats

The beautiful hats which the women wear to church on Sunday are a Cook Islands speciality. These hats are woven of *rito* (fine, bleached pandanus leaves); the best ones come from Rakahanga and Penrhyn. Prices start at about NZ$90.

Baskets & Woven Pandanus

Some good-quality basket work is still done, although you'll see some plastic-carton strapping and other man-made materials creeping into use. Traditional woven pandanus products such as mats, purses and fans are now rarely made on Rarotonga, since the pandanus that used to grow on this island has mostly died off, but you can find these products in the arts and crafts shops. On the other islands of the Southern Group (except 'Atiu), all the traditional pandanus items are still made for everyday use. If you visit the outer islands, you'll see pandanus products everywhere.

Pearls

Pearls, a very important product in the Cook Islands economy, are farmed on the Northern Group islands of Manihiki and Penrhyn, and sold on Rarotonga. Black pearls, golden pearls, white pearls, pearls embedded in their mother-of-pearl shells, and mother-of-pearl products are all available on Rarotonga (see Shopping under Avarua in that chapter). Black pearls, very rare in the world, are a speciality of the Cooks.

Shells & Shell Jewellery

A lot of shell jewellery is produced, as well as larger items like shell lamps. Some of this work is imported, principally from the Philippines, but some fine shell work is produced locally. *Pupu ei*, long necklaces made of tiny yellow or white snail shells collected on the *makatea* of Mangaia, are a sought-after item; you can buy these necklaces individually or by the dozen on Rarotonga and on Mangaia, where they are less expensive.

Before you rush off to buy shells, remember that something has to be evicted to provide the shell, and conservationists are worried about some species being collected to extinction.

Tivaevae

These colourful and intricately sewn appliqué works are traditionally made as burial shrouds, but are also used as bedspreads, and smaller ones for cushion covers. They're rarely seen for sale on most islands; if you do find a full-size *tivaevae* for sale, you'll find they cost upwards of several-hundred dollars due to the enormous amount of time required to make them. Smaller wall hangings, cushion covers, or clothing using *tivaevae*-inspired patterns are cheaper.

The **Atiu Fibre Arts Studio** (w *www .adc.co.ck*) on 'Atiu is the only place in the Cook Islands where *tivaevae* are commercially produced and always available. If you stop by, you can see a selection of *tivaevae*, wall hangings, clothing and more; *tivaevae* are on sale there and at the Beachcomber Gallery on Rarotonga.

Other Souvenirs

There's a multitude of other things you can buy as souvenirs of the Cooks. Pure coconut oils and coconut oil-based soaps (from NZ$12) come either in their natural state or scented with local flowers, including *tiare maori* (gardenia), frangipani, starfruit flower and jasmine. The Perfume Factory and Perfumes of Rarotonga, both on Rarotonga, sell quality perfumes made from these local flowers (from about NZ$10 a bottle), for both men and women.

Colourful *pareu* (sarongs) come in many styles and thicknesses; original tie-dyed ones of very thin material (costing about NZ$12) are the most popular and the best for the warm climate.

A kilogram or two of 'Atiu coffee (there are two brands available) is another good souvenir. Liqueurs made from local fruits or coffee beans are also a popular souvenir and can be tasted and bought at The Perfume Factory and Perfumes of Rarotonga. Rarotonga has a few resident artists, and their paintings and other artwork are on sale, often at very reasonable prices.

A few souvenirs made outside the Cooks – woodcarvings produced in the Solomon Islands, for example – are sold in some Avarua shops. If you specifically want a Cook Islands souvenir, and you're not sure where something comes from, just ask if a piece is local or made elsewhere. You'll always get a straight answer.

Getting There & Away

Most destinations in the South Pacific are relatively expensive to get to. Considering the cost of getting to the Cook Islands, it might be worth including other Pacific islands in your travel plans. Unless you have unlimited funds, some careful route-planning will be necessary. Remember that all visitors arriving in the Cooks need an onward air ticket (or a yacht-owner's guarantee that they will be departing on the same boat they arrived on).

AIR

Air New Zealand and Aloha Airlines fly to the Cook Islands, connecting Rarotonga with Auckland (New Zealand), Fiji, Tahiti and Hawaii.

Airports

Since Rarotonga is the only island in the Cooks with an international airport, that's where you'll land. The Rarotonga international airport is a rather simple airport by international standards. Queues can move pretty slowly once you're inside the building, but Jake Nanumanga (a virtuoso on ukulele and Casiotone) will keep you entertained, and the music, along with the tropical warmth and general sense of excitement, usually creates a festive feeling rather than the angst and stress you'll find at faster-moving airports.

You'll be given a free 31-day visitors permit upon arrival, which can later be extended (see Visas & Visitors Permits in the Facts for the Visitor chapter for details). You'll be asked to fill in an arrival form, including details of where you'll be staying. This is important information, because the Cook Islands has a 'prior booking requirement' and technically you can be turned away and sent back to the plane if you haven't booked a place to stay, at least for the first night of your visit (see Accommodation in the Facts for the Visitor chapter for details). You'll also be asked to show an onward or return ticket.

After you've collected your bags and passed through customs, you'll be greeted and asked where you're staying. A fleet of minibuses and taxis meets each flight, and you will be directed to the one going to the place you're staying. See Getting Around in the Rarotonga chapter for more on airport-transport options.

The Westpac bank at the airport is open for all arriving and departing flights. If you need to change money, you can do it here (or in town). If you have New Zealand dollars (NZ$) you won't need to change money, as NZ and Cook Islands money is used interchangeably in the Cooks. There's an ANZ bank ATM on your left as you exit, and there are two baggage-storage options (see Information in the Rarotonga chapter). Booking offices for a few interisland tours are nearby, but these places also have offices in town if you just want to get to your hotel and get some sleep.

Airlines

Air New Zealand flies to Rarotonga from NZ, Fiji and Tahiti, and Aloha Airlines connects Rarotonga with Hawaii. Thus, through onward flights, travel to the Cooks from Australia, NZ, Hawaii and the US west coast is fairly straightforward. From anywhere else, however, you will have to get to one of these connecting points before heading on to the Cooks.

Air New Zealand (W www.airnewzealand.com)
Australia: (☎ 132 476)
Cook Islands: (☎ 682-26300, fax 23300,
e airnzcookislands@airnz.co.nz) Rarotonga
international airport
Fiji: (☎ 679-301 671)
French Polynesia: (☎ 689-540 747)
New Zealand: (☎ 0800-737 000, 09-336 2480)
UK: (☎ 020-8600 7600)
USA: (☎ 310-615 1111)
Aloha Airlines (W www.alohaairlines.com)
Canada: (☎ 800-367 5250)
Hawaii: (☎ 808-484 1111)
Mainland USA: (☎ 800-367 5250)

Buying Tickets

It's possible to visit the Cooks as a single destination, as a stopover when you're travelling across the Pacific, or as part of a round-the-world or Circle Pacific ticket. Depending on where you're coming from, it may not cost much more to visit the Cooks along with other Pacific islands than it would to visit the Cooks, or the other destinations, alone.

Although there aren't that many flight options or airlines to choose from, it is still a good idea to research your flights carefully, either with a travel agent or the airline itself.

Both Air New Zealand and Aloha Airlines have online ticket sales, and many travel agencies around the world have websites, making the Internet a quick and easy way to compare prices. There is also an increasing number of online agents that operate only on the Internet.

High- and low-season air fares apply for flights to the Cooks. The low season is from mid-April to late August, and the high season is from December to February. There is a heavy demand for flights from NZ to the Cooks around Christmas, and in the opposite direction in January. Check your dates and options carefully when you book your ticket; going just a day or two earlier or later can make a big difference in cost.

Travellers with Special Needs

If warned early enough, airlines can often make special arrangements for travellers, such as wheelchair assistance at airports or vegetarian/vegan/kosher meals on the flight. Children under two years travel for 10% of the standard fare on Air New Zealand, and for free on Aloha Airlines.

They don't get their own seat or a baggage allowance, but car seats and prams are usually carried free. Baby food and nappies can be provided by the airline if requested in advance and skycots are available (but usually cannot be booked). Children aged between two and 12 years can usually occupy a seat for 50% to 80% of the full fare, and do get a baggage allowance.

The disability-friendly website W www.everybody.co.uk has an airline directory that provides information on the facilities offered by various airlines.

Departure Tax

There's a NZ$25 departure tax when you fly out of the Cook Islands. For children (aged two to 12 years) it's NZ$10. You can pay the tax at the airport, where the Westpac branch is open for all international flights, or at the Westpac bank in Avarua.

Round-the-World & Circle Pacific Tickets

Round-the-world (RTW) tickets offered by the various airline alliances give travellers an almost endless variety of airline and destination combinations. RTW tickets can be excellent value; expect to pay around US$2100, A$2650 or UK£1250 for a RTW ticket that takes in Rarotonga. Star Alliance (a code-sharing group of airlines that includes Air New Zealand) offers RTW deals for travel in the Pacific.

Circle Pacific tickets use a range of airlines to circle the Pacific – combining Australia, NZ, North America and Asia, and allowing stops at a number of South Pacific islands. Circle Pacific fares are the best value if you are travelling to Australia and the Pacific from the USA, but are not such a good option from Australasia. From North America, Circle Pacific fares that include Rarotonga start from around US$1272 (see The USA, later, for more information).

New Zealand

Air New Zealand has seven flights per week between Auckland and Rarotonga. Return fares are NZ$1100/1375 in the low/high season.

It's almost always cheaper to travel from NZ to the Cook Islands on a package deal (a combination of air fare and accommodation booked through a travel agent). In fact, packages can work out cheaper than just buying the air fare alone. Nine-night packages start as low as NZ$959, and once your nine nights are up, you can always move somewhere else and stay on to see more of the country (usually up to a maximum one-month stay). Useful travel agents in NZ include the following.

Air New Zealand (☎ 09-377 7999, **w** www.airnewzealand.co.nz)

Flight Centre (☎ 0800-24 35 44, fax 09-524 9960, **w** www.flightcentre.co.nz)

Talpacific Holidays (☎ 09-914 8728, **w** www.talpacific.com)

Other Pacific Islands

Apart from NZ, the only Pacific islands with direct flight connections to Rarotonga are Fiji (F$870 return), Tahiti (39,000 CFP return) and Hawaii (US$950 return). If you want to visit any other island, you'll have to fly via one of these. **Air Zealand** (*w* www.airnz.co.nz*) operates connecting flights to Hawaii, Fiji and Tahiti, and **Aloha Airlines** (*w* www.alohaairlines.com*) operates flights to Hawaii; check their websites or contact your travel agency for schedules and routes.

Australia

There are no direct flights between Australia and Rarotonga, but getting to the Cooks is relatively straightforward with a connecting flight in Auckland. Air New Zealand return flights from Sydney, Melbourne or Brisbane are A$999/1350 in the low/high season.

Like NZ, it's almost always cheaper to travel to the Cook Islands from Australia as part of a flight/accommodation package deal. Seven-night packages start at around A$1350. Agents for fares and packages include the following.

Hideaway Holidays (☎ 02-9743 0253, fax 9743 3568, **w** www.hideawayholidays.com.au)

Pacific Specialist Holidays (☎ 1800 226 442, fax 02-9080 1699, **w** www.pacificholidays.com.au)

Talpacific (☎ 1300 137 727, fax 02-9262 6318, **w** www.talpacific.com)

Asia

The easiest option for travellers from Asia to the Cook Islands is to fly into Auckland and connect there with an Air New Zealand

flight to Rarotonga. The other less direct options are to travel via Nadi (Fiji) either directly to Rarotonga (one flight per week) or via Auckland.

Most Asian countries offer fairly competitive air-fare deals, with Bangkok, Singapore and Hong Kong the best places to shop around for discount tickets. **STA Travel**, which is reliable, has branches in Hong Kong (☎ *2390 0421*), Tokyo (☎ *03-5391 2922*), Singapore (☎ *737 7188*) and Bangkok (☎ *02-236 0262*).

The USA

Air New Zealand's flights from the USA to the Pacific depart from Los Angeles (LA). There are daily flights (except for Tuesday) to Rarotonga and one flight per week also stops at Tahiti. Return fares start from around US$890/1620 in the low/high season.

Air New Zealand offers an excellent stopover deal that allows for four stopovers in the Pacific en route to Auckland. The options are Honolulu, Nadi (Fiji), Pape'ete (Tahiti) and Rarotonga. In the low season, expect to pay around US$1300 for a return fare to Auckland, including one free stopover. Extra stopovers cost US$150 each. Check with Air New Zealand or your travel agent for ticket options and restrictions.

Aloha Airlines has direct flights from Burbank, Oakland and Orange County airports to Honolulu, connecting with its flights to Rarotonga. Aloha flies from Honolulu to Rarotonga twice a week between November and April, and once a week at other times of the year. From mainland USA, return fares start from US$870/1085 in the low/high season, and from Honolulu fares start from US$445/625 in the low/high season.

Circle Pacific fares can be good value for travellers from the USA. Options include a straightforward LA–Rarotonga–Auckland–LA fare for US$1272, or a multidestination LA–Pape'ete–Rarotonga–Nadi–Auckland–Sydney–Tokyo–LA fare for approximately US$2139.

For online fare bookings there are plenty of good sites, such as **w** www.orbitz.com, **w** www.cheaptickets.com and **w** www.expedia.com.

Flight/accommodation package deals can work out to be remarkably good value. Packages start at US$1390 (seven nights) – barely more than the cost of a ticket alone!

Contact your travel agent for more information or try one of the following agencies that specialise in Pacific travel.

Pacific-for-Less (☎ 808-249 6490, **w** www
.pacific-for-less.com)
South Seas Adventures (☎ 800-576 7327,
w www.south-seas-adventures.com)
Sunspots International (☎ 800-334 5623,
w www.sunspotsintl.com)

Canada

Travel options from Canada are much the same as those from the USA. From Vancouver, Air New Zealand return fares to Rarotonga (via Seattle and Los Angeles) start from C$1625/2250 in the low/high season. Canadian travellers can also connect with Air New Zealand's stopover flights (see The USA, previous) in either Los Angeles or Honolulu.

Aloha Airlines' flights from Vancouver, via Honolulu, start from C$1590/2200 in the low/high season.

Travel CUTS (☎ 800-667 2887; **w** www
.travelcuts.com) is Canada's national student travel agency. For online fare bookings, try **w** www.expedia.ca and **w** www.travel
ocity.ca. **Goway** (☎ 800-387 8850; **w** www
.goway.com) is a Toronto-based Pacific islands travel specialist.

South America

Lan Chile airline has three flights a week between Santiago (Chile) and Pape'ete (Tahiti), where you can connect with Air New Zealand's weekly Pape'ete–Rarotonga flight. Return flights from Santiago start from US$1260.

Europe

Considering how far Rarotonga is from Europe, a RTW ticket could be the most economical way to get to Rarotonga, plus you'll get to see a whole lot of the rest of the world (see Round-the-World & Circle Pacific Tickets earlier for fares). For those travelling only to Rarotonga, Air New Zealand flights from London via Los Angeles are the most straightforward option. Return fares from London start from around £960/1200 in the low/high season.

Packages from the UK are between £970 and £1500 for seven nights. For flights or flight/accommodation packages from the UK, the following travel agencies are recommended.

All Ways Pacific Travel (☎ 014-9443 2747,
w www.all-ways.co.uk)
Bridge the World (☎ 087-0444 7474, **w** www
.b-t-w.co.uk)
Trailfinders (☎ 020-7938 3939, **w** www.trail
·finders.co.uk)

From Germany there are a number of airlines, including Air New Zealand, that have direct flights to Los Angeles, where travellers can connect with Air New Zealand flights to Rarotonga. Expect to pay around €1200 for a return flight from Frankfurt in the low season.

Travellers from other parts of Europe are most likely to fly directly to Los Angeles, or via London or Frankfurt, where they can connect with Air New Zealand flights to Rarotonga.

In the Netherlands, **My Travel** (☎ 1900 10
20 300; **w** www.mytravel.nl) has good fare deals, and **Wereldcontact** (☎ 0343-53 05
30; **w** www.wereldcontact.nl) has flight/accommodation packages.

In Germany, **Adventure Travel** (☎ 97 99
555; **w** www.adventure-holidays.com) and **Art of Travel** (☎ 089-21 10 760; **w** www
.artoftravel.de) specialise in South Pacific travel.

Recommended agencies for fares in France include **OTU Voyages** (☎ 0820 817
817; **w** www.otu.fr) and **Nouvelles Frontières** (☎ 0825 000 747; **w** www.nouvelles-fron
tieres.fr). Both **Iles Du Monde** (☎ 01 43 26 68
68; **w** www.ilesdumonde.com) and **Ultra-
marina** (☎ 0825 02 98 02; **w** www.ultramarina
.com) specialise in travel to the Pacific.

SEA

The only regularly scheduled passenger ship connecting the Cook Islands with the outside world is the small *World Discoverer* cruise ship (see following). The luxury-liner cruise ship passes through the Cooks, stopping for only a day or two, but only very infrequently. If you're coming by sea, it usually means you'll be coming on a private yacht.

The Cook Islands is not a major Pacific yachting destination like French Polynesia, Tonga or Fiji. Nevertheless, a steady trickle of yachts pass through the islands, except during the November-to-March cyclone season. Official entry points are Rarotonga and Aitutaki in the Southern Group and Penrhyn and Pukapuka in the Northern Group. Many yachties only visit the practically uninhabited atoll of Suwarrow, which is OK with the authorities even though it's not a port of entry. Yachties are under the same entry and exit regulations, including paying departure tax, as those who arrive and depart by air.

The **harbour master** (☎ 28814, fax 21191; e hrbrmstr@oyster.net.ck; Avatiu Harbour, Avarua) on Rarotonga should be the first person you talk to once you arrive; you can deal with customs and immigrations formalities in his office. Leave your Q flag up until you've been cleared by Port Health. The harbour master can sell you marine charts for the Cook Islands, Northern Group, Southern Group and Rarotonga. The new Harbour Master/Ports Authority building is between Avatiu Harbour and the road, conveniently across from the Coconut Bar.

It doesn't happen often, but there's a remote chance that you can catch a yacht sailing from the Cooks to other nearby destinations such as Tonga, Samoa, Fiji, French Polynesia or NZ. Check with the Ports Authority at Avatiu Harbour on Rarotonga, and on its bulletin board downstairs, as yachties sometimes use this as a message board.

The *World Discoverer*

The *World Discoverer* is a small cruise ship that includes the Cook Islands in its South Seas itineraries each year, from approximately March to October. Cruises, ranging from nine to 17 days long, travel to French Polynesia, the Cook Islands, Fiji, the Samoan islands and elsewhere in the Pacific. Prices, which include return air fare to/from Los Angeles and activities such as land tours, snorkelling and scuba diving, are between US$2020 and US$4760 per person.

The only way you can get to Rarotonga on the *World Discoverer* is via Los Angeles; you can't just see the ship in the harbour somewhere along its journey and jump on. Contact **Society Expeditions** (☎ 800-548 8669; w www.societyexpeditions.com; 2001 Western Ave, Suite 300, Seattle, WA 98121 USA) or check its website.

Getting Around

There are basically two ways of getting from island to island around the Cooks (unless you have a yacht): in the Southern Group you can fly with Air Rarotonga or you can take the interisland cargo ships; in the Northern Group, only Manihiki, Penrhyn and Pukapuka have airstrips – for the other Northern Group islands, the only option is the interisland cargo ships.

Note that flights to Manihiki and Penrhyn are scheduled only once a week and adverse circumstances, such as bad weather, limited fuel supplies and too few bookings, can sometimes cause them not to operate. Check that your travel insurance covers unavoidable delays. Flights to Pukapuka operate not on any particular schedule, but only as needed.

AIR
Domestic Air Services

Air Rarotonga is the only commercial interisland air service in the Cooks. The **Air Rarotonga office** (☎ 22888, fax 23288; e bookings@airraro.co.ck; w www.airraro .com) is at the Rarotonga international airport, where you can make bookings and buy tickets. The **administration office** (☎ 22890) is off to one side.

Flights go several times a day between Rarotonga and Aitutaki, several times a week between Rarotonga and the other Southern Group islands, and only once a week between Rarotonga and the Northern Group islands of Manihiki and Penrhyn. There are no flights on Sunday on any of Air Rarotonga's routes.

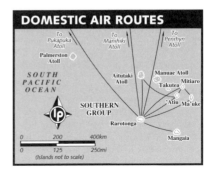

DOMESTIC AIR ROUTES

Tickets bought from outside the Cook Islands are substantially more expensive than resident fares (bought and paid for at the Air Rarotonga office at Rarotonga airport). However, if you wait until you're on the island to buy the cheaper resident-fare tickets, you risk all the flights being sold out!

One-way/return fares are listed in the table.

A 'Super Saver' fare is offered on flights between Rarotonga and Aitutaki (one way/ return NZ$123/246). You must depart on the last flight of the day from Rarotonga to Aitutaki, and when you return it must be on the first flight of that day. It's available only if you book and purchase your ticket locally, in cash.

Air Passes

Air Rarotonga offers a Rarotonga–Aitutaki–'Atiu–Rarotonga service (NZ$367), using a Discovery Pass. You can add a return

One Way/Return Fares

route	normal fares NZ$ (one way/return)	resident fares NZ$ (one way/return)	duration
Rarotonga–Aitutaki	184/368	154/308	50 minutes
Rarotonga–'Atiu	165/330	138/237	45 minutes
Rarotonga–Mitiaro	184/368	154/255	50 minutes
Rarotonga–Ma'uke	184/368	154/255	50 minutes
Rarotonga–Mangaia	165/330	138/237	40 minutes
Rarotonga–Manihiki	618/1244	-	4 hours
Rarotonga–Penrhyn	683/1374	-	4 hours
Rarotonga–Pukapuka	683/1374	-	4¼ hours
Aitutaki–'Atiu	165/330	138/276	50 minutes

Flying in the Cooks

With people travelling back and forth among the islands for many different reasons, there's often quite a motley collection of passengers on any flight. Around December and January, large numbers of people fly to and from the outer islands, as relations living in Rarotonga, New Zealand, Australia and other places return to the outer islands to spend Christmas at home. If you're travelling at this time, book a seat as early as possible; despite additional scheduled flights, finding an available seat can still be difficult.

The tradition of bedecking necks and heads with *ei* (traditional flower necklaces) whenever people arrive and depart is alive and well on the outer islands. It's still practised on Rarotonga too, but much more so on the outer islands where, to many people, it would be inconceivable for a guest to arrive or depart without being garlanded with flowers. Sometimes, as in the case of important figures, so many *ei* are draped around the neck that the recipient is practically buried in flowers. The small planes end up resembling mobile florist shops, and the aroma can be quite overwhelming!

flight to Mangaia for an extra NZ$115. For more flexibility, the Paradise Island Pass offers travel to any of the Southern Group islands, with a minimum of two islands (NZ$128 per sector/flight). Both passes are valid for 30 days.

Note that there are no direct flights between 'Atiu and Ma'uke, so if you want to fly between these two islands you have to pay two sectors – 'Atiu to Mitiaro, then Mitiaro to Ma'uke – so you might as well stay for a while in Mitiaro! At the time of writing, no passes included the Northern Group islands.

Package Deals

All the Rarotonga-based travel agents (see the Rarotonga chapter) offer package tours to the Southern Group islands, which include air fare plus accommodation. You can visit just one island this way, or several; a popular combination is to visit 'Atiu, Mitiaro and Ma'uke all in one go. If you book these packages on Rarotonga, they work out even

cheaper than if you do the booking yourself. Booking from overseas is more expensive – the trade-off is that you are unlikely to get the flights and/or accommodation you want if you leave it until you're in the country!

Several travel agents also offer flight/accommodation packages to the Northern Group islands of Manihiki and Penrhyn (see the Northern Group chapter for details).

BOAT

Shipping services have had a colourful history in the Cooks: companies have come and gone, ships have run onto reefs, and fortunes have been made, but more often lost. Despite the increasing use of air services, shipping is still vital to the islands for supplies. Most of the Northern Group islands are only served by ship, and throughout the islands, ships are necessary to bring in commodities and export produce.

Shipping services on the islands face two major problems. First, there are simply too few people and they're too widely scattered to be easily and economically serviced. From the ship owners' point of view, shipping between the islands is only feasible with a government subsidy. From the islanders' point of view, it's difficult to produce export crops if you can't be certain a ship will be coming by at the appropriate time to collect them.

The second problem is that the islands generally have terrible harbours. The Northern Group atolls' reef passages are generally too narrow or shallow to allow large ships to enter, and at the Southern Group islands (apart from Rarotonga) the passages through the fringing reefs are too small. Ships have to anchor outside the reef and transfer passengers and freight to shore by barge. At some of the islands it's not even possible to anchor offshore, because the ocean is too deep, so freighters have to keep their engines running while loading and unloading.

If you plan to explore the outer islands by ship, you need to be flexible and hardy. Schedules are hard to pinpoint and unlikely to be kept to – weather, breakdowns, loading difficulties or unexpected demands can all put a kink in the plans. Just ask any outer islander waiting for supplies to arrive and you'll hear how unreliable the interisland ships are. It's not unknown for a passenger's one-month stay on one of the Northern Group islands to stretch out to two months or longer. If you think that's annoying when you're planning your holiday, imagine how annoying it is if you're waiting for a new part for your diesel generator, or have export crops rotting on the wharf.

At each island visited, the ship usually stays just long enough to discharge and take on cargo. Travellers get the chance to spend a few hours visiting each island before taking off again – or you can jump off and stay for a month (or more) until the next ship. Outside of Rarotonga, only the northernmost island of Penrhyn has a wharf; at all the others, you have to go ashore by barge.

On board the ships, conditions are adequate, but these are *not* luxury cruise liners. They're also small and the seas in this region are often rough. If you're at all prone to seasickness you'll definitely spend a bit of time hanging your head over the side.

Despite the discomforts, travelling by ship through the Cook Islands does have its romantic aspects. This may be one of the last places in the world that you can sleep out on the deck of a South Pacific island freighter, savouring the wide horizon, chatting with your fellow passengers and the captain and crew, watching the moon rise up out of the ocean and the stars above you in the velvety-warm air.

Just hold that thought when the weather turns rough!

Interisland Shipping Companies

Two shipping companies provide interisland passenger and cargo services for the Cooks; both travel from Rarotonga to each of the populated islands except Palmerston. Both companies are based at Rarotonga's Avatiu Harbour. Information, schedules and booking services are available at:

Mataroa Shipping (☎ 29018, fax 29019, e mata roa@oyster.net.ck) The office is inside a large building straight ahead as you approach Avatiu Wharf

Taio Shipping (☎ 24905, 24912, fax 24906, e taio@oyster.net.ck) The office is near Punanga Nui Market, on your right as you arrive at Avatiu Wharf

There are two classes of passenger service: cabin and deck. Deck passengers sleep on decks, which can be covered for protection from sun and rain, while the cabins offer more shelter while you slumber. There's only limited cabin space and some ships have no cabins at all. You can bring your own food or pay for it beforehand. Showers and toilets are available to all passengers.

It takes about a day for ships to get from Rarotonga to any of the other Southern Group islands, and costs NZ$65 per day. The Rarotonga–Mangaia–Ma'uke–Mitiaro–'Atiu–Rarotonga service takes about four days (NZ$260). The ships only rarely travel to Aitutaki. It takes about 3½ days for ships to get to the Northern Group islands; there's a regular monthly Rarotonga–Manihiki–Rakahanga–Penrhyn–Rarotonga service that takes 10 to 12 days (NZ$600 to NZ$800).

The people of Palmerston Atoll own a boat, *Marsters Dream*, which is used for fortnightly trips to Rarotonga. See the Palmerston Atoll chapter for details.

LOCAL TRANSPORT

On Rarotonga there's a bus service and taxis, and you can hire cars, motorbikes and bicycles. Aitutaki and 'Atiu have rental cars, motorbikes and bicycles (note 'Atiu has rental bicycles sometimes only). Ma'uke and Mitiaro have rental bicycles and motorbikes. Mangaia has only one pick-up truck and a few motorcycles for rent. On other islands you don't really need wheels – they're small enough to get around on foot – although you might need to borrow a boat to get around the atolls. See the individual island chapters for more information.

Car & Motorcycle

The main form of transport in the Cook Islands, for locals and travellers alike, is the motorbike. Usually small 70cc to 100cc motor scooters, they achieve a good fuel-consumption rate (important when petrol is selling for NZ$2.30 per litre!) and are much cheaper to freight in from New Zealand than a car.

Road Rules To rent a motorbike or car in the Cook Islands you need a driving licence (see the Getting Around section in the Rarotonga chapter for details). Cook Islanders drive on the left-hand side of the road. The speed limit for motorbikes is 30km/h in town and 40km/h out of town (10km/h faster for cars). If you stay below the speed limit, you're not required to wear a helmet – any faster and you risk fines for both speeding and not wearing a helmet!

Rental There are motorbikes to rent on all of the major Southern Group islands (from NZ$15 to NZ$30 per day). Cars (including jeeps and vans) can be rented on Rarotonga, Aitutaki and 'Atiu (upwards of NZ$50 per day). Usually, you have to be 18 years or older to rent a vehicle, but ask around and you might find someone who'll accommodate you.

Bicycle
Roads tend to be narrow and when unsealed can be tough going, but traffic is light and motor vehicles generally move pretty slowly, so riding a bicycle is fairly safe. If you feel more secure wearing a helmet, you're better off bringing one of your own.

Hitching
Hitching is never entirely safe in any country in the world, and we cannot recommend it. Travellers who decide to hitch should understand that they are taking a small but potentially serious risk.

However, if you're going to hitch anywhere in the world, this is one of the safest places to do it. At least you needn't worry too much about attacks, although you're as likely to encounter unsafe driving here as anywhere (and seat belts in cars around here are usually jammed down the side of the back seat from lack of use).

Many people do choose to hitch in the Cooks; if you've missed your bus or run out of petrol, it's an excellent last resort. Hitch-hiking is not the custom here, though; if you see someone hitching, it will be a foreigner, not a local. However, it's not illegal, only rather cheeky, and if you do hitchhike you'll almost certainly get a ride in no time.

ORGANISED TOURS
There are various interesting tours you can take in the Cooks. On Rarotonga the circle-island tours provide a good introduction to the island and its history, culture, people, agriculture, economy and more. Circle-island tours are also offered on Aitutaki, 'Atiu, Ma'uke and Mangaia. More specialised tours (such as cave tours) are mentioned in the individual island chapters.

Day tours are available from Rarotonga to Aitutaki (see the Aitutaki chapter). Also, travel agents on Rarotonga can organise one-island or multi-island package tours. See Air, earlier in this chapter.

Rarotonga

pop 8100 • area 67.2 sq km

Rarotonga is not only the major island and population centre of the Cook Islands, it's also virtually synonymous with the whole island chain, like Tahiti is to French Polynesia.

Rarotonga is extravagantly beautiful – it's spectacularly mountainous and lush green. The interior is rugged, virtually unpopulated and untouched – the narrow valleys and steep hills are simply too precipitous and overgrown for easy settlement. In contrast, the coastal region is fertile, evenly populated and neat, clean and pretty – like a South Pacific Switzerland. You almost feel as though somebody zips around the island every morning making sure the roads have all been swept clean and the flowers all neatly arranged and watered. Fringing this whole Arcadian vision is an almost continuous, clean, white beach with clear, shallow lagoons and, marked by those ever-crashing waves, a protective outer reef.

History

Numerous legends across eastern Polynesia touch upon the early existence of Rarotonga, which was clearly one of the best-known and most important of the Polynesian islands.

Ancient oral histories say that the first person to discover Rarotonga was Io Tangaroa from Nuku Hiva in the Marquesas Islands, now part of French Polynesia. He came by canoe about 1400 years ago, but didn't stay; he went back to Nuku Hiva and never returned to Rarotonga. He told his people about the new land, though, and his sons and grandsons visited on their own journeys. Io Tangaroa's son, Tongaiti, gave the island its first name: Tumu Te Varovaro (Source of the Echo).

Settlers from both the Marquesas and nearby Society Islands eventually made Rarotonga their home, although there was still a lot of journeying back to the Society Islands for trading and to pay respects at the great marae (ancient religious meeting ground) of Taputapuatea on Ra'iatea, near Tahiti. The Ara Metua inland road, also called Te Ara Nui o To'i (The Great Road of

Highlights

- Enjoying traditional dance, music and delicious local cuisine at an island-night dinner and show
- Relaxing on pristine, white-sand beaches
- Learning about the Cook Islands' culture, environment and history at the Cultural Village
- Snorkelling in beautiful lagoons or diving beyond the reef
- Taking one of the circle-island tours
- Hiking across the island and discovering the interior's mountains, streams and valleys

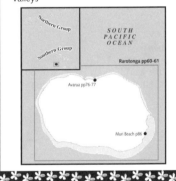

To'i) was built around the 11th century, though no-one today knows precisely who To'i was.

A pivotal event in the history of the island's settlement was the simultaneous arrival, in the early or mid-13th century, of Tangi'ia from Tahiti and Karika from Samoa, both men leading settlers to establish communities on the island. Tangi'ia settled in the area that still bears his name, Ngatangi'ia (in the southeast); Karika settled where Avarua is today. The story of these two settlers is told in the 'Cook Islands Myths & Legends' special section.

Tangi'ia and Karika divided the land among six tribes, each headed by an *ariki* (high chief or king). One *ariki* title, Kainuku Ariki, belonged to the first settlers, those who Tangi'ia and Karika had defeated in battle. Pa Ariki (based in Ngatangi'ia) and

RAROTONGA

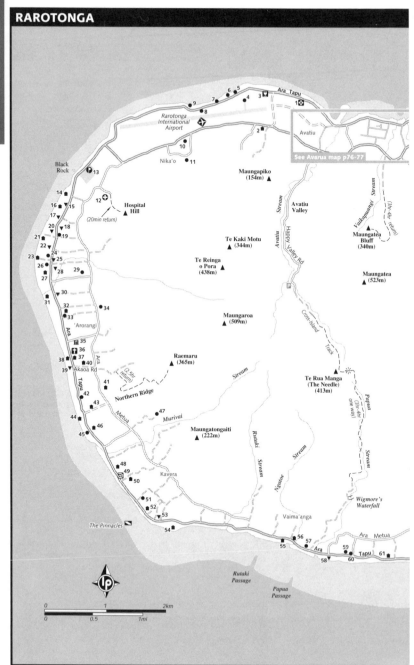

Ara Tapu

Rarotonga
International
Airport

Avatiu

See Avarua map p76-77

Black
Rock

Nika'o

Maungapiko
(154m)

Avatiu
Valley

Avatiu
Stream

Happy Valley Rd

Waikapuangi Stream
(3hr 4hr return)

Hospital
Hill
(20min return)

Te Kaki Motu
(344m)

Maungatea
Bluff
(340m)

Te Reinga
o Pora
(438m)

Maungatea
(523m)

Ara Tapu

'Arorangi

Maungaroa
(509m)

Cross-Island Track

Raemaru
(365m)

(2.5hr return)

Ara

Akaoa Rd

Northern Ridge

Metua Stream

Te Rua Manga
(The Needle)
(413m)

Papua Stream

(3hr 4hr one way)

Murivai

Maungatongaiti
(222m)

Rutaki Stream

Ngatoe Stream

Kavera

Vaima'anga

Wigmore's
Waterfall

The Pinnacles

Ara Metua

Ara Tapu

Rutaki
Passage

Papua
Passage

0   1   2km
0   0.5   1mi

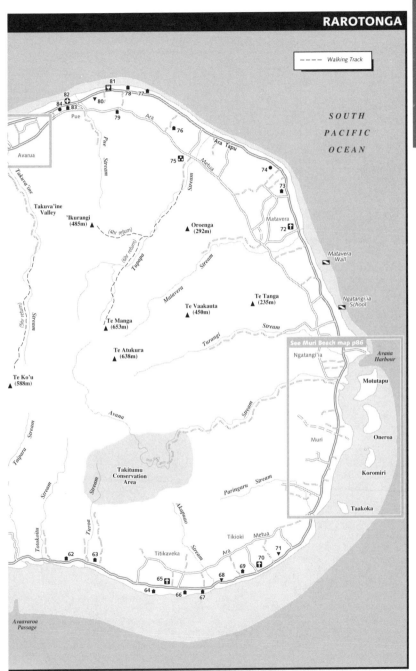

RAROTONGA

PLACES TO STAY
2	Tiare Village Hostel
14	Reefcomber Sunset Motel
16	Rarotongan Sunset
21	Edgewater Resort
23	Aunty Noo's Beach Lodge
27	Crown Beach Resort; Windjammer Restaurant
31	Manuia Beach Hotel; Seashells Apartments
32	Are Renga Motel
37	Mama Ru's Guesthouse
38	Ati's Beach Bungalows
40	Maria's Backpackers; Exham Wichman's Studio
41	Rarotonga Backpackers
43	Manuae & Daughters Hostel
44	Sunhaven Beach Bungalows
46	Etu Bungalows
48	Puaikura Reef Lodge
50	Backpackers International Hostel
52	Lagoon Lodges
54	Rarotongan Beach Resort
55	Piri's Hostel & Cottage
56	Daydreamer Accommodation
61	Palm Grove Lodges
62	Maiana Guest House; Saltwater Cafe
63	Beach Lodge; QR's Residence
64	Takitumu Villas
66	Moana Sands Hotel
67	Little Polynesian
69	Raina Beach Apartments
73	Royal Palms
76	Ariana Bungalows & Hostel
77	Kii Kii Motel
78	Club Raro
79	Sea View Lodge
83	Lovely Planet

PLACES TO EAT
15	Kikau Hut; Oasis Village
17	Alberto's Steakhouse & Bar
18	Hopsing's Chinese Restaurant
20	Spaghetti House
22	Tumunu Bar & Restaurant
25	Priscilla's Takeaways
28	The Flamboyant Place
30	Moko Cafe; Island Car & Bike Hire
39	Bunny's Diner
53	Kaena Restaurant
58	Vaima Restaurant & Bar
68	Maire Nui Gardens & Café
71	Fruits of Rarotonga; Tikioki Rentals
80	Just Burgers

OTHER
1	CITC Supermarket; CITC Liquor Store; Longline Bar & Grill
3	Nu Bar
4	Airport Terminal
5	Cemetery
6	RSA Club
7	Rarotonga Rentals
8	Tipani Tours
9	Parliament
10	Tereora College
11	National Stadium
12	Hospital
13	Golf Course
19	Tipani Rentals
24	Snowbird Laundromat
26	Dive Rarotonga
29	Cook Island Divers
33	BT Rentals
34	Cook Islands Cultural Village
35	Tinomana Palace
36	'Arorangi CICC
42	Pacific Arts
45	Hugh Henry Travel & Tours
47	Highland Paradise
49	Kavera Central; Cafe Maohi
51	Esther Honey Foundation
57	Sheraton Resort Site
59	Wigmore's Superstore; Eat Inn-Take Out
60	Raro 4x4 Adventures
65	Titikaveka CICC
70	Roman Catholic Church
72	Matavera CICC
74	Perfumes of Rarotonga; Pottery Shop
75	Arai-Te-Tonga Marae
81	Cook Islands Game Fishing Club
82	Outpatient Clinic
84	Niki's Surf Shop

Tinomana Ariki (in 'Arorangi, in the west) are descended from Tangi'ia's people. The two or three Makea titles (in Avarua) descend from Karika (a dispute rages over whether the third Makea title has *ariki* rank). There were three *vaka* (districts) on the island, which still remain today: Te Au O Tonga on the northern side of the island, Takitumu on the eastern and southeastern side, and Puaikura on the western side.

Conflicts and wars over land and other issues were frequent among the tribes, and the people did not live on the low coastal plain as they do today; they lived at the higher elevations where they could better defend themselves from attack, only venturing down to the sea in armed groups for fishing. Inland they practised agriculture and raised livestock, including pigs.

From AD 1000 to AD 1400, Rarotonga was the island from which canoes departed to settle New Zealand (NZ) – some of these canoes came from the Society Islands; some

were Rarotongan. They followed the sailing directions of Kupe, an early Polynesian navigator who had discovered and named Aotearoa (The Land of the Long White Cloud, NZ) around AD 800, explored it, then returned and told about the land and how to get there. The people on these canoes became the great ancestors of the NZ Maori tribes, with many of these tribes taking the names of the canoes the ancestors arrived on as their tribal names (eg, the Tainui tribe, the Te Arawa tribe).

European Contact Interestingly, considering its historic importance and that it is the largest and most populous of the Cook Islands, Rarotonga was one of the later islands to be found by Europeans. The first European sighting was probably by the mutineers on the *Bounty*, who happened upon Rarotonga in 1789, after the mutiny, while they were searching for a remote where they could hide. However, hardly surprisingly, the mutineers didn't come forward to tell about their important discovery.

In 1813 a piece of sandalwood floating in the sea was picked up by a passing ship and taken to Australia. The idea that the island might have sandalwood – a valuable commodity – led directly to the visit of the next European visitor. Philip Goodenough, captain of the *Cumberland*, showed up in 1814 and spent three fairly violent months on Rarotonga. During their stay, at Ngatangi'ia, the crew got involved in some local squabbles that resulted in the deaths of a number of the crew – including Goodenough's female companion, Ann Butcher (the first European woman to come to the island), and also numerous Rarotongans. Eventually the *Cumberland* left Rarotonga with some haste.

In 1823, Papeiha, a Polynesian missionary from Ra'iatea in the Society Islands, came to Rarotonga from Aitutaki, where he had done remarkably well at introducing Christianity. Rarotonga proved elusive; the missionaries arrived via Mangaia, 'Atiu, Ma'uke and Mitiaro. Finally, an 'Atiuan *ariki*, Rongomatane, whose people had invaded Rarotonga on occasions, gave the missionaries sailing directions that turned out to be spot on. Papeiha was left on Rarotonga to convince the islanders to give up their religion and take on the new one. As on Aitutaki, he succeeded with surprising speed; a little more than a year after his arrival, Christianity had taken firm hold.

The first permanent London Missionary Society (LMS) missionaries arrived in 1827. They translated the Bible into Maori, and established the village of 'Arorangi, which was to be a model for new villages on the island (the missionaries wished to gather the previously scattered population together in order to speed the propagation of Christianity).

As elsewhere in the Pacific, previously unknown diseases were introduced by the new arrivals, and the population plummeted – from around 6000 at the time of European arrival on Rarotonga to less than 3000 within 20 years, and to less than 2000 about 20 years after that.

Although the missionaries tried to exclude other Europeans from settling, whalers and traders visited the island – as one missionary's wife lamented, men of 'some wealth and little religious principle'. Unable to deter the traders, the missionaries did at

Rarotonga's Name

There are various stories relating to how the island got its present name, Rarotonga. *Raro* means 'west' or 'down', and *tonga* means 'south', so *'raro tonga'* could mean 'southwest'. From the point of view of the early discoverers and navigators from the Marquesas and Society Islands, Rarotonga was certainly to the southwest.

Some claim that the explorer Tangi'ia named Rarotonga after sailing down too far (raro) to the south (tonga) before finding it. See the 'Cook Islands Myths & Legends' special section for why he went wrong.

A third theory has Tangi'ia's contemporary, Karika, naming the island after his marae back home in Samoa.

least warn the Rarotongans to beware the French, who had taken over Tahiti in 1843. The dangers of Papism were a major worry for the LMS!

In 1865 the paramount Rarotongan *ariki*, Makea Takau, alarmed by rumours of French expansionism in the Pacific, requested British protection for the first time. This request was turned down. In the following years the missionaries' once absolute power declined, as more Europeans came to the island and trade grew. Finally in 1888 a British protectorate was formally declared over the Southern Group islands, and Rarotonga became the unofficial capital of the group.

Geography

Rarotonga is the only high volcanic island in the Cook Islands. The inland area is mountainous with steep valleys, razorback ridges and swift-flowing streams. Most of this area is covered with dense jungle.

Rarotonga is the youngest of the Cook Islands: the volcanic activity that thrust it above sea level occurred about two million years ago, more recently than on any of the other islands. The island's major mountains are the remains of the outer rim of the cone. The cone is open on the northern side and Maungatea rises in the centre.

The narrow coastal plain with its swampy area close to the hills is somewhat like the *makatea* (raised outer coral fringe) of several other islands in the Southern Group, though on Rarotonga the coastal plain is fertile, sandy loam rather than the jagged razor-sharp coral of true *makatea*.

The lagoon within Rarotonga's outer reef is narrow around most of the island but widens out around the southern side, where there are the best beaches. Muri Lagoon, fringed by four *motu* (lagoon islets), is the widest part of the lagoon, although even here it is very shallow in most places. There are few *ava* (natural passages through the reef) – where water that has entered the lagoon over the top of the reef rushes back into the open sea.

Orientation
Finding your way around Rarotonga is easy – there's a coastal road (the Ara Tapu), another road about 500m inland (the Ara Metua) going most of the way around the island, and a lot of mountains in the middle. Basically it's that simple. A number of roads connect the Ara Tapu to the Ara Metua and a few roads lead into inland valleys. If you want to get all the way into the middle, or cross the island from one side to the other, you must do it on foot.

Maps The (now defunct) New Zealand Department of Lands & Survey produced excellent 1:25,000 topographical maps of each of the Cook Islands. The Rarotonga map (last updated in 1989) shows all the roads, a number of walking trails, the reefs and the villages, and has a separate enlargement of Avarua. These maps are available for about NZ$10 at many shops in Avarua – check at the CITC Shopping Centre, Bounty Bookshop and Island Craft.

The tourist office in Avarua hands out a number of free publications containing good maps: *Jason's* has a large fold-out map of Rarotonga and Aitutaki. The *What's On* booklet, *Cook Islands Sun* and *Raro Magic* magazine also contain maps.

Rarotonga's Mountain Tracks and Plants (available at various book outlets for NZ$25), by Gerald McCormack & Judith Künzlé, contains detailed maps for a number of walking tracks.

Information
Tourist Offices Located in a bright yellow office right in the middle of Avarua is the

Cook Islands Tourist Authority (☎ 29435, fax 21435; W www.cook-islands.com; open 8am-4pm Mon-Fri). It has the usual sort of tourist information and can help you with everything from accommodation, nightspots and 'island nights' to interisland flights and shipping services.

The office has free copies of *What's On in the Cook Islands*, an annually produced information-and-adverts booklet guide to Rarotonga and Aitutaki, and *Jason's*, a foldout advertisement sheet with good maps of both of these islands. Also free here is the tourist magazine *Raro Magic*, and the *Cook Islands Sun* newspaper and map.

Money The two travellers' banks on Rarotonga, Westpac and ANZ, are both in Avarua, on the main road. **Westpac** (☎ 22014; e bank@westpac.co.ck; open 9am-3pm Mon-Fri, 9am-midday Sat) is beside the Foodland supermarket and **ANZ** (☎ 21750, fax 21760; open 9am-3pm Mon-Fri, 9am-midday Sat) is between the CITC Shopping Centre and the Banana Court. Travellers cheques and cash (major currencies) can be changed at either bank. They also give cash advances on Visa, MasterCard and Bankcard, and do telegraphic transfers.

There's another Westpac branch at the airport, open for all international flights, and a third at Punanga Nui Market (open 8am-11am Sat).

ANZ has three ATMs: one in Avarua, one at the airport and one at Wigmore's Superstore on the south coast. They're linked to the international Cirrus/Maestro systems so you might be able to access your home bank account (for a healthy fee). Some European cards don't work here; check with your home bank.

Travellers cheques and major currencies in cash can also be changed at some of the larger hotels, but the banks offer a better rate of exchange. Most of the larger stores, hotels and rental-car companies accept Visa, MasterCard and Bankcard.

Post & Communications Just inland from the traffic circle in central Avarua is the **post office** (☎ 29940; open 8am-4pm Mon-Fri). Poste restante is handled here; they will receive and hold mail for you for 30 days. It should be addressed to you, c/o Poste Restante, Avarua Post Office, Rarotonga,

Glass-bottom boat on Muri Lagoon

View from Te Manga (653m), Rarotonga

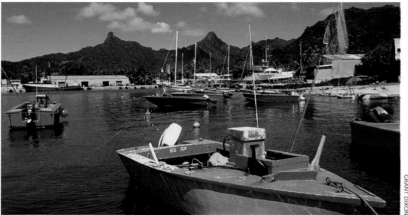
'Ikurangi (485m) and Te Manga (653m) beyond Avatiu Harbour, Rarotonga

Kayaking in the waters off Muri Beach, Rarotonga

Poinciana trees, Rarotonga

A resort on Rarotonga

Cook Islands. You can send mail from here or **Telepost** *(☎ 29940, ext 273; beside the CITC Shopping Centre, Avarua)*. There are also postal 'depots' at several small shops around the island, where you can buy stamps, and post and receive letters.

You can make an international collect phone call from any phone on the island, but if you want to pay for the call yourself, you must either find someone who will allow you to do it on their telephone, use a card phone, or go to **Telecom** *(☎ 29680; Tutakimoa Rd, Avarua; open 24hr)* or Telepost in Avarua.

'Kiaorana' phonecards, costing NZ$5, NZ$10, NZ$20 or NZ$50, can be purchased at the post office, Telecom, Telepost and many shops. Local, interisland and international phone calls can all be made using these cards. Public telephones in Avarua can be found outside the post office in Avarua; on the outside wall of the CITC Shopping Centre, opposite Cook's Corner; and outside Telepost, at the other end of the CITC Shopping Centre. There are other public phones dotted around the island.

Email/Internet access is available at the following places on Rarotonga. They all charge around NZ$1.80 for five minutes or NZ$0.30 per minute.

Blue Rock Cyber Cafe (☎ 23531) Muri Beach. This place has coffee, smoothies and snacks available.

The Internet Cafe (☎ 27242) Muri Beach. Coffee, Gameboy and bicycle hire are all here.

Kavera Central (☎ 20012) Kavera. You can buy groceries and Cook Islands music CDs here.

Pacific Computers (☎ 20727) Browne's Arcade, Avarua. This place has offline printing and a fast Internet connection.

Ronnie's Bar & Grill (☎ 20823) Ara Maire Nui, Avarua. You can get beer at Ronnie's.

Telecom (☎ 29680, fax 26174) Tutakimoa Rd, Avarua; open 24 hours. You can receive phone calls (on the big red Batphone; ☎ 23942) and faxes, and it has the fastest Internet connection in the Cook Islands.

Telepost (☎ 29940, ext 273, fax 29873) Beside the CITC Shopping Centre, Avarua. Postal services are available and you can receive faxes.

Travel Agencies The two 'big' travel agencies on Rarotonga are Island Hopper and Jetsave Travel, but shopping around at the others might find you some good deals.

Cook Islands Tours & Travel (☎ 28270, after hours ☎ 20270, fax 27270, ⓦ www.cook islandstours.co.ck) Rarotonga international airport

Hugh Henry Travel & Tours (☎ 25320, fax 25420, ⓔ tours@hughhenry.co.ck) 'Arorangi

Island Hopper Vacations (☎ 22576, fax 22036, ⓦ www.islandhoppervacations.com) Banana Court, Avarua

Jetsave Travel (☎ 27707, fax 28807, ⓦ www .jetsave.co.ck) Ara Maire Nui, Avarua

Tipani Tours (☎ 25266, fax 23266, ⓔ tours@ tipani.co.ck, ⓦ www.tipanitours.com) Ara Tapu, near the airport

Bookshops Rarotonga's book outlets are all in Avarua.

The **University of the South Pacific** *(USP; ☎ 29415; Makea Tinirau Rd)* sells all the books published by USP at prices much lower than anywhere else – check here first. There are lots of books about Cook Islands history, literature, legends, poetry, arts and crafts, politics and culture etc.

CITC Shopping Centre *(☎ 22000; Ara Maire Nui)* has a wide selection of general-interest paperback books as well as a small selection of Cook Islands/Pacific books. There are kids' books here too.

Bounty Bookshop *(☎ 26660)*, near the post office, has a good selection of foreign magazines, the *New Zealand Herald* and local newspapers, and a variety of books, including titles on the Cook Islands and other Pacific destinations.

There's often a good selection of Cook Islands books in Treasure Chest stores, along with lots of tacky souvenirs. You'll see their shops at the resorts and in Mana Court, Avarua.

There are only a few books for sale at the **Cook Islands Library & Museum Society** *(☎ 26468)* and the **National Library** *(☎ 20725)* at the National Culture Centre, but you can access all their books, including extensive Pacific collections, by signing up for a temporary borrower's card. For more information, see the individual sections under Avarua later in the chapter.

Laundry Charging NZ$4 per washload, including soap and softener, **Snowbird Laundromat** *(☎ 21952; Ara Tapu, Avarua; open 8am-4pm Mon-Fri, 8am-noon Sat • ☎ 20952; Ara Tapu, 'Arorangi)* also hits you for NZ$5.50 to dry. The 'Arorangi shop is open almost 24 hours.

Toilets Rarotonga has only a few fully 'public' toilets. One at the airport, and four in Avarua: in the Ports Authority Building near Avatiu Harbour, at either end of Punanga Nui Market and another behind Banana Court (this one is usually locked; ask at the Blue Note Cafe for the key). Other public toilets tend to be slowly claimed by whoever's building they are in – you'll find such semi-public toilets at Avatiu Harbour, in Cooks Corner Arcade and Paulina's Polynesian Restaurant.

Around the island are a few other equally private public toilets. The ones at Black Rock, opposite Kavera Central, and at Avana Harbour are usually unlocked.

One government official we asked about public toilets suggested 'the bush' as the best option (fine for the boys, but stay clear of waterways and watch out for falling coconuts). You can almost always use the facilities at restaurants and pubs if you ask.

Left Luggage If you're heading to the outer islands and want to shed some weight, you can leave bags in dented old lockers at the airport, leaving the keys with the 24-hour **airport rescue fire service** (☎ 25890) for NZ$4 per locker per day. Another option is **Cook Islands Tours & Travel** (☎ 28270, after hours ☎ 20270), for NZ$4 per bag per day. Its airport office is only open weekday mornings and one hour before international flight arrivals, but they have a 24-hour service.

A far more simple option is to ask the place you're staying at on Rarotonga to look after your bags. Many do it for free, but some charge a fee.

Medical Services Rarotonga's **hospital** (☎ 22664; open 8am-4pm Mon-Fri, 24hr emergency service) is on a steep hill up behind the golf course, west of the airport. A sign on the main road marks the turn-off. There's also an **outpatient clinic** (☎ 20065; open 8am-6pm Mon-Fri, 8am-11am Sat) on the main road at Tupapa, about 1km east of Avarua.

Several **private doctors** practise on Rarotonga; you'll pay NZ$20 to NZ$30 for a consultation. They all operate normal business hours.

Dr Uma Kush (☎ 27727) Cooks Corner Arcade, Avarua

Dr Wolfgang Losacker (☎ 23306) Banana Court, Avarua
Dr T Noovao (☎ 20835) Ara Metua, behind the airport
Drs Uka and Strickland (☎ 23680) Ingram House, opposite Punanga Nui Market, Avarua

There's an **optometrist** (☎/fax 26605; Mana Court, Avarua), and several **dental studios** listed in Telecom's Yellow Pages.

Emergency The **police station** (☎ 22499) is on the main road in the centre of Avarua. Emergency phone numbers are:

Ambulance & Hospital (☎ 998)
Fire (☎ 996)
Police (☎ 999)

Hiking

You don't have to get very far into the interior of Rarotonga to realise the population is almost entirely concentrated along the narrow coastal fringe. The mountainous interior is virtually deserted and can be reached only by walking tracks and trails.

Rarotonga's Mountain Tracks and Plants by Gerald McCormack & Judith Künzlé is an excellent book that is very useful if you plan to walk any of the mountain tracks. (Yellow tags on the trails correspond to points of interest and trees listed in the book.) The same authors have also published a separate colour-illustrated booklet, *Rarotonga's Cross-Island Walk*. These publications give much more detail about each walk (including information on geology, plants, animals and other natural features) than we have space to include here.

The valley walks are easy strolls suitable even for older people and young children, and the scaling of the hill behind the hospital is also easy and short, although a bit steep.

Most of the mountain walks are hard work, often involving difficult scrambling over rocky sections. Apart from the cross-island track by the Needle, and the ascent of Raemaru behind 'Arorangi village (both of which have individual sections later in the chapter), most of the mountain walks are a cross between scaling Everest and hacking your way through the Amazon jungle.

The interior of Rarotonga is surprisingly mountainous, with some steep slopes and sheer drops. Keep an eye out for these drops, as you can stumble across them quite suddenly. Although the trails are often difficult to follow, Rarotonga is too small for you to get really lost (unless you try; people have managed in the past!). You can generally see where you're going or where you've come from. If you do get lost, walk towards the coast on a ridge crest. (Streams often have sprawling hibiscus branches, making progress very slow.)

Walking will generally be easier if you follow the ridges rather than trying to beat your way across the often heavily overgrown slopes. Rarotonga has no dangerous wild animals, snakes or poisonous insects, but the valleys and bushy inland areas do have plenty of very thirsty mosquitoes, so bring repellent.

Shorts are cool and easy for walking, but you may want to wear some sort of leg or ankle protection, as you can easily get pretty scratched up forcing your way through fern or scrub. Wear adequate walking shoes or boots, not thongs or sandals, as the trails can often be challenging. They can also be quite muddy and slippery, particularly after rain; don't underestimate the danger of this when you're on a steep incline. Carry plenty of drinking water with you; hiking on Rarotonga can be thirsty work.

Most importantly, be sure to observe the basic tramping safety rules of letting someone know where you're going and when you expect to return, and *don't go alone*. The mountain tracks are no walk in the park. There have been numerous instances of trampers getting injured or lost in the mountains. If you slip and injure yourself it could be a very long time before anyone finds you. Don't be paranoid (the Cook Islands Tourist Authority recommends *never* walking without a guide – which *is* being paranoid), but do take sensible precautions.

Walking times quoted are for a complete trip from the nearest road access point and do not allow for getting lost – which on most trails is a distinct possibility.

Organised Walks The popular Cross-Island Trek is organised through local travel agents and private guides. They only go in fine weather, as the track is very slippery when wet. If you'll only be staying on the island for a short time and you want to do a cross-island walk, it's sensible to do it as soon as you can upon arriving. Guaranteed – if you plan to do it on your last day, it'll be raining.

The **Takitumu Conservation Area** (*TCA*; ☎ 29906, fax 29906; **e** *kakerori@tca.co.ck; Ara Tapu, Avarua*) is a private reserve in Rarotonga's southeast. The nonprofit organisation administering the area leads easy walking tours on Tuesday and Thursday and bird-watching tours by prior arrangement. A four-hour tour costs NZ$45/20 for adults/children.

You're almost guaranteed to see a *kakerori* (flycatcher), the tiny bird that the TCA has saved from extinction by setting up the conservation area and eliminating pests. Tours include the story of the *kakerori*, a description of the traditional uses of plants, and light lunch and transportation. Ian Karika at the TCA might be able to help you arrange guides for other walks on Rarotonga as well.

Pa Mountain Trekking (☎ 21079) is run by Pa – a big, friendly dreadlocked fellow who leads tours over the Cross-Island Track as well as less-strenuous walks up Matavera Stream. Pa discusses the fauna, flora and medicinal plants of the island. Tours take place from Monday to Saturday and cost NZ$50/25 for adults/children.

Bill Tschan runs **Bill's Mountain Treks** (☎ 22244) and leads two-hour, easy walks through Takuva'ine Valley (NZ$20) and more-strenuous, four-to-five-hour climbs of Te Ko'u (NZ$35). Learn about history and nature, and enjoy a cup of tea in Bill's mountain-top hut.

Diving

Diving is good outside the reef. There's coral, canyons, caves and tunnels and the reef drop-off goes from 20m to 30m right down to 4000m! Most diving is about 3m to 30m, where visibility is 30m to 60m (100ft to 200ft) depending on weather and wind conditions; it's seldom less than 30m.

In addition to the brilliant visibility, other special features of diving on Rarotonga include shipwrecks, the largely unspoiled reef with several varieties of colourful, living coral, and the very short boat trip to reach the diving grounds. The fact that Rarotonga is a small, round island means that regardless of where the wind is coming from there's practically guaranteed to be good diving somewhere around the island. For the novice diver, the sheltered lagoon makes an excellent learning and practising ground.

Rarotonga has three diving operators:

Cook Island Divers (☎ 22483, fax 22484,
  w www.cookpages.com/CookIslandDivers/)
  'Arorangi
Dive Rarotonga (☎ 21873, **w** www.diveraro
  .com) 'Arorangi
Pacific Divers (☎/fax 22450, **w** www.pacific
  divers.co.ck) Muri Beach

All offer morning and afternoon diving trips outside the reef for certified divers. Dives cost around NZ$60 to NZ$75, with discounts for multiple dives, two dives in one day, or if you have your own gear. Snorkellers can go along for around NZ$20, including gear, if there's enough room on the boat.

Cook Island Divers and Pacific Divers offer 3½-day diving courses leading to internationally recognised PADI or NAUI certification for NZ$499. They also offer PADI-approved resort courses (two-hour Discover Scuba courses designed to give an initial feel for diving) in the lagoon for NZ$75. Ask about night dives.

Snorkelling

Rarotonga's lagoon is wonderful for snorkelling, with lots of colourful coral and tropical fish. The lagoon is shallow all the way around, but the south side, from the Rarotongan Beach Resort to Muri Lagoon, has some great snorkelling.

The lagoon roughly in front of the Raina Beach Apartments, the Little Polynesian Motel and Moana Sands Hotel has the best snorkelling on the island. The water is deep here and there are many, many fish, protected by the two *ra'ui* (traditional bans on fishing for the purpose of conservation) that have been placed on this area. Other *ra'ui* areas are near the Rarotongan Beach Resort, Black Rock, opposite Parliament and at the northern end of Muri Lagoon.

Snorkelling gear can be rented from the following places for around NZ$10 per day.

Beside the Rarotonga Sailing Club is **Captain Tama's AquaSportz Centre** (☎ 27350; *Muri Beach*). Nearby, and a little cheaper, is the Beach Hut at the **Pacific Resort** (☎ 20427; *Muri Beach*).

On the South Coast, beside Fruits of Rarotonga, is **Tikioki Rentals** (☎ 21509). The lagoon here is probably *the* best snorkelling spot on Rarotonga. If the water's rough or the wind's cold, they close up the shop.

If you decide to purchase instead of rent, **Dive Shop Avarua** (☎ 24496; *Mana Court, Avarua*) is well stocked, with fins from NZ$39; masks and snorkels from NZ$35.

The lagoon boat tours (see later) include snorkelling on their trips. A few accommodation places have snorkelling gear available for their guests, so be sure to ask at the place you're staying before you spend money to hire it. All the diving operators (see Diving, earlier) will take snorkellers along on their diving trips outside the reef if there's room on the boat for around NZ$20, equipment included.

Reef to See (☎ 22212) does two three-hour trips every day (NZ$50), taking snorkellers outside the reef.

Avoid the temptation to feed the fish to improve your view. Breadcrumbs and such (sold at a couple of the snorkel-rental operations) are not part of a fish's normal diet, and bread-fed fish can become susceptible to bacterial diseases.

Deep-Sea Fishing

Deep-sea fishing is excellent right off the reef, and with the steep drop-off there's no long distance to travel out to the fishing grounds – within two minutes of leaving the dock you're already in deep water and you can start fishing. World-class catches include fish such as *ma'i ma'i* (or *mahi mahi*) and tuna (found in Rarotongan waters from October to May), wahoo and barracuda (April to October), sailfish and marlin (November to March).

Several boats are available to take you deep-sea fishing. Prices vary so it pays to compare; also ask if lunch is included. In particular, ask beforehand whether you can keep your fish (on some boats the fish are divided among the passengers, but on others the boat operators keep the fish to sell to restaurants, particularly fish over 7kg). This can be a cause of considerable tension if you haven't worked it out before you go fishing!

Most fishing trips are from 4½ to five hours. All of the following operators have full safety gear.

BECO's Fishing Charters (☎ 21525, 24125; NZ$100) 29ft catamaran. Fish usually stay with the boat.

Fisher's Fishing Tours (☎ 23356; NZ$70) 26ft Polynesian-style catamaran. Fish are shared.

Manutea Fishing Charters (☎ 22560; NZ$85) 20ft motorised cruiser. Fish are shared; whale-watching is available in season.

Mateu's Fishing Charter (☎ 21237; NZ$100) 26ft motorised cruiser. You keep the smaller fish.

Pacific Marine Charters (☎ 21237; NZ$100) 26ft motorised cruiser. You keep most of the fish.

Sea Hunter's Game Fishing Charters (☎ 25254; NZ$65 per person) 23ft cabin cruiser. You usually get to keep some smaller fish.

Seafari Charters (☎ 20328; NZ$100) 34ft motorised cruiser. You keep the smaller fish.

The **Cook Islands Game Fishing Club** (☎ 21419) – see Entertainment under Around the Island – is a popular hang-out for fishing folk; they can help you arrange fishing trips.

Surfing

On Rarotonga, surfing is for the experienced only – reef-break rides tend to be short, thrilling and, if you get it wrong, can end with a painful landing on the reef itself. Surfing is safest for a couple of hours either side of high tide. You'll see a scattering of surfers trying their luck (and savouring their solitude) on the waves at Avarua (right in front of the traffic circle), near Club Raro, at Avana Harbour, Matavera (near the Matavera School), Black Rock and near the airport.

Niki's Surf Shop (☎ 26240; w www.cook islandsurf.co.ck; Ara Tapu), east of Avarua, sells surfing supplies (mostly après-surf supplies) and distributes wisdom about Rarotonga's best surfing spots (also see the website).

It's unlikely you'll find surfboards for sale or rent on Rarotonga, so if you're determined to surf, bring your own – and check your travel-insurance policy, dude.

Other Sports

Muri Lagoon is the best place for a variety of other water sports, including windsurfing, sailing and kayaking, and of course it's also good for swimming. Sailing races are held every Saturday at 1pm from the Rarotonga Sailing Club on Muri Beach. Muri Beach is also the departure point for

glass-bottom boat tours (see Lagoon Boat Tours later).

Captain Tama's AquaSportz Centre (☎ 27350; Muri Beach) is beside the Rarotonga Sailing Club and has kayaks (singles/doubles NZ$7/12 per hour, NZ$15/20 for three hours), windsurfers (NZ$15 per hour) and reef runners (small motorised inflatable boats with see-through bottoms; NZ$35 per hour). They also give windsurfing lessons (NZ$35).

The **Pacific Resort** (☎ 20427; Muri Beach) hires kayaks (singles/doubles NZ$7/15 per hour) and windsurfers (NZ$20 per hour). Short windsurfing lessons are free.

On the south coast, beside Fruits of Rarotonga, is **Tikioki Rentals** (☎ 21509; Ara Tapu). Single kayaks cost NZ$7 per hour.

There are **tennis courts** and rental gear available at the **Edgewater Resort** (☎ 25435); many public tennis courts dotted around the island can be used for free if you have your own gear. The Edgewater also has **squash courts** to rent; or you could use the **Rarotongan Squash Club** (☎ 21056, 29180), near St Joseph's Catholic Cathedral in Avarua.

You can usually find a **volleyball** game on the beach at the Rarotongan Beach Resort or at Muri Beach. **Lawn bowling** is held at the **Rarotonga Bowling Club** (☎ 26277; Moss Rd) in Avarua most Saturdays. The greens are usually free on weekdays. There's a nine-hole **golf course** (☎ 20621) – see that section later – southwest of the airport.

Whale-Watching

Humpback whales visit the Cook Islands each year from July to October; you might be able to see them just outside the reef. The **Reef Sub** – see Lagoon Boat Tours later – and **Manutea Fishing Charters** (☎ 22560) offer whale-watching trips in season.

Check out the **Cook Islands Whale Education Centre** (☎ 21666; w www.whale research.org; Ara Metua, Atupa), west of Avarua, for more information about whales.

Horse Riding

Horse-riding tours are offered by **Aroa Pony Trek** (☎ 21415), just inland from Kaena Restaurant, near the Rarotongan Beach Resort. On morning and afternoon weekday rides you go along the beach, inland up to Wigmore's Waterfall for a swim, then back

RAROTONGA

Weddings

If the romantic sunsets (or the absence of thirsty cousins) put you in a matrimonial mood, there are a number of organisations on Rarotonga that can help you tie the knot. They will help organise any type of wedding you can think of. Ministers/celebrants, certificates, witnesses, music, photos, video, dancers, flowers and food can all be arranged. Here are a couple of companies that can help you:

Captain Tama's AquaSportz Centre
  (☎ 27350, fax 23810, e weddings@cook islands.co.ck) Muri Beach
Maire Nui Gardens & Café (☎ 22796)
  Titikaveka

Resorts and other top-end accommodation that arrange weddings for their guests include **Castaway Beach Villas**, **Club Raro**, **Crown Beach Resort**, **Edgewater Resort**, **Pacific Resort**, **Rarotongan Beach Resort** and **Takitumu Villas**. See Places to Stay for contact details.
  Try **Island Photo** (☎ 27023) for photographic evidence to prove you did it and **Cook Island VIP Services** (☎ 27303) if you want to turn up in a Rolls Royce (although a scooter would be so much more 'Cook Islands'!).

again. Rides (adults/children NZ$30/15) take 2½ hours and bookings are essential.

Lagoon Boat Tours

There are two options for glass-bottom boat tours and snorkelling on Muri Lagoon, anothe for nonglass-bottom tours, and, for those wanting to go beyond the lagoon, a semi-submersible sub that goes out past the reef. The first three cruise out to some fine snorkelling spots (snorkelling gear is provided) and then to Koromiri Island in Muri Lagoon for a meal. The tours last from 11am to about 3pm and go every day except Sunday. Bookings are essential.
  The **Pacific Resort** (☎ 20427; Muri Beach) operates glass-bottom boat cruises (with/ without lunch NZ$37/20), including snorkelling, fish feeding and the option of a truly delicious lunch. Kids cost NZ$18/12. **Captain Tama's AquaSportz Centre** (☎ 27350; Muri Beach) also does glass-bottom boat tours (NZ$60), including a stop at a small pearl farm in the lagoon, followed by an

umukai (earth-oven meal) on Koromiri, and entertainment. Hotel transfers are available.
Tarina Lagoon Tours (☎ 20067) has a small catamaran, and tours include snorkelling and fishing, followed by a barbecue on Koromiri (NZ$49).
  Another option is the **Reef Sub** (☎ 25837), a semi-submersible viewing vessel that goes beyond the reef, enabling you to see coral formations, shipwrecks, fish, turtles and whatever else that might be outside the reef. Sometimes sharks can be seen. One-and-a-half to two-hour cruises depart twice a day (10am and 2pm) every day from Avatiu Harbour (NZ$35). Whale-watching trips are available in season.

Sailing Trips & Boat Cruises

There are a couple of options for sailing trips – either do-it-yourself trips on small yachts or old-fashioned cruises.
  The **Rarotonga Sailing Club** (☎ 27349; Muri Beach) has small yachts for NZ$30 per hour, NZ$50 for two hours. The 64ft topsail schooner Silent Lady (☎ 23104) departs from Avana Harbour, Ngatangi'ia at 10am on Mondays, Wednesdays and Fridays. Two-hour cruises cost NZ$55 and include refreshments.
  Hotel California (☎ 23577) is a huge trimaran that does deep-sea cruises out of Rarotonga, and Akura (☎ 54355) does day trips.

Scenic Flights

Scenic flights are great for working out exactly where those mountain trails go and where the good diving spots are. The national airline **Air Rarotonga** (☎ 22888; w www.airraro.com) offers 20-minute flights (adults/children NZ$65/35), with a minimum of two passengers and a maximum of three. Flights take place from 8.30am to 3.30pm daily and bookings can usually be made on the day of the flight.

Organised Tours

You must do a circle-island tour sometime during your stay on Rarotonga. Several interesting and informative tours are available, and they provide insight into many aspects of Rarotongan history and culture, both ancient and modern, that you'll never learn riding around on your own.
  The **Cook Islands Cultural Village** (☎ 21314; e viltours@oyster.net.ck; Ara Metua)

operates a three-hour circle-island tour (NZ$55) that starts off with an island-style lunch and a show of legends, song and dance. Tours take place on Monday, Wednesday and Friday. You can combine the circle-island tour with a tour of the village itself; see the Cultural Village entry later for details.

Areiti Taxis & Tours (☎ 23012, 55752; *Muri Beach*) does three-hour tours daily (NZ$50), following the Ara Metua (back road) and stopping at historical spots, plantations and other places of interest.

The **Mountain Bike Association** (☎ 22627) has guided mountain-bike tours that leave from near the Punanga Nui Market in Avarua. Three-hour tours (NZ$30) take place Monday, Tuesday, Wednesday and Sunday. The five-hour tour (NZ$50) is on Sunday.

Papa Ken (☎ 23752) runs travellers around the island, spinning tales that combine ancient legends with modern anecdotes. Three-hour tours cost NZ$25.

Raro Mountain Safari Tours (☎ 23629; w *www.rarosafaritours.co.ck*) is opposite Punanga Nui Market. It runs three-hour 4WD Jeep expeditions daily (adults/children NZ$60/30), which get right off the beaten track, going on the back roads, through inland valleys and up the mountains for good views.

Appealing to the petrol-head in all of us, **Raro 4x4 Adventures** (☎ 22200, 55584; *Ara Tapu, Vaima'anga*) runs tours in which you can ride a four-wheel quad bike through local plantations and bush. Instructions are given first. Tours run from Monday to Saturday and cost NZ$50.

In their comfortable buses, **Raro Tours** (☎ 25325; e *coaches@rarotours.co.ck; Rarotonga international airport*) offers a daily 3½-hour circle-island historical tour, arts and crafts tour, Saturday market/circle-island tour and Sunday church/circle-island tour. Tours cost between NZ$25 and NZ$45.

See also Organised Walks under Hiking earlier in this chapter for information about Pa Mountain Trekking, Bill's Mountain Treks and walks in the Takitumu Conservation Area.

Cook Islands Tours & Travel (☎ 28270; w *www.cookislandstours.co.ck; Rarotonga international airport*) offers personalised island orientation tours for two to six passengers. The tours are available anytime,

at your own convenience. A three-hour tour costs NZ$45 per person.

Getting There & Away

See the Getting There & Away chapter earlier for information on getting to Rarotonga from overseas, and the Getting Around chapter for interisland transport within the Cooks.

Getting Around

To/From the Airport Most hotels, motels and hostels send vans to the airport to meet international flights. If you've booked your accommodation, you'll probably be met by a van from your hotel (usually pickup from the airport is free – being dropped off at the airport costs around NZ$10).

If your accommodation doesn't include transport, you can use **Raro Tours** (☎ 25325), which meets all international flights and charges NZ$18 one-way to anywhere on the island. Or you can phone a taxi (see later in this section).

The last option, available during the day (ie, not for most international arrivals, which almost all turn up in the middle of the night) is the (anticlockwise) Cooks Passenger Transport bus (see Bus later). Note that the clockwise bus goes along the Ara Metua and doesn't pass the airport terminal building.

Many accommodation places won't pick up from domestic flights, so you're limited to Raro Tours, taxis or the bus.

Bus Operating a round-the-island bus service that runs along Ara Tapu is **Cook's Passenger Transport** (☎ 25512, *after hours* ☎ 20349). The bus is a good way of getting around, and an easy way to do a complete round-the-island circle to get an initial feel for the place. The complete trip takes 50 minutes.

The bus departs from the bus stop at Cook's Corner in Avarua. Daytime buses going clockwise around the island depart every hour on the hour from 7am to 4pm Monday to Saturday, and from 8am to midday and 2pm to 4pm Sunday. Buses going anticlockwise depart at 25 minutes past every hour, 8.25am to 4.25pm on weekdays and 8.25am to 12.25pm Saturday. There's no anticlockwise bus on Sunday.

The service runs pretty much on time so you can work out relevant arrival times around the island, or you can flag down the bus anywhere along its route. If buses get too full (which often happens on rainy days or when school is let out) an extra bus will run.

The same buses operate at night, but on a more limited schedule. Most go around the island in a clockwise direction. Departure times from Cook's Corner are at 6pm, 7pm, 9pm and 10pm Monday to Saturday, with additional late-night buses departing at midnight on Friday and 1.30am and 11pm Saturday.

The bus fare is NZ$2.50 for one ride, NZ$4 for a return trip (two rides) or NZ$17 for a 10-ride ticket. There's also a NZ$9 all-day bus pass (the family pass, for two adults and two kids, is NZ$16).

Bus timetables are printed in the *What's On* tourist booklet, *Raro Magic* magazine and *Cook Islands Sun*, all available free from the tourist office. The bus drivers also have timetables. Or ring Cook's Passenger Transport for information.

Car & Motorcycle Before you can rent a car or motorbike you must obtain a local driving licence from the police station in Avarua. It's a straightforward operation taking only a few minutes and costing NZ$10. Even an international driving permit is not good enough for the Cooks, and if your home licence does not include motorbikes you'll have to pay another NZ$5 and take a (fairly easy) practical driving test to get a Cook Islands motorbike licence. You can get your licence any day from 8am to 3pm. You must present your home driving licence or passport as identification.

You don't need to hire anything very big on Rarotonga – the farthest place you can possibly drive to is half an hour away and even on a 70cc motorbike you can reach the open-road speed limit (40km/h) in a few seconds.

Small motorbikes are the principal mode of transport on Rarotonga and there are lots of motorbikes to hire, mostly 70cc to 100cc models. All of the car-rental agencies rent motorbikes; ring around to find the best deal or just walk up the main road in Avarua and pop in to ask. The lowest rates are about NZ$20/90 per day/week (most places offer discounts for weekly rentals). Many hotels also rent motorbikes. Budget is the only company with safe-looking helmets.

Rates are around NZ$50/65 per day for a small/medium car and NZ$70 per day for a jeep, with discounts for three- to five-day rentals and even further discounts for rentals of a week or more. Baby capsules can be rented at Budget for NZ$5/25 per day/week, and child seats are available at Avis and Budget for NZ$5 per day.

It's worth phoning around to check the prices; many companies will have special deals going. Check if insurance and the 12.5% value-added tax (VAT) are included in the stated cost.

Avis Rental Cars
Avarua: (☎ 22833, fax 21702, **w** www.avis .co.ck) Bicycles, motorbikes and cars are available
Airport: (☎ 21039)
BT Rentals (☎ 23586) 'Arorangi. You can rent bicycles, motorbikes and cars here.
Budget Rent-a-car
Main office, Avarua: (☎ 20895, after hours ☎ 20895, 55019, fax 20888, **w** www.budget .co.ck) Motorbike helmets, motorbikes and cars are available
Downtown office, Avarua: (☎ 26895)
Airport: (☎ 21039) Open for international-flight arrivals/departures only
Edgewater Resort: (☎ 21026)
Rarotongan Hotel: (☎ 20838)
Island Car & Bike Hire
'Arorangi: (☎ 22632, 55278, **w** www.island carhire.co.ck) Ara Tapu. Motorbikes and cars are available.
Avarua: Ara Maire Nui, opposite the Punanga Nui Market
Niki's Surf Shop (☎ 26240) Ara Tapu, east of Avarua. Cars can be rented here.
Rarotonga Rentals
Airport: (☎ 22326, after hours ☎ 20126, 55204, fax 27236, **w** www.rarotongarentals.co.ck) Motorbikes, cars and 'fun' vehicles such as scootcars are available
Avarua: (☎ 22326)
Tara's Rental Bikes (☎ 20757) Muri Beach. You can rent motorbikes here.
Tipani Rentals (☎ 22382) 'Arorangi, opposite Edgewater Resort. Motorbikes are available.
TPA Rental Cars (☎ 20611, 20610) 'Arorangi. Cars can be rented here.
Vaine's Rental Bikes (☎ 20331) Muri Beach, near Vara's Beach House. Bicycles are available here.

There are few surprises for drivers on Rarotonga. The driving is reasonably sane (except late on Friday and Saturday – the two nights when there's heavy drinking) and there's no reason to go fast, as there's

Who Let the Dogs Out?

Forget gravel roads and fellow drivers. The road hazard that brings the most motorbike riders to grief on Rarotonga is dogs. The island has thousands of dogs and, particularly on quieter roads, they have a nasty habit of running out onto the road just when you're at full throttle around a difficult gravel corner. As well as toppling motorcyclists, Rarotonga's canines spend each night competing with the cockerels to disturb your slumber.

One of the first things you notice about Rarotonga's dogs (apart from their lack of traffic sense or singing ability) is their shape: you've never seen so many chubby, short-legged, stumpy dogs in your life! And they're all sorts of breeds too – Alsatians, Labradors, Border collies…they all have that same round body and those same stumpy little legs, often with the paws turned outwards. Perhaps a couple of dachshunds (a breed that carries a form of hereditary dwarfism) were introduced during some kind of genetic bottleneck in the island's canine past? No-one seems to know.

The number of dogs on the island worries many Rarotongans too, and two organisations, in particular, are trying to do something about it. The **Esther Honey Foundation** (EHF; ☎ 22336; e ehclinic@oyster.net.ck; Kavera) neuters dogs for free, and over time this has reduced the canine population considerably. The **Cook Islands SPCA** (☎ 25003; Ara Maire Nui, Avarua) operates a system of free registration, as long as the animal gets neutered.

However, dog registration and neutering are not enough to satisfy Rarotongans sick of swerving around stumpy pooches on the road and throwing boots at them during the night. Here the SPCA and EHF differ – the SPCA wants to put down unwanted dogs, while the EHF would rather just neuter them.

If, like many visitors, you are worried by the dog situation, there are a few ways you can help.

- Report ownerless/nuisance dogs to the SPCA or EHF (but be aware the dogs might be destroyed)
- If you have a car, take a few mutts to the EHF in Kavera to be neutered
- Contribute money to the SPCA and/or EHF
- Adopt a mutt and take it home (talk to the SPCA and EHF for advice)

It's rare for the Rarotongan canine army to hassle pedestrians – it seems to be motorbikes that get it riled. But if you are caught on foot, there's one good thing about their stumpy legs: they can't run very fast!

not far to go wherever you're going. The speed limit is 30km/h (19mph) in town, 40km/h (25mph) out of town. Drive on the left-hand side of the road.

There are two important rental-car rules: don't leave the car windows open, not because of the risk of theft, but because of the chances of an unexpected tropical downpour leaving the car awash; and don't park under coconut palms, because a falling coconut can positively flatten a tiny Japanese car.

Taxi You can phone for a taxi any time between 6am and 10pm. Rates (which are government controlled) are NZ$2.50 per kilometre, so it will cost around NZ$40 to go from Muri to the airport. Taxi operators include:

Areiti Taxis & Tours (☎ 23012, 55752) Muri Beach. 24-hour service.
BK Taxis (☎ 20019) Avarua
JP Taxis (☎ 26572, 55147) 'Arorangi. 24-hour service.
Lazaro Tekii (☎ 20529) 'Arorangi
MLT Taxis (☎ 21397) 'Arorangi
Muri Beach Taxis (☎ 21625) Muri Beach
Ngatangiia Taxis (☎ 22238) Ngatangi'ia
Parekura Taxis (☎ 26490) Avarua
Pokoinu Cab (☎ 20529) Pokoinu

Bicycle Mountain bikes are readily available for hire on Rarotonga and generally cost around NZ$5 to NZ$10 a day, with discounts for weekly rentals. The island is compact enough, and the traffic is light and slow enough to make riding a pleasure, particularly on the inland roads. (But watch out for stray dogs!)

The **Internet Cafe** (☎ 27242) at Muri Beach and **Tikioki Rentals** (☎ 21509) at Titikaveka rent bicycles. Also see the Car & Motorcycle section earlier for companies that rent both vehicles and bicycles.

The **Mountain Bike Association** (☎ 22627) do guided mountain-bike tours (see Organised Tours earlier).

Avarua

Avarua, the capital of the Cook Islands and Rarotonga's principal town, lies in the middle of the north coast, about 2km east of the airport. Until about 10 years ago it was just a sleepy little port – very much the image of a south-seas trading centre. The town had a face-lift to spruce it up for the international Maire Nui festival in October 1992. It's now more attractive and has more businesses, but its relaxed, friendly ambience still remains.

Avarua doesn't demand a lot of your time but it does have all the basic services (post office, banks, supermarket, shops and restaurants) and some interesting places to visit. If you're looking for nightlife, Avarua is probably where you'll find it.

ORIENTATION

Finding your way around Avarua is no problem; there's only one main road, the Ara Maire Nui (which turns into the island-circling Ara Tapu at both ends of town). The Ara Maire Nui, usually referred to as either Marine Drive or 'the main road', runs right along the waterfront; a grassy strip down the middle offers plenty of shady trees.

A landmark you can use to orient yourself is the traffic circle, on the main road near the Takuva'ine Stream and the Avarua Harbour entrance.

Standing at the traffic circle, to your east you'll see a group of seven tall coconut trees arranged in a circle – this is the 'Seven-in-One Coconut Tree'. Look inland and you'll see the post office on the right side of the road; the Philatelic Bureau and the New Zealand High Commission are in the two-storey building next door. Heading inland down this road past the post office brings you to Papeiha's Stone and then the road heading up the Takuva'ine Valley.

The commercial centre of town is just west of the traffic circle. The Banana Court

Bar (which you can see from the traffic circle), with the Blue Note Cafe on the veranda, is a Rarotongan landmark. Just west of the Banana Court is the Tourist Authority visitor information office. The large CITC Shopping Centre is on the corner, there's a petrol station on the opposite corner, and just a few doors inland from there is Cook's Corner Arcade, where there's a bus stop. Keep heading inland down this road to reach the Telecom office.

West on the main road are banks, shops, cafés, a supermarket and police station. A couple of long blocks down, on the seaward side of the road, is the Punanga Nui open-air market, with fruit and vegetable stalls, arts and crafts, and takeaway-food caravans. Just past this is Avatiu Harbour, where the interisland passenger freighter ships are based. The airport is 1km or so further west.

INFORMATION

For details about things such as banks, post and communications, and medical services in Avarua, see the Information section at the beginning of this chapter.

SEVEN-IN-ONE COCONUT TREE

Just to the east of the traffic circle is a group of seven tall coconut trees growing in a perfect circle. The circle of trees marks an important boundary between two *ariki*.

Tradition has it that the seven trunks are really all one tree! Supposedly in the distant past an amazing coconut with seven sprouts was found on the island of Takutea, near 'Atiu, and brought here to be planted.

PAPEIHA'S STONE

A block further inland, the stone upon which Papeiha stood on 26 July 1823 and preached the gospel on Rarotonga for the first time sits atop a raised traffic circle. The occasion is remembered with an annual holiday, Gospel Day, when Papeiha's walk from Avatiu Harbour to this spot is re-enacted, and a sermon is again preached from Papeiha's Stone.

PARA O TANE PALACE

About 200m east of the traffic circle on the inland side of the main road is Para O Tane Palace (not open to the public). It is the traditional residence of the most senior *ariki* in the Avarua area, Makea Nui Teremoana Ariki.

This whole area where the church and palace were built is called Taputapuatea. Named after a marae in the Society Islands, Taputapuatea was once the largest, most sacred marae on Rarotonga. When Christian missionaries wanted to take over and replace the old religion, they destroyed the marae; today nothing remains of it.

BEACHCOMBER GALLERY

One long block east of the traffic circle on the sea side of the main road, facing the CICC, the Beachcomber Gallery (☎ 21939) occupies a building constructed in 1845 by the LMS for its Sunday school. The building, which had been worn down to a ruin, was restored in 1992 and converted into a gallery for Cook Islands arts, crafts, jewellery, pearls and other items of interest. You can visit the workshop in the back to see how the black-pearl jewellery and shell carvings are made.

Avarua also has several other galleries; see Shopping later.

CICC

The CICC (Makea Tinirau Rd) is a fine, old, white coral building, much in the same mould as other CICCs in the Cooks. It was built in 1853, when Aaron Buzacott was the resident missionary. The interesting graveyard around the church is worth a leisurely browse. At the front you'll find a monument to the pioneering Polynesian missionary, Papeiha. Just to the left (as you face the church) is the grave of Albert Henry, the first prime minister of the independent Cook Islands. You can't miss it – it's the one with a life-size bust of the man himself. Other well-known people buried here include author Robert Dean Frisbie.

You're welcome to attend services; the main service of the week, as at all of Rarotonga's CICCs, is Sunday from 10am to 11.30am. See the Religion section in the Facts about the Cook Islands chapter for advice about attending a CICC.

LIBRARY & MUSEUM SOCIETY

Inland behind the Para O Tane Palace is the small Cook Islands Library & Museum Society (☎ 26468; Makea Tinirau Rd; open 9am-1pm Mon-Sat, 4pm-8pm Tues), which has friendly staff and a good collection of Pacific and general-interest books. Visitors are able to borrow books: a library card costs NZ$15, plus a NZ$10 deposit (refunded when you leave Rarotonga). The library also houses a collection of rare books and literature on the Pacific. If you ask, you might be able to inspect and read the collection, but only on the premises.

The small museum (admission NZ$2) has an interesting collection of ancient and modern artefacts – basketry, weaving, musical instruments, wooden statues of various gods, adzes, shells and shell fishhooks, spears, tools and a beautiful old outrigger canoe.

If you're going to 'Atiu, check out the large tumunu (hollow coconut-tree stump) pots here in the museum. You can read more about tumunu ceremonies in the boxed text 'Tumunu – Bush-Beer Drinking Sessions' in the 'Atiu, Ma'uke & Mitiaro chapter, and attend a tumunu if you visit 'Atiu. (Actually, most tumunu on 'Atiu use a plastic bucket these days – not as aesthetically pleasing but less prone to leakage).

And no, the large iron pot on the veranda wasn't used in cannibal rites – it's an old whaling pot, used for boiling down blubber to make whale oil. When people were eaten in the Cooks, they were baked in ovens.

UNIVERSITY OF THE SOUTH PACIFIC (USP)

The USP, based in Suva, Fiji, has a **Cook Islands Centre** (☎ 29415; Makea Tinirau Rd) in the building opposite the Library & Museum Society. Most classes are taught externally from the main campus. A wide selection of books on the Cook Islands and other parts of the Pacific, published by the university, are on sale in the office. If you're planning a lengthy stay in the Cooks, you can ask here about classes for learning the Cook Islands Maori language (NZ$60 for 20 hours of instruction).

NATIONAL CULTURE CENTRE

One block inland from the Paradise Inn is the large Sir Geoffrey Henry National Culture Centre (W www.culture.gov.ck). Conceived by Prime Minister Sir Geoffrey Henry, the complex was formally opened on 14 October 1992. The centre is home to the National Auditorium, the National Museum, the National Library, the Conservatory &

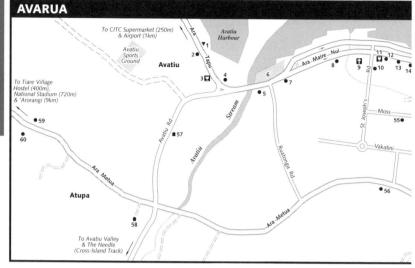

National Archives and the Ministry of Cultural Development.

The **National Auditorium** is the venue for large-scale concerts and other events. The **National Museum** (☎ 20725; admission free, donations appreciated) has a well-presented selection of Cook Islands and South Pacific artefacts, including a traditional *vaka* (canoe) from Pukapuka, Mangaian *toki* (adzes) and photos of some Maori artefacts that the British Museum kindly looks after on behalf of the Cook Islands.

Visitors to the **National Library** (☎ 20725) can get borrowing privileges by paying a NZ$10 refundable bond plus a NZ$20 fee. There's a good Pacific collection here, including such valuable reference books as Lonely Planet's *South Pacific*.

WRECK OF THE *MAITAI*

West of the traffic circle and directly offshore from the centre of Avarua is the wreck of the SS *Maitai*, a 3393-ton Union Steam Ship vessel that used to trade between the Cook Islands and Tahiti. She ran onto the reef, fortunately without loss of life, on 24 December 1916. Her cargo included a number of Model T Fords. All that remains today is her rusted boiler, just off the edge of the fringing reef. In the 1950s a couple of enterprising New Zealanders brought up one of the ship's bronze propellers.

PUNANGA NUI MARKET

On the main road and beside the waterfront near Avatiu Harbour, Punanga Nui (☎ 29370) is an outdoor market. The fruit and vegies here are among the best you'll find in Avarua, and early Saturday morning (very early!) you can often buy whole fresh fish. There are also some takeaway-food caravans, and stalls selling *pareu* (sarongs), clothing and handicrafts.

Wednesday is 'arts and crafts day', when you'll sometimes see craft demonstrations. Friday is 'feast night', with various meals available and live entertainment. The biggest market day is Saturday (morning), when everyone brings their fresh produce to sell.

RAROTONGAN BREWERY

The Cook Islands' national beer, Cooks Lager, is brewed at the Rarotongan Brewery (☎ 21007), behind Bond's Liquor Store opposite the Punanga Nui Market. You can do a free tour of the brewery at 2pm Monday to Friday. If you're inspired to buy a T-shirt to commemorate the tour, walk across the road to the market where they cost NZ$12 instead of NZ$18 (that's a saving of three glasses of Cooks Lager).

AVATIU HARBOUR

This small harbour at the western end of Avarua is Rarotonga's principal harbour. An

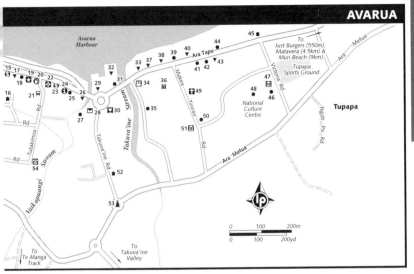

RAROTONGA

AVARUA

PLACES TO STAY
16 May's Downtown Guesthouse
45 Paradise Inn
52 Central Motel
57 Sharn's Guesthouse
58 Atupa Orchid Units

PLACES TO EAT
1 Palace Takeaways
17 Mama's Cafe; Foodland Supermarket
26 Banana Court; Blue Note Cafe; Arasena Gallery; Banana Court Bar; Island Hopper Vacations; Bergman & Sons Crafts Store
29 Paulina's Polynesian Restaurant; T's Tatts
32 Trader Jack's
33 Browne's Arcade; Waterfront Café; Pacific Supplies; Pacific Computers
37 The Café; TJ's Nightclub
38 Staircase Restaurant & Bar; Tuki's Pareu
40 Japanese Sushi Restaurant
43 Portofino

OTHER
2 Snowbird Laundromat
3 Coconut Bar
4 Ports Authority; Harbourmaster
5 Rarotonga Rentals

6 Punanga Nui Market
7 Island Car & Bike Hire; Rarotongan Brewery; Bond's Liquor Store; Raro Mountain Safari Tours
8 Kenwall Gallery
9 St Joseph's Catholic Cathedral; Rarotongan Squash Club
10 Budget Rent-a-car main office
11 Ronnie's Bar & Grill
12 Jetsave Travel; Vonnia's Store
13 Mana Court; Dive Shop Avarua; Optometrist; Treasure Chest; Maui Pearls
14 Island Craft
15 Westpac Bank
18 Budget Rent-a-car downtown office
19 Police Station
20 Petrol Station; SPCA
21 Cook's Corner Arcade; Cook's Corner Cafe; Mae Jo's Takeaways; Hideaway Bar; Turtle's; Bergman & Sons Pearl Store; Bus Stop
22 CITC Shopping Centre; CITC Pharmacy; Cocophoto; SS Maitai; Telepost; Avis Rental Cars
23 ANZ Bank
24 Cook Islands Tourist Authority
25 Pearl Factory; Honorary German Consul

27 Ministry of Foreign Affairs & Immigration
28 Post Office; Bounty Bookshop; Philatelic Bureau; New Zealand High Commission
30 The Rock; Seven-in-One Coconut Tree
31 Ministry of Marine Resources
34 Empire Theatre; Raro Records
35 Cook Islands Environment Services
36 Para O Tane Palace
39 Beachcomber Gallery
41 Perfumes of Rarotonga
42 Rarotonga Realty
44 Takitumu Conservation Area Office; Shekinah Homes
46 National Library
47 National Museum
48 National Auditorium
49 Avarua CICC
50 University of the South Pacific (USP)
51 Cook Islands Library & Museum Society
53 Papeiha Stone
54 Telecom
55 Rarotonga Bowling Club
56 The Perfume Factory; Marama Lounge
59 Michael Tavioni's Studio
60 Cook Islands Whale Education Centre

international freighter or two, one or two interisland passenger freighters, a collection of fishing boats and yachts, and the occasional visiting ship are all often seen here.

PLACES TO STAY

May's Downtown Guesthouse (*☎ 21877, fax 23088; e mayshome@oyster.net.ck; rooms per person NZ$20*) is right in the middle of downtown Avarua, on a hard-to-find back street. The delightful May Kavana's house has four rooms for travellers. It's the same cost whether you stay in a share, twin or double room. The guesthouse isn't signposted, but all the neighbours know where May lives, so just ask someone.

Paradise Inn (*☎ 20544, fax 22544; e paradise@oyster.net.ck; PO Box 674; budget singles NZ$57, split-level singles/doubles/ triples NZ$77/96/112, family units NZ$123*) is a short walk east of the centre of town on the main road. The beach is rocky and shallow here – no good for swimming – but the amenities are great, with a large lounge area, informal bar and a barbecue area on the seafront patio. Most of the units are townhouse-style and spacious, with a double bed in the ample sleeping loft and sitting room, kitchen and bath areas downstairs. The family unit sleeps four. Paradise Inn doesn't accept children under 12 years.

Atupa Orchid Units (*☎ 28543, fax 28546; w www.atupaorchids.co.ck; singles NZ$35, bungalow doubles/triples/quads NZ$65/75/ 90, share rate NZ$22*) is about 500m inland from Avatiu Harbour. These units are quiet and peaceful, yet close to town. They are run by the ebullient Ingrid Caffery. The six bungalows have one, two or three bedrooms, a well-equipped kitchen, sitting room, bathroom (hot shower) and veranda.

Lovely Planet (*☎/fax 25100; Ara Tapu; rooms per person from NZ$20*) is only a short walk from town. Lovely Planet (no relation) has several rooms, with insect screens, and a large common/kitchen area. There is free laundry use and luggage storage.

Central Motel (*☎ 25735, fax 25740; e stopover@centralmotel.co.ck; Takuva'ine Rd; units per person NZ$65*), half a block inland from the post office, has 14 spotless units, three of which can be interconnected. It's a favourite of visiting businesspeople,

with IDD telephones, minibars, secretarial/ fax/Internet services and a large outdoor spa pool for those business negotiations.

Sharn's Guesthouse (*☎ 23370; Takuva'ine Rd; singles/doubles NZ$15/26*), three doors down from the small shop on this road, is a bright-yellow, family-oriented guesthouse and a delightful place to stay. Each room has a double bed (luxury!), and facilities include a kitchen and hot showers.

PLACES TO EAT
Restaurants

There is a fantastic selection of restaurants in Avarua.

Blue Note Cafe (*☎ 23236; breakfast NZ$8-17, all-day menu NZ$10-13, dinner mains NZ$13-23*), on the veranda of the Banana Court building, near the traffic circle, is a fine place to catch the breeze, have a coffee, lunch or a snack and watch the world go by.

Trader Jack's (*☎ 26464; entrees from NZ$8, mains NZ$11-26, snacks from NZ$10*) sits on the waterfront near the traffic circle. 'Traders', as it's known to its friends, is one of Rarotonga's most popular bar-and-grill restaurants. The indoor tables, as well as those on the outside deck, all have great sea views (in fact the deck tables are mere metres from the waves at high tide). The bar here (see Entertainment) is popular with Rarotonga's more genteel crowd.

Waterfront Café (*☎ 20260; mains NZ$13-15*), a quiet open-air café/bar a couple of doors east of Trader Jack's, hidden away in Browne's Arcade, is a nice retreat from the hustle and bustle of busy Avarua. Dinner is served from 6pm. Try the Waterfront pizza.

Longline Bar & Grill (*☎ 26079; Ara Tapu; breakfast NZ$7-11, lunch NZ$7-17*) is in the CITC Supermarket car park. Pleasant and breezy and with a unique view (of parked cars), this is a good spot for lunch after a hard shopping session.

Staircase Restaurant & Bar (*☎ 22254; Ara Tapu; dinner NZ$12-15*) is upstairs behind the Topshape Health & Fitness Centre. It has reasonable-quality food at low prices, a dinner special that changes every night, plus à-la-carte options. There's live music nightly and an island-night show on Thursday (with/without dinner NZ$20/5). Dinner reservations are preferred.

Ronnie's Bar & Grill (☎ 20823; Ara Maire Nui; mains NZ$13-19, snacks from NZ$9.50), on the airport side of Avarua, is a pleasant restaurant/bar serving tasty, reasonably priced meals, and bar snacks all day. On Thursday and Friday nights the bar at Ronnie's can get pretty crowded.

Paulina's Polynesian Restaurant (☎ 28889; burgers NZ$5-7, dinner dishes NZ$7-15), in an open-walled building near the traffic circle, serves good, cheap Polynesian and European meals. Brightly coloured and festooned with plants and flowers, Paulina's always has a festive feel and is popular with locals and travellers alike.

SS Maitai (☎ 22215; mains NZ$11-15, pizza NZ$9-39, ice cream from NZ$2.50), in the CITC Shopping Centre, is named after the rusting shipwreck in the sea off Avarua. It serves a variety of snacks and meals, including excellent wood-fired pizzas.

Marama Lounge (☎ 29993; Ara Metua; meals NZ$10-15), beside the Perfume Factory, is a popular backpackers bar a couple of nights a week and does a variety of meals. Friday's seven-course lunch is good value at NZ$20. Sunday's roast is designed to appeal to homesick Poms – complete with overcooked vegetables and Yorkshire puddin'. Hotel transfers are NZ$1.50 each way.

Japanese Sushi Restaurant (☎ 25045; Ara Tapu; meals NZ$15-23) serves magnificent Japanese dishes. Nevertheless, this little restaurant is usually almost deserted. If you can't decide what to try, the sushi/sashimi set platters (NZ$23/20) won't disappoint.

Portofino (☎ 26480; Ara Tapu; pasta NZ$16-20, pizza NZ$12-25, mains NZ$27-35) specialises in Italian dishes.

Cafés & Fast Food

As well as the following cafés, many of the restaurants in Avarua (see earlier) also serve snacks during the day.

Mama's Cafe (☎ 23379; Ara Maire Nui; hot breakfasts from NZ$5.50), beside the Foodland supermarket in central Avarua, is a popular café with inexpensive meals and snacks, plus an ice-cream counter.

The Café (☎ 21283; Ara Tapu; breakfast NZ$7-11, lunch NZ$9-11), across the road from Para O Tane Palace, has some tasty meals and the *best* coffee (roasted on the premises) in the Cook Islands. Ground coffee is available for NZ$4 per 100g.

Portofino (☎ 26480; Ara Tapu; pizzas from NZ$12, burgers NZ$5.50, pasta NZ$11-14) delivers all over Rarotonga (free for orders over NZ$40, otherwise NZ$3) or you can pick up.

Cook's Corner Cafe (☎ 22345; Tutakimoa Rd; snacks from NZ$3, mains NZ$10-18), a popular hangout even when you're not hungry, is just a few metres from where the bus stops at Cook's Corner. It does desserts and milkshakes – just the thing for a cool refuge on a hot day.

Mae Jo's Takeaways (☎ 26621; Cook's Corner Arcade; burgers NZ$5, meals NZ$12-$29) is most popular late at night when the nearby Hideaway Bar is open. This place serves burgers and other takeaway fare. There are some tables here in case you want to eat in.

Punanga Nui Market (see that section earlier) has a couple of stalls selling basic takeaway, with picnic tables where you can relax and eat. One of the most popular is **Moana Takeaway** (☎ 22536), which has Chinese food as well as burgers and fish and chips.

Palace Takeaways (☎ 21438; Avatiu Harbour; burgers NZ$4-8, meals NZ$10-13) is a popular takeaway joint with a few picnic tables out front. Try the legendary Palace Burger.

Before eating at some of Avarua's less-salubrious takeaway venues (not listed here), check that your travel-insurance policy covers food poisoning.

Markets & Supermarkets

Avarua's two large supermarkets have a good selection of food. Wherever you're staying on Rarotonga, if you have a lot of food shopping to do, it can be worth taking a trip into Avarua to do it. Packaged and imported food is cheaper (and a little less likely to be past its use-by date) here in town than at the tiny local grocery shops dotted around the island.

Foodland Supermarket (Ara Maire Nui) has produce that is less likely to be past its use-by date than anywhere else on the island. **CITC Supermarket** (Ara Tapu), halfway to the airport, shares the grounds with Café Kotuku and the CITC Liquor Store.

See the **Punanga Nui Market** section earlier for information on shopping for fresh produce and fish.

RAROTONGA

ENTERTAINMENT
Island Nights

See the boxed text 'Island Nights' under Entertainment in the Around the Island section to see where you can experience a cultural food-and-dance island night.

Bars & Clubs

There's a good selection of places to go out in Avarua, especially on Friday night – the big party night. Once you get into town you can easily walk from one to another. They tend to attract different crowds – one place might attract young backpackers and locals, another an older and more upmarket crowd. Popularity of watering holes changes rapidly; the place that 'everybody' was going to last year may be eclipsed by some new place this year.

Though Friday night is the big partying night, most of the places mentioned also have entertainment on Saturday nights; a couple have music every night. Typically, all these places stay open until around midnight most nights, and later on Friday nights (until around 2am). On Saturday night they have to shut bang on midnight (so as not to be revelling on the Sabbath).

There are a couple of 'organised' Friday-night pub crawls, put on by the **Rarotongan Beach Resort** (☎ 25800; with/without dinner NZ$45/25) as well as the **Edgewater Resort** (☎ 25435; NZ$45/25). Some hostels, **Aremango Guesthouse** (☎ 24362) and **Backpackers International** (☎ 21847) among them, run less-organised Friday-night tours. **Mama Josie** (☎ 27242) is another option.

Trader Jack's (☎ 26464), on the waterfront near the traffic circle, is very popular with Rarotonga's upmarket set – both tourists and locals (at NZ$5 a can, you won't find the peasants drinking here). There's live music in the bar every night.

The Rock (☎ 27625; Ara Tapu), east of the traffic island, was *the* social spot at the time of writing.

Staircase Restaurant & Bar (☎ 22254; Ara Tapu), upstairs in the rear of the Topshape Health & Fitness Centre building, has live music Tuesday to Friday night. Friday and Saturday here are pumping – with the DJs catering for the diverse crowd by alternating fairly recent techno (for the backpackers and younger locals) and 1970s hits and reggae (for the oldies). A sign at the door requests

an 'excellent' standard of dress, but it allows in scruffy travel writers who haven't washed for a week – so it's not very fussy!

Hideaway Bar (☎ 22224; Cook's Corner Arcade; beers from NZ$2.50, spirits from NZ$3.50) is a small, intimate bar in the centre of Avarua. There are good live bands on Friday and Saturday nights and DJs on Wednesday and Thursday. The Hideaway can get pretty raucous on busy nights – when it really gets humming there's lots of wobbly dancing and general hilarity.

Ronnie's Bar & Grill (☎ 20823; Ara Maire Nui) is a popular drinking spot, especially on Friday night, when its large garden patio is packed with drinkers.

Waterfront Café (☎ 20260), in Browne's Arcade, is another popular restaurant/bar near the waterfront.

TJ's Nightclub (☎ 24722; Ara Tapu; cover charge Fri & Sat NZ$2), a locals' nightspot with ear-splittingly loud music and UV lights, proudly claims to match 'all the sounds and lighting of any overseas disco'. It's *very* popular with the 18-to-25 age group on Friday and Saturday night.

Banana Court Bar (☎ 23397) is near the traffic circle in Avarua. This was once the best-known drinking hole and dance hall in the Cook Islands, possibly in the whole South Pacific. However, these days, the recently renovated Banana Court is but a well-behaved shadow of its former self. There are well-patronised late-night (starting at 10pm or 11pm) island-night performances on Friday in the tourist season, and startlingly empty, but loud, discos on Saturday.

Marama Lounge (☎ 29993; Ara Metua) is beside the Perfume Factory. Wednesday and Thursday nights are huge, with vanloads of backpackers pouring in from all around the island (transfers NZ$1.50 each way). Dive for free pearls in the swimming pool.

Coconut Bar (☎ 29879; Ara Tapu), opposite Avatiu Harbour, is popular with sailors. There are tables outdoors and under cover.

A few other bars within a (long) walk of Avarua are listed under Entertainment in the Around the Island section.

Cinemas

The **Empire Theatre** (☎ 23189; Ara Tapu; adult/child NZ$5/3) is the only cinema in town. It shows films nightly, usually double features. There's a two-for-one special on

Tuesdays (and entertainment from the crowd itself is free).

SHOPPING
Traditional Arts & Crafts

Island handicrafts are available at several stalls in the **Punanga Nui Market** (see that section earlier).

Michael Tavioni's Workshop (☎ 24003; *Ara Metua, Atupa*) is open 'all the time, mate. We live here.' One of the Cook Islands' most skilful and renowned carvers, Michael shows a wide variety of top-quality woodcarvings at his studio. Other carvers use his workshop too, including the next generation of carvers from local schools. Michael has a shop at the Punanga Nui Market as well. He and his brother, the late Taputu Tavioni, worked on the large stone carvings at Punanga Nui Market and the area around the Sir Geoffrey Henry National Culture Centre.

Island Craft (☎ 22009; *Ara Maire Nui*) has an excellent selection of very good Cook Islands arts and crafts, including an impressive collection of masks and spears from around the Cook Islands and the Pacific, with plenty of dramatic examples from the Solomon Islands. There are also nontraditional paintings from local artists.

Beachcomber Gallery (☎ 21939; *Ara Tapu*) has a wide selection of excellent local handicrafts and artwork of all kinds. The gallery sells weavings, *tivaevae* (appliqué works), paintings, jewellery and plenty more. For more information, see the Beachcomber Gallery section earlier.

Bergman & Sons Crafts Store (☎ 21901; *Banana Court*) is a prominent store with some excellent carvings and other Cook Islands crafts. The quality of their merchandise is first-rate, but don't expect to pick up a low-cost giveaway here. Even if you don't want to spend lots of money, it's worth visiting to see what they've got.

Modern Arts & Crafts

Modern Cook Islands art is displayed at **Pacific Arts** (☎ 20200; *Ara Tapu*) in 'Arorangi, the **Beachcomber Gallery** (see earlier), as well as the following places in Avarua.

Arasena Gallery (☎ 23476; *Banana Court*) displays local artists' works. It's tucked behind the Blue Note Cafe.

Kenwall Gallery (☎ 25526; *Ara Maire Nui*) offers a variety of local artists' works, mostly paintings. If you wish to discover your inner Gauguin while you're here, Kenwall stocks art supplies.

Judith Künzlé (☎ 20959) sells watercolours of local landscapes and seascapes, and drawings and paintings of Cook Islands dancers, from her home studio, Beachcomber Gallery and Island Craft. Her drawings appear in many books and posters in the Cook Islands.

Books

There are some excellent Cook Islands books for sale, including coffee-table books full of beautiful images (just in case your own photos don't turn out as planned). A Cook Islands Maori Bible makes a novel souvenir. See Bookshops, earlier in this chapter, and Books in the Facts for the Visitor chapter.

Music

If you want to take the sound of Rarotonga's heavy drums or frantic ukuleles home with you, try **Raro Records** (☎ 25927; **W** *www.rarorecords.musicpage.com; Ara Tapu*), near the Empire Theatre, or check out some of the stalls at the **Punanga Nui Market** (☎ 29370; *Ara Maire Nui*).

Kavera Central (☎ 20012; *Kavera*), on the west coast of the island, has a great selection of Cook Islands CDs.

Pearls & Jewellery

Pearls are a speciality of the Cook Islands. The Northern Group islands of Manihiki and Penrhyn are important producers of black pearls (which are among the rarest pearls in the world), but pearls in other colours, including gold and white, are also produced in the Cooks and sold on Rarotonga. Being on Rarotonga gives you the chance to see a fine selection of pearls and buy them at much better prices than you'll find elsewhere in the world.

Several shops in Avarua sell pearls – loose pearls, pearl jewellery, pearls still embedded in their shells, mother-of-pearl shells and many other innovative creations. There is no shortage of pearl shops on Rarotonga! The big ones include **Bergman & Sons Pearl Store** (☎ 21902; *Tutakimoa Rd*), between Cook's Corner and the petrol station, **Beachcomber Gallery** (☎ 21939; Ara Tapu) and **Maui Pearls** (☎ 26066; Ara Maire Nui), which has a pearl information show at 10.30am and 2pm weekdays. **The Perfume Factory** (☎ 22690; Ara Metua) is not a bad place for cheap pearls, as are the multitude of sellers operating from their homes.

A single pearl could cost you anything from NZ$5 (irregular and stunted) to well over NZ$1000. For NZ$25 to NZ$30 you can get pearls that don't look too shabby.

Perfumes, Soaps & Coconut Oil

Locally made perfumes (from NZ$10) and soaps (NZ$15) made from pure coconut oil are sold direct from the manufacturers at **The Perfume Factory** (☎ 22690; Ara Metua) and **Perfumes of Rarotonga**, which has a small **outlet** (☎ 24238; Ara Tapu) near the Avarua CICC. The Perfume Factory also sells locally produced liqueurs (from NZ$20) made from various combinations of co-conut, pineapple and 'Atiu coffee – the Tangaroa bottles are a wonderfully kitsch touch. Perfumes of Rarotonga's **main shop and factory** (☎ 26238; Ara Tapu) is in Matavera village.

Pure coconut oil (from NZ$12), good for skin and hair, is sold at many places around Avarua, including the two perfume shops mentioned earlier, **Island Craft** (☎ 22009; Ara Maire Nui), the **CITC Pharmacy** (☎ 29292) in the CITC Shopping Centre, and the **Punanga Nui Market**. You can buy it plain or scented with various local flowers and herbs. Ma'uke Miracle Oil contains a special medicinal herb, *pi*, which gives protection from the sun and is good for healing cuts.

Pareu & Other Clothing

A common item of clothing on Rarotonga is the *pareu*, worn mostly by women and chil-dren (it's rare to see men wearing them). A *pareu* is simply a length of fabric, which you wrap around yourself. It can be tied in a variety of ways – a book has even been published showing some of the many ways of tying *pareu*. Called by different names in different countries, the *pareu* serves as the general all-purpose garment of the Pacific islands.

Most popular are tie-dyed *pareu*, often with overlays of breadfruit leaves and other designs. Printed *pareu* are also popular. You can buy *pareu* for around NZ$15 at many

places around Rarotonga. At least a dozen shops in Avarua, including **Punanga Nui Market**, sell them; circle around the island on Ara Tapu and you'll see many other places selling *pareu*.

Printed souvenir T-shirts and singlets (from NZ$10 to NZ$25) and Hawaiian-style printed men's shirts (from NZ$20 to NZ$95) are sold in many shops around Avarua. There's a wide selection and good prices – shop around before you buy. Good places to start looking are **Vonnia's Store** (☎ 20927; Ara Maire Nui), **Tuki's Pareu** (☎ 25537; Ara Maire Nui) and the **Punanga Nui Market**. If you want to spend more, try **Turtle's** (☎ 27133) in the Cook's Corner Arcade. For a big old *muu muu* (Mother Hubbard dress), Tuki's Pareu is probably the best bet.

If you want to buy brightly coloured fab-ric to stitch up your own creation, there are great selections of material at Tuki's Pareu and Vonnia's Store.

Stamps & Coins

Cook Islands stamps, coins and bank notes are all collector's items. **Cook Islands Philatelic Bureau** (☎ 29336), next door to the post office, beside the traffic circle, sells uncirculated mint and proof sets of coins and bank notes, plus collector editions of Cook Islands stamps.

Tattoos

The word 'tattoo' is actually a derivative of *tatau*, the Tahitian word for this traditional Polynesian craft. Early missionaries tried to stamp it out, but it's returning to favour now. Even the most respectable of Cook Islanders, such as Pa Upokotini Marie Ariki (one of Rarotonga's premier *ariki*), sport traditional designs.

T's Tatts (☎ 25157) is behind Paulina's Polynesian Restaurant. Tetini Pekepo ('T') will give you an all-original Maori design from NZ$40.

Around the Island

Most island attractions are on or near the coastal road, the Ara Tapu (Sacred Road), which encircles Rarotonga. It is a wide, well-surfaced route, paralleled by a second road, the Ara Metua (Ancient Road), which is slightly inland.

The Ara Metua, also called 'the back road', follows the path of an ancient road originally built of coral blocks around AD 1000. Historically it was known as Te Ara Nui o To'i (The Great Road of To'i), although who exactly To'i was has been lost in history. None of the old road remains in an original state; most of it was surfaced or built over during WWII, and a road-improvement campaign in the early 1990s took care of the rest.

If you hire a vehicle or take a circle-island tour and go around Rarotonga on the Ara Metua, you'll see another side to the island – swampy taro fields, white goats and black pigs grazing in pawpaw patches, citrus groves, men on ancient tractors or even digging out entire fields with shovels, and graves of the ancestors off to one side of the houses.

The following descriptions move around the island anticlockwise, starting from Avarua; distances from the centre of Avarua are indicated.

AIRPORT (2.5KM)

The Rarotonga international airport was officially opened in 1974 and tourism in the Cooks really started at that time. With limited space available, the runway is fairly short (Rarotongans joke that the reason all the planes land here in the middle of the night is so you can't see how short the runway is). Public roads running right past the ends of the runway allow thrill seekers to get either directly beneath departing aircraft, or directly behind them when they drop the hammer. Lonely Planet does not recommend such dangerous, immature recreation…but what a buzz!

See the Getting There & Away chapter for practical information about the airport.

Behind the airport is the **National Stadium**, where many of Rarotonga's big sporting events are held.

CEMETERY (2.5KM)

Opposite the airport terminal is a small graveyard known locally as 'The Brickyard'. Milan Brych (pronounced 'brick'), a controversial Australian cancer-cure specialist, set himself up on Rarotonga after being chucked out of Australia. When his patron, Prime Minister Sir Albert Henry, was run out of office in 1978, Brych was soon run out of the country as well. Cancer patients who died despite his treatment are buried in this graveyard, which is adjacent to the Returned Servicemen's Association (RSA).

Tom Neale, the hermit of Suwarrow Atoll, is also buried opposite the airport. He died in 1977 and his grave is in the front corner of the RSA cemetery, with its 'Lest We Forget' sign.

PARLIAMENT (3.5KM)

The Cook Islands Parliament (☎ 26500) is opposite the Air Rarotonga terminal. The building was erected in 1974 as a hostel for the New Zealanders who came to work on the construction of the airport. The offices of the prime minister and other ministers are in the former bedrooms, with a few walls rearranged.

Parliament meets at various times throughout the year, according to need; it's usually in session from around August to January, but there is no fixed schedule. Stop by or ring the parliament building to find out when parliament will be in session. You are welcome to watch the proceedings from the cosy public gallery. You'll be sitting about 3m from the prime minister, so behave yourself. Ensure you're properly dressed, and don't take photos.

If you wander in when parliament is not in session, one of the staff will give you a short tour of the building. Sergeant at Arms Gavin Aratangi has even been known to collar passers-by and *insist* they look around.

GOLF COURSE (5.5KM)

The **Rarotonga Golf Club** (☎ 20621; open *8am-4pm Mon-Fri, members only Sat*) welcomes well-dressed visitors (no jandals or singlets) to play on its nine-hole course. The nine radio masts dotted around the course make an interesting extra hazard. (If you hit one by accident, replay the ball; if you hit one on purpose, great shot!) The bar here is open from 8am on weekdays. Green fees are NZ$15 a round, and you can hire a set of golf clubs for NZ$15.

BLACK ROCK (6.5KM)

Just beyond the golf course and down on the beach is Black Rock (Turou), where the missionary Papeiha is supposed to have swum ashore, clasping the Bible over his head. Actually, he was rowed ashore in a small boat! Traditionally, Turou was the departure point from where the spirits of the dead commenced their voyage to 'Avaiki (the afterworld). If you follow the track up behind the hospital there are good **views** (see Other Mountain Tracks, later in this chapter).

CULTURAL VILLAGE (7KM)

The Cook Islands Cultural Village (☎ 21314; e viltours@oyster.net.ck; Ara Metua, 'Arorangi) is a delightful experience; you'll learn more about traditional Cook Islands culture in one day here than you probably will for the rest of your stay.

Guided tours through the village, beginning weekdays at 10am, visit a number of traditional huts and include information and demonstrations of many aspects of Cook Islands culture, including history, Maori medicine, ancient fishing techniques, weaving, coconut husking, woodcarving, traditional firemaking and cooking, costume making and dancing. The tour is followed by a feast of traditional foods, with your tour hosts and the people from the various huts all getting together for a rousing show of traditional music, dance and chants, lasting until about 1.30pm. The morning village tour alone costs NZ$54, including the lunch and show, plus NZ$4 for transport if you need it, with discounts for children 11 years and under.

In the afternoon, the Cultural Village offers a circle-island tour around Rarotonga, which features history, agriculture, culture and many other aspects of Rarotongan life. The tour ends around 4pm. You can take the tour by itself, with the lunch, show and transfers included (NZ$55), or combine the tour with a visit to the Cultural Village (NZ$85).

A minimum of 25 people are required for village tours – ring well in advance to make bookings and arrange transport. Don't let their telephone manner put you off; they're much friendlier in person!

'ARORANGI (8KM)

On Rarotonga's west coast, 'Arorangi was the first missionary-built village and was conceived of as a model village for all the others on the island.

The main place of interest in 'Arorangi is the 1849 **CICC** – a large, white building that

still plays an important role in village life. The missionary Papeiha, the first to preach the Christian gospel on Rarotonga, is buried here, right in the centre front of the church; a huge monument to him has been raised by his many descendants.

To the left of the church is the old **Tinomana Palace**, built for the Tinomana Ariki by the British. The name of the palace is Au Maru, meaning 'The Peace Brought by Christianity'.

Interestingly, Tinomana, the chief who first accepted the message of Christianity from Papeiha, is not buried in the church graveyard, although he is honoured by a memorial plaque inside the church, which is built on land he gave to the missionaries. He later became Papeiha's father-in-law when the missionary married one of his daughters. Tinomana is buried on the hill behind 'Arorangi, near his old marae. Did he have second thoughts about his adopted religion?

Rising up behind 'Arorangi is the flat-topped peak of **Raemaru**. See Raemaru under Other Mountain Tracks later in the chapter for details on the climb to the top, and the Aitutaki chapter for the traditional story of why the mountain is flat-topped and what happened to the rest of it!

Pacific Arts (☎ 20200; e merkens@oyster .net.ck; Ara Tapu) is a small roadside studio where artist Andi Merkens sells prints and originals of her vibrant oil paintings. A small card-mounted print is only NZ$4, while larger prints cost upwards of NZ$15.

Exham Wichman (☎ 21180) is a fine Cook Islands carver who has a shop out behind his house where he displays all types of carved wooden handicrafts. It's at Maria's Backpackers (see Places to Stay – Budget later).

There are a number of popular places to stay and eat in 'Arorangi. Along the road are numerous small shops, and a branch of the Snowbird Laundromat.

HIGHLAND PARADISE (9KM)

High atop a slope behind 'Arorangi, Highland Paradise (☎ 24477, 20610; admission NZ$10) is on the site of the original village of the Tinomana people, where they lived before the arrival of Christianity. Raymond Pirangi, a descendant of Tinomana Ariki, takes visitors on a tour of the site and tells stories of the old days. The tour starts at 10am and includes a visit to the extensive botanical garden, the marae and other historical places. The two-hour tour, including lunch, costs NZ$30, and transfers are NZ$5.

SOUTH COAST (12KM TO 20KM)

The south coast of Rarotonga has the best beach and the best **swimming** and **snorkelling** possibilities. The reef is much further out, the sea bottom is relatively free from rocks, and it's sandier than the other beaches. There are lots of good places to stop for a swim, particularly from around the 16km to 20km mark. Opposite **Fruits of Rarotonga** (☎ 21509; *Ara Tapu*), a small jam shop whose owners will mind your bags while you swim, is perhaps Rarotonga's *best* snorkelling spot. There's a snorkel-rental operation here too (see Snorkelling earlier).

You can't miss the **Sheraton resort site** (*Ara Tapu*) – the echoing, abandoned remains of an ambitious government programme in the early 1990s. Cook Islanders laugh it off as yet another politicians' stuff up, but this strange colossus is responsible for about half of the country's national debt!

On the eastern edge of the Sheraton site, a road leads inland to **Wigmore's waterfall**, a lovely little waterfall dropping into a fresh, cool, natural swimming pool. You can drive all the way up to the waterfall, though the last stretch of road is quite rugged and is probably most suitable for 4WD vehicles or sturdy motorbikes. Otherwise, it makes a pleasant walk from the coast road up to the waterfall and back. If you do the Cross-Island Trek (see later) you will come to the waterfall near the end of your journey – a lovely spot to cool off – but be warned: there are more mosquitoes here than anywhere else on Rarotonga!

There's a picturesque **CICC** at Titikaveka, with some interesting old headstones in the graveyard. The church was built, in 1841, of coral slabs, hewn by hand from the reef at Tikioki and passed to the site at Titikaveka hand-to-hand in a human chain.

MURI (22KM TO 25KM)

Muri Beach, at Muri Lagoon on the southeast side of the island, is particularly beautiful. The shallow water has a sandy bottom

dotted with countless sea cucumbers and some coral formations making it interesting for snorkelling. Out towards the reef are four *motu* (lagoon islets): Taakoka, Koromiri, Oneroa and Motutapu. Taakoka is volcanic, the other three are sand cays. The welcoming **Rarotonga Sailing Club** (☎ 27349) includes **Sails restaurant**, which has a great view of the lagoon. A few doors down, the **Pacific Resort** (☎ 20427) also has restaurants. **That's Pasta** (☎ 22232) is a recent, and excellent, addition to Muri's culinary options.

Water-sports equipment and lagoon cruises are available from a couple of places here; see Other Sports and Lagoon Boat Tours earlier in this chapter. The beach between the Pacific Resort and the Rarotonga Sailing Club is especially popular; at low tide you can easily wade out to Koromiri – it's a great place to spend a windy day, since the lagoon side is sheltered from the offshore breeze.

Shells & Craft (☎ 22275), a small shop by the main road in Muri, is the pet project of a retired shell collector, Terry Lambert.

AVANA HARBOUR (25KM)

Beside Motutapu, the northernmost of the four Muri Lagoon *motu*, is the comparatively wide and deep reef passage into Avana Harbour (sometimes called Ngatangi'ia Harbour). It's a popular mooring spot for visiting yachts and small fishing boats.

Matu Rori

Sea cucumbers *(bêches-de-mer)* are an Asian delicacy and many Rarotongans find them delicious. Called *rori* in Maori, the creature's innards look rather like spaghetti, and around here a reference to eating spaghetti might refer to either *rori* or That's Pasta. *Matu rori* (fat *rori*) are best cooked with butter, garlic and spices, but the locals are equally happy to eat them raw. It's not uncommon to see someone pick one up in the lagoon, tear the skin open, squeeze the guts out as if from a tube of toothpaste, toss the black skin away and eat the 'spaghetti' on the spot. Surprisingly, the animal survives – a couple of weeks later, the same animal can yield the same harvest of 'spaghetti' all over again.

RAROTONGA

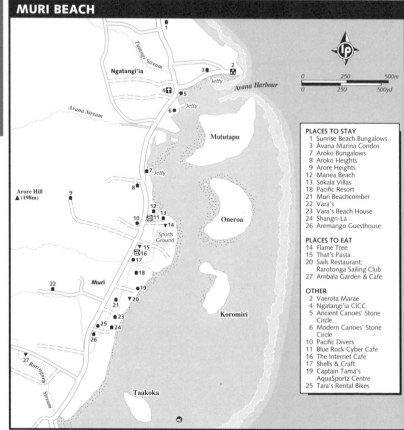

MURI BEACH

PLACES TO STAY
1 Sunrise Beach Bungalows
3 Avana Marina Condos
7 Aroko Bungalows
8 Aroko Heights
9 Arore Heights
12 Manea Beach
13 Sokala Villas
18 Pacific Resort
21 Muri Beachcomber
22 Vara's
23 Vara's Beach House
24 Shangri-La
26 Aremango Guesthouse

PLACES TO EAT
14 Flame Tree
15 That's Pasta
20 Sails Restaurant;
   Rarotonga Sailing Club
27 Ambala Garden & Café

OTHER
2 Vaerota Marae
4 Ngatangi'ia CICC
5 Ancient Canoes' Stone
   Circle
6 Modern Canoes' Stone
   Circle
10 Pacific Divers
11 Blue Rock Cyber Cafe
16 The Internet Cafe
17 Shells & Craft
19 Captain Tama's
   AquaSportz Centre
25 Tara's Rental Bikes

This harbour is historically significant as the departure point for the Maori canoes that set off in the 14th century to settle NZ. In the park opposite the **Ngatangi'ia CICC**, a **circle of seven stones** with a historical plaque commemorates seven of the canoes that completed the journey (see the boxed text 'The "Great Migration"' in the Facts about the Cook Islands chapter). On the point of land to your left as you gaze out through the harbour passage is **Vaerota Marae**. On this large, well-preserved marae the mariners were given their blessing for the journey and human sacrifices were made to the gods. Vaerota, the traditional marae of the Kainuku Ariki, is just past Avana Marina Condos.

A little further south, near the public toilets, another **circle of stones** commemorates

the arrival here of many traditional Polynesian canoes during the 6th Festival of Pacific Arts in 1992. If you're lucky, a couple of those vessels may be hauled up here, including the magnificent double voyaging canoe, *Te Au o Tonga*, sometimes called the Cook Islands' flagship, which still frequently sails across the Pacific.

MATAVERA (27.5KM)

The old CICC at Matavera, also made of coral, is beautiful at any time, but especially lovely at night when the outside is all lit up. The scenery inland of the stretch of road between Matavera and Avarua is particularly fine.

Perfumes of Rarotonga (*☎ 26238*), on the main road in Matavera, makes its own perfumes and colognes (from NZ$10) from local flowers; liqueurs (from NZ$16) from local mangoes, bananas and coffee; and coconut-oil soap (NZ$15) from the local coconuts. Some crafts from the outer islands are also on sale. There's a **pottery shop** at the rear. Perfumes of Rarotonga also has an outlet in Avarua, opposite the Beachcomber Gallery.

ARAI-TE-TONGA MARAE (30KM)

Just before you arrive back in Avarua, a small sign points off the road to the most important marae site on the island. Marae were the religious ceremonial gathering places of pre-Christian Polynesian society; the *koutu*, similar in appearance, were political meeting grounds where *ariki*, the great chiefs of premissionary Rarotonga, held court. The ceremonial offerings to the ancient gods were collected on the *koutu* before being placed upon the marae.

When you meet the Ara Metua there's a stone-marked *koutu* site in front of you. This whole area was a gathering place, and the remains of the marae, *koutu* and other meeting grounds are still here. Arai-Te-Tonga has the remains of an oblong platform 4m long. At one end stands the investiture pillar, a square basalt column 2m high, which extends an equal distance down into the ground. You may have to peer through the bush to see it. Don't walk on the marae; it's still a sacred site.

There are other marae in the area – a large one on your right as you come from the Ara Tapu to the Ara Metua, and another on your right (the inland side) if you walk southeast along the Ara Metua from Arai-Te-Tonga.

INLAND DRIVES

Two inland drives on the northern side of the island give you an opportunity to see the lush fertile valleys of Rarotonga, with mountains towering above on every side. Both drives follow streams and are in areas which were populated by the Rarotongan people before the missionaries came.

The drive along Avatiu stream begins at Avatiu Harbour – just turn inland at the harbour and keep going straight ahead. The road extends about 3.5km inland; at the end is the beginning of the Cross-Island Track, which must be continued on foot past this point.

The other drive is through the Takuva'ine Valley, which is reached by going inland on the road past the post office in Avarua and continuing inland. It's a wonderfully peaceful place. The Happy Valley Road extends inland for about 2km; a walking track continues inland and climbs up to the summit of Te Ko'u mountain.

CROSS-ISLAND TREK

The trek across the island, via the 413m Te Rua Manga (also known as 'the Needle'), is the most popular walk on the island. It can also be done as a shorter walk from the northern end to near the Needle and back again, rather than continuing all the way to the south coast. It's important that you do the walk in a north–south direction, as the chances of taking a wrong turn are much greater if you try it from the other direction. Wear adequate shoes and take enough drinking water with you. There are several places on this walk that get extremely slippery, and therefore dangerous, when there's been wet weather.

The road to the starting point runs south from Avatiu Harbour (the Cook's Passenger Transport bus can drop you off near here – see Getting Around earlier). If you're driving, continue on the road through the Avatiu Valley until you reach a prominent sign that marks the point past which vehicles cannot be taken. After this point, a private vehicle road continues for about 1km.

A footpath takes off from the end of the vehicle road. It is fairly level for about 10 minutes, then it drops down and crosses a small stream. Don't follow the white plastic power cable track up the valley; instead, pick up the track beside the massive boulder on the ridge on your left, after the stream crossing.

From here the track climbs steeply and steadily all the way to the Needle, about a 45-minute walk. If it wasn't for the tangled stairway of tree roots, the path would be very slippery in the wet. At the first sight of the Needle there's a convenient boulder right in the middle of the path, where you can rest and admire the view.

A little further on is a very obvious T-junction. A track to the Needle goes off to the right, but after a severe landslide in 2001 this track was closed indefinitely; Wigmore's Waterfall is a 90-minute walk to the left. Up to now you've been ascending a ridge running in a north–south direction; at this junction it intersects with another ridge, running in an east–west direction. Resist the temptation to approach or climb the Needle; two large pieces fell off it in 2001 and it would be a shame for that to happen while you were standing under it.

After about 30 minutes the track meets the Papua stream and follows it down the hill, zigzagging back and forth across the stream several times. After about 45 minutes of following the stream, the track emerges into fernland. Here the track veers away from the stream to the right, passing clearly through the fernland. Be sure to stick to the main track; there are several places where newer, minor tracks seem to take off towards the stream, but don't take these, as they will bring you out at dangerous spots upstream from the waterfall. After about 15 minutes the main track turns back towards the stream, bringing you to the bottom of the beautiful Wigmore's Waterfall. If you're hot, sweaty and muddy by this time, the pool under the fall is a real delight.

A rough dirt road comes from the south coast up to Wigmore's Waterfall. Walking down this road brings you to the coast road in about 15 minutes, passing alongside the eastern edge of the large, deserted Sheraton resort site.

You can flag the Cooks Passenger Transport bus down when you reach the coast road at the end of the track. Note, however, that on Sunday the last daytime bus departs from Avarua at midday. If you come on an organised trek across the island, hotel transfers will be provided at both ends; see Organised Walks, earlier in this chapter.

TAKITUMU CONSERVATION AREA

In the southeast of the island, this 155-hectare area of forested hills is the home of the once all-but-extinct *kakerori* (flycatcher; see Ecology & Environment in the Facts about the Cook Islands chapter). In 1996 the landowners recognised that the survival of the *kakerori* depended on conservation of this area, so they set it aside as a reserve. From the tracks through the forest there are great views of southern Rarotonga's valleys and hills, and you're almost guaranteed to see a *kakerori*. However, you can only enter

the area as part of a guided tour led by the staff of the **Takitumu Conservation Area** (☎ 29906). See Organised Walks earlier for details. The price of the tour goes towards further conservation work.

OTHER MOUNTAIN TRACKS

There are several other good mountain tracks on Rarotonga. Instructions for the easier ones are given here, but look for *Rarotonga's Mountain Tracks and Plants* by Gerald McCormack & Judith Künzlé if you want to do some real mountain trekking. The Cook Islands Natural Heritage Project, publisher of the book, in concert with the Cook Islands Environment Services, upgrades and maintains Rarotonga's inland tracks. Some signs are posted, to clarify the routes, and particularly difficult spots – going up vertical rock-faces, for example – have been made safer with the help of good ropes and other safety gear.

Raemaru

Flat-topped Raemaru (365m) rises directly behind 'Arorangi village on Rarotonga's west coast. For most of its length, this track has some of Rarotonga's easiest bush walking; the climb up a rock face on the southwest side of the summit is the only challenge, and excellent safety gear makes this quite safe – if you take it easy. See the Aitutaki chapter for the legend explaining why this mountain, unlike all the others on Rarotonga, is flat-topped.

Turn off Ara Tapu onto Akaoa Rd, about 200m south of the 'Arorangi CICC, and then turn right (south) onto the Ara Metua. There's a small road immediately on the left; park on the Ara Metua and walk up this small road, passing a couple of houses on the hill to your right, veering to the right and then following the road as it makes a left turn.

About 30m past this turn, find the walking track leading off to the right (yellow marker number 2), then walk uphill through a grove of avocado trees. The track doubles back and forth across the hill a couple of times as it heads uphill. Be careful, as the steeper sections can be slippery even in dry weather; they are quite hazardous when wet.

The place where you scale the rock face is about 15m high. Safety equipment has been installed on the rock face, but you must still be careful. Finally you emerge onto an open grassy area that slopes gently to the top. From the far end you can look across a valley to Maungaroa (509m) and Te Rua Manga (413m), the easily recognised peak also known as 'the Needle'. Looking back you can see along the coast all the way from south of 'Arorangi to the airport runway in the north. The return walk takes around two to 2½ hours.

Maungatea Bluff

Maungatea (523m) is the peak behind that impressively sheer cliff-face directly overlooking Avarua. The climb brings you to the top of the 340m bluff at the top of the cliff face, not to the top of the mountain itself, which is very difficult to reach and affords no great view once you get there. The bluff, on the other hand, offers a great view over Avarua and the north coast. The track is muddy and extremely slippery when wet. The track begins from the Ara Metua behind Avarua, beside the Tauvae Store. The return walk takes three to four hours.

Te Ko'u

More or less in the centre of the island, Te Ko'u (588m) is interesting because there is a volcanic crater at the top that you can traverse. The walk offers spectacular views of Rarotonga's inland mountains and of the south coast. It starts off with an easy one-hour walk through the Takuva'ine Valley behind Avarua, followed by a more challenging 1½-hour, steep climb up the mountain, which is treacherous when wet. The return walk takes about five hours.

'Ikurangi

The ascent of 'Ikurangi (485m) is a vigorous climb to a spectacular view of the north coast, Avarua and the Takuva'ine Valley. It's easier than the Te Ko'u walk, but not much. The track starts from the Ara Metua just to the east of Arai-Te-Tonga and takes about four hours return – a half-hour walk through the Tupapa Valley following Tupapa Stream, followed by a 1½-hour ascent of the mountain. A couple of small rock faces are encountered on the way to the summit.

Hikurangi, the sacred mountain of the Ngati Porou tribe on NZ's East Coast, was named in honour of this peak when the Ngati Porou's ancestors arrived from Rarotonga in the 14th century.

Te Manga

Rarotonga's highest mountain, Te Manga (653m), is probably the most difficult to scale on the island – the long, strenuous climb has several sections that are difficult and very steep. Starting at the same place as the 'Ikurangi walk, the return walk to Te Manga takes about six hours, with a one-hour walk through the valley following Tupapa Stream, followed by a two-hour ascent up the mountain.

Hospital Hill

About the easiest way to climb up to a good viewpoint is to drive up the hill to the hospital, just behind the golf course, park in the car park there and continue on foot. It's a fairly easy walk, although steep in places. The walk to the top takes about 15 minutes; the view is beautiful and unobstructed, with the airport on one side, a lush agricultural valley stretching inland from there between mountain ridges and, on the other side, 'Arorangi village. The different colours of water in the lagoon, much deeper blue out past the reef, the wide vista of ocean stretching off into the distance and the fresh breezes all make it a nice change from the lowlands.

VALLEY WALKS

The mountain walks on Rarotonga are hard work. If you want something easier, consider the valley walks, such as the stroll along the Avana stream from Ngatangi'ia. You can drive quite a distance up the road beside the stream and then follow the trail, repeatedly crossing the stream until you reach a pleasant picnic spot at the main intake. A similar walk follows the Turangi stream a little north of Ngatangi'ia. Matavera stream, further north, makes another good walk. Be prepared for mosquitoes.

Two other beautiful valleys are Avatiu, inland from Avatiu Harbour, and Takuva'ine, behind Avarua. See details on these under Inland Drives earlier. They also have walking tracks extending up into the valleys beyond where the roads end.

PLACES TO STAY

Rarotonga has a wide variety of places to stay in every budget range. It also has an official policy that every arriving visitor should be booked into a place to stay before arriving on the island. See the Accommodation section in the Facts for the Visitor chapter for details on this requirement.

Most of the places to stay on Rarotonga have some sort of kitchen or cooking facilities where guests can prepare their own food – much cheaper than restaurants and requiring a lot less travel each night. The large resorts and a few other hotels don't have kitchens in the rooms, so eating out will be an extra expense if you stay at one of these.

If you're looking for the most beautiful beaches on the island, choose accommodation on Muri Beach, or along the southern side of the island. The beaches along the southern and western sides of the island are all good for swimming, but not those on the northern and eastern sides, where the reef is too close to shore, making the beaches rocky and the lagoon too narrow for swimming. If you want to see the sunset from your hotel, then of course you must stay on the western side of the island. Der.

A 12.5% VAT is charged on virtually every economic transaction in the Cook Islands, including the price of accommodation; all prices given here include VAT. Most places provide free airport pick-up, and have laundry facilities available for guests.

Many of these places have their own websites, with pictures of the rooms and grounds, and information on specials. Check out **w** www.ck and **w** www.yellowpages .co.ck for listings.

Renting a House

Some of the best deals, especially if you're staying on the island for a while, are houses rented by the week. Fully equipped two-bedroom houses cost upwards of NZ$250, but more usually NZ$400, per week. The following organisations should be able to help with renting a house:

Cook Islands Tours & Travel (☎ 28270, **w** www .cookislandstours.co.ck) Rarotonga international airport
Jetsave Travel (☎ 27707, **w** www.jetsave.co.ck) Ara Maire Nui, Avarua
Nana Short (☎ 20064, **w** www.homerent.co.ck) Titikaveka
Nikao Holiday Homes (☎/fax 20168, **e** aretai@ oyster.net.ck)

Rarotonga Realty (☎/fax 26664, **w** www.raro realty.co.ck) Ara Tapu, Avarua
Shekinah Homes (☎/fax 26004, **w** www.shek inah.co.ck) Takitumu Conservation Area office, Ara Tapu, Avarua

Also with houses to rent are **Aroko Heights** (☎ 24922), in the Muri Beach area (NZ$350 to NZ$400 per week); and the **Kii Kii Motel** (☎ 21937), in the 'Arorangi and Muri Beach areas (NZ$435 per week plus power).

Check the classified section of the *Cook Islands News* (**w** www.cinews.co.ck) and *Cook Islands Herald* (**w** www.ciherald .co.ck), where rental houses might be listed. Placing a classified newspaper advert of your own well in advance of your visit might help you find something. Or you may have the best luck simply by asking around; there are plenty of houses available that are not advertised.

PLACES TO STAY – BUDGET

Rarotonga has a healthy number of budget-accommodation choices. All of the following places have kitchen facilities for guests to use, and are listed in an anticlockwise order around the island starting from outside Avarua, in the northeast. Unless otherwise stated they're on, or just off, the Ara Tapu (main road).

Near Avarua

These places are within a long walk, or a short ride, of town.

Ariana Bungalows & Hostel (☎/fax 20521; **e** bobh@ariana.co.ck; *dorm beds NZ$18, singles/doubles NZ$30/40, 1–3-person bungalows NZ$60-65*), with buildings spaced around a peaceful, green garden, is about 300m inland from the coast road, 3km east of Avarua. There's a pool, barbecue area, a small shop for your groceries and beer, self-service laundry and a small recreation room. As well as self-contained bungalows, each with its own kitchen, there's hostel-type accommodation. There's a healthy discount for week-long stays (35% to 40%).

Tiare Village Hostel (☎ 23466, ☎/fax 21874; **w** www.tiarevillage.co.ck; *singles/ doubles NZ$25/44, poolside units NZ$70*), a comfortable backpackers, is about 3km from the centre of Avarua behind the airport. The large house has two triple rooms and one four-bed room (share rate NZ$20), all sharing a common sitting area, kitchen and two bathrooms. There are also three separate, self-contained A-frame chalets (each with one triple, one double and one pokey little single bedroom). Guests share a TV lounge, board games and a library for entertainment on rainy days. Bring mosquito coils.

'Arorangi/West Coast
Some people pay a lot of money for the west coast's quiet beaches and beautiful sunsets, but you don't have to.

Aunty Noo's Beach Lodge (☎ 21253, fax 22253; share rate NZ$10-12, doubles NZ$26) has quite basic accommodation, but many budget-minded young backpackers love it. It's near the beach, the sunset and it's fun.

Are Renga Motel (☎ 20050, fax 29223; e arerenga@oyster.net.ck; share rate NZ$20, singles/doubles NZ$30/50) is about 8km from Avarua. Most accommodation is in tiny, self-contained, one-bedroom apartments, but there are also a few larger rooms with shared kitchen and sitting areas. The apartments are rather basic, but if you're looking for a low-priced motel you might not mind.

Mama Ru's Guesthouse (☎ 23278, 23279; singles NZ$15) has five small rooms and shared facilities. It's pretty basic accommodation, as you'd expect at that price.

Maria's Backpackers (☎ 21180; dorm beds NZ$15, doubles NZ$30, units per person NZ$18) is behind the family home of Exham and Maria Wichman – turn inland at the sign on the main road opposite Bunny's Diner and go about 200m. The two self-contained units have everything you need, including a large shared veranda. There are weekly discounts. Exham has a home workshop where he carves Tangaroa figures and wooden drums, and makes ukuleles and other island crafts.

Rarotonga Backpackers (☎ 21590; w www.rarotongabackpackers.com; dorm beds NZ$20, singles NZ$30, doubles & twins NZ$44-48) is a great new hostel in the hills backing up to Raemaru.

Manuae & Daughters Hostel (☎ 24110, fax 24988; e poko@oyster.net.ck; singles/doubles NZ$15/28, flat NZ$45), a small hostel on an unsealed side road, has shared facilities for the hostel rooms and a self-contained flat suitable for families.

The **Backpackers International Hostel** (☎ 21847, fax 21849; e annabill@backpackers.co.ck; singles NZ$26, doubles & twins NZ$32, beds in 8-bed dorm NZ$15) offers rooms in a large concrete building – a bit of a prison cell block from the outside but nice enough inside. Upstairs rooms get more light but they're noisier. There's a large, fun, communal kitchen, indoor and outdoor lounge areas, a rooftop sundeck and a famous Monday-night island buffet (NZ$20/25 for guests/nonguests). The Friday Nite Life tour (pick up and drop off NZ$5) gets rave reviews. Look for the sign pointing inland near Kavera Central; the hostel is the first two-storey house on your right. Discounts are given for stays of a week or more.

South Coast
There are two budget places on the south coast, both on the main road.

Piri's Hostel & Cottage (☎/fax 20309; dorm beds NZ$15, twins & doubles NZ$36, cottage NZ$50) has shared kitchen and bathroom facilities in the small, basic hostel; the cottage is self-contained. Women should not stay here.

Maiana Guest House (☎/fax 20438; w www.maianaguesthouse.co.ck; share rate NZ$18, twins & doubles NZ$40, triples NZ$54), a new hostel, has been very popular with all who have stayed there. It's spotlessly clean, has good cooking facilities and a lively common lounge; the owners, Ina and Mano, are lovely.

Muri Beach/East Coast
Beautiful Muri Beach is (understandably) popular with sun-seeking backpackers and there are a few cheap options here.

Aremango Guesthouse (☎ 24362, fax 24363; e aremango@oyster.net.ck; dorm beds NZ$22, twins & doubles NZ$44, triples NZ$58), on the coast side of the main road at Muri Beach, is a friendly, clean guesthouse, with a large shared kitchen and outdoor sitting areas. It has 10 spacious bedrooms, each sleeping between two and five people. Aremango's Friday-night pub crawl is a big hit.

Vara's (☎ 23156, fax 22619; w www.varas.co.ck; dorm beds NZ$25, singles NZ$40, doubles & twins NZ$48, doubles with en suite NZ$75, units NZ$90-140) has several buildings on or near Muri Beach. Vara's beach house has a reputation for overcrowding, poor facilities, late-night parties and a lot of coming and going. For cleaner rooms and a little peace and quiet – not to mention great views – go up the hill. Dorms sleep three to five people. There are discounts for stays over three nights.

PLACES TO STAY – MID-RANGE
Near Avarua

The following places are a few kilometres east of town.

Kii Kii Motel (☎ 21937, fax 22937; W www.kiikiimotel.co.ck; budget singles/ doubles NZ$77/99, deluxe singles/doubles from NZ$132/165, family unit singles/ doubles/triples/quads/quints NZ$95/120/ 155/185/215), a 24-room motel, is on the beachfront – it's no good for swimming right here but there's a nice little pool in a grassy area between the units. There's a choice of studio and one-bedroom units, all with kitchens.

Club Raro (☎ 22415, fax 24415; W www .clubraro.co.ck; garden rooms per 1-2 adults NZ$165, poolside/beachfront rooms NZ$210/ 340 plus per extra adult NZ$60) is right on the waterfront (although the beach here is no good for swimming). The motel-like rooms, surrounded by a sea of concrete, have tea-and-coffee-making facilities but no kitchens; beachfront rooms have air-con. Children under 12 years are free. The two bars and dining areas (see Places to Eat later), not to mention the pool, are available for nonguests as well.

Sea View Lodge (☎ 26240, fax 26241; e reuther@oyster.net.ck; doubles NZ$100 plus per extra person NZ$25) is a luxurious two-bedroom home on the Ara Metua. Amenities include a Jacuzzi on the veranda, which has a great view of the sea, and a well-equipped kitchen, sitting room and office.

'Arorangi/West Coast

Mid-range accommodation includes the following.

Reefcomber Sunset Motel (☎ 25673, fax 25672; W www.soltel.co.ck; studios/bunga-lows NZ$175/200) is smallish and modern, with eight studios and four self-contained bungalows sitting around a small garden. Ask about a two-island package, which includes a stay at Maina Sunset Motel on Aitutaki. No kids allowed.

Oasis Village (☎ 28213, fax 28214; W www.oasis.co.ck; singles/doubles/triples NZ$135/150/185), shady and quiet, is just south of the golf course. Its free-standing, one-room studio cabins all have air-con, TV and private bathrooms; there's tea-and-coffee-making facilities but no kitchens (breakfast is included in the prices listed, and there's a small restaurant on site). There's a pool and the beach isn't far away.

Rarotongan Sunset (☎ 28028, fax 28026; e welcome@rarosunset.co.ck; studio rooms NZ$150-225, 1-/2-bedroom suites NZ$266/ 399) is a pleasant beachfront motel with 19 self-contained studio units, all with air-con, well-equipped kitchens and private ver-andas. Breakfast is served in the poolside bar, and there's a Sunday barbecue. No kids under 12 years allowed.

Seashells Apartments (☎ 24317, fax 24318; W www.seashells.co.ck; doubles NZ$185 plus per extra person NZ$35) is a block of four modern, self-contained, two-bedroom apart-ments. Kids under 12 stay for free.

Castaway Beach Villas (☎/fax 21546; W www.castawayvillas.com; standard doubles/ triples NZ$130/170, poolside or beachfront doubles NZ$200) sits on a great stretch of beach with a good view of the sunset. There's a small bar and restaurant, as well as a pool for guests only.

Etu Bungalows (☎/fax 25588; e anietu@ oyster.net.ck; bungalow singles & doubles NZ$70 plus per extra person NZ$20) has sev-eral free-standing, self-contained bungalows in a quiet, peaceful garden behind a family home. It's right opposite a good beach and you can help yourself to all the fruit you like. You could squeeze a fourth person in (NZ$80) if you were very good friends.

Puaikura Reef Lodge (☎ 23537, fax 21537; W www.puaikura.co.ck; units NZ$135-140), on the southwestern side of the island, has 12 modern, well-equipped units, each with kitchen and dining area, and sleeping up to two adults and two children. The family units are great if you're with children, as the main sleeping area has a concertina door which you can slide across to shut off the living area. The beach, narrow but pleasant and with good swimming, is only a few steps away across the main road. There's also a swimming pool, a barbecue off to one side and a small honesty-system bar for guests.

Lagoon Lodges (☎ 22020, fax 22021; W www.lagoonlodges.com; studio units NZ$180, 1-bedroom bungalows NZ$205, 2-bedroom standard/deluxe villas NZ$245/315, 3-bedroom lodge NZ$575) stretches back from, rather than along, the coast road, so there's little traffic noise. There are 21 spacious bungalows and villas in a large garden setting, with a trampoline, barbecue and swimming pool. Several of the bungalows are larger one- or two-bedroom units – spacious, with kitchens and living rooms, large verandas and your own virtually private garden. If you have children, these larger units are among the best options on Rarotonga. The listed prices, apart from the lodge, are for two adults; extra adults/children are NZ$35/20 each. Complimentary snorkelling equipment and kayaks are available.

South Coast

The quiet south coast has several mid-range places.

Daydreamer Accommodation (☎ 25965, fax 25964; e byoung@daydreamer.co.ck; 1-/2-bedroom units NZ$120/150) has five clean, modern and pleasant units opposite a fine stretch of beach. All are spacious, airy and well-equipped with fans, kitchen, TV and phone.

Palm Grove Lodges (☎ 20002, fax 21998; e beach@palmgrove.co.ck; studio units NZ$205, 1-bedroom standard/superior garden bungalows NZ$220/250, 2-/3-bedroom bungalows NZ$285, beachfront studio units NZ$315) has free-standing, self-contained bungalows beside and opposite a fine stretch of beach good for swimming and snorkelling. Studio units sleep up to three; standard one-bedroom garden bungalows sleep four; superior one-bedroom garden bungalows sleep three; the two- and three-bedroom bungalows sleep up to five and six, respectively; and beachfront studio units sleep two. Prices are for up to two people – each extra person costs NZ$45. Kids under five are free, but aren't accepted in the beachfront studios. A bar/bistro serves breakfast (free for guests) and dinner.

Beach Lodge (☎ 28270, 20270, fax 27270; e raroinfo@citours.co.ck; apartments per night/week NZ$90/600) has three self-contained, two-bedroom apartments next door to the official residence of the Queen's Representative (QR) in Titikaveka. This beautiful spot is opposite a white sandy beach good for swimming and snorkelling.

Moana Sands Hotel (☎ 26189, fax 22189; W www.moanasandshotel.co.ck; superior beachfront/beachfront suites singles & doubles NZ$315/495, superior beachfront triples NZ$370) has 17 rooms, each with a veranda facing directly onto the beach. Complimentary canoes and snorkelling gear (this is one of Rarotonga's best snorkelling beaches) are available, and other activities can also be arranged with the help of the very efficient, very friendly staff. Rooms each have a small kitchen, there's a barbecue area and there's also a restaurant and bar. Children under 12 years can stay (free) in the superior beachfront rooms, but not in the beachfront suites.

Little Polynesian (☎ 24280, fax 21585; e littlepoly@beach.co.ck; beachfront studio units NZ$250, lagoonside cottage NZ$290) is right on the beach at Titikaveka Lagoon. It's secluded and private, with eight units and a lagoonside cottage, each with full kitchen. The usual resort-style amenities include swimming pool, barbecue hut, picnic tables, and hammocks stretched under the palms.

Raina Beach Apartments (☎ 23601, fax 23602; W www.raina.com; 1–2-person units NZ$150 plus per extra person NZ$25), a curious-looking three-storey concrete structure, is opposite a good snorkelling beach. Two one-bedroom family units downstairs can sleep up to six people each. Upstairs units are smaller, without a separate bedroom. No children under two years are accepted. The rooftop garden has a sundeck and a 360-degree view overlooking the lagoon and the mountains.

Muri Beach/East Coast

These places, on Rarotonga's most beautiful lagoon, are listed south to north.

Muri Beachcomber (☎ 21022, fax 21323; W www.beachcomber.co.ck; unit singles/doubles/triples NZ$224/250/327, villas NZ$300/320/408) has 16 self-contained, one-bedroom, seaview units, plus a couple of larger, poolside, one-bedroom garden units and three luxury one-bedroom villas. Children under 12 years can stay in the garden units, but not in the seaview units or villas. The spacious grounds have a swimming pool, barbecue areas and a relaxing lily pond.

Arore Heights *(☎ 20337; doubles/triples NZ$90/100)* has three self-contained bungalows sitting high, *very* high, on the hill behind Muri Beach. Needless to say, the view is unrivalled, but you'll need wheels.

Aroko Bungalows *(☎ 21625, 23625, fax 24625;* **w** *www.bungalows.co.ck/; single, twin & double garden/lagoon-view bungalows NZ$100/120 plus per extra adult NZ$30)* has one of the most tranquil and beautiful settings on Rarotonga, on the shore of Muri Lagoon, with a view across to Oneroa and Motutapu. It's a simple place with 11 small-ish but cosy self-contained bungalows, each sleeping two to three people. Beachfront bungalows have verandas overlooking the lagoon, and the communal lagoonside platform and pier looks specially designed for evening gin and tonics. No kids under 12 years accepted.

Sunrise Beach Bungalows *(☎ 20417, fax 24417;* **w** *www.sunrise.co.ck; bungalow doubles/triples from NZ$95/105, units NZ$115)* has eight nice self-contained bungalows, some right on the beach with an ocean view; there are also a couple of units. Kids aged between one and five years stay free, and cots are available (NZ$10). The beach here is not so good for swimming, but there's a small swimming pool for cooling off and it's not too far to walk to Muri Lagoon.

Royal Palms *(☎ 22838, fax 22836;* **w** *www.royalpalms.co.ck; bungalows NZ$140)* has three self-contained bungalows, tranquilly set amongst lush gardens inland between Muri Beach and Avarua. You'll need wheels.

PLACES TO STAY – TOP-END

Rarotonga has some excellent places to stay in the top-end range. If you're booking directly, ask about 'earlybird' (usually 30 days) payment discounts, which can be quite substantial. The following places are on the Ara Tapu unless stated otherwise.

'Arorangi/West Coast

Facing the sunset, 'Arorangi has three top-end lodgings.

Crown Beach Resort *(☎ 23953, fax 23951;* **w** *www.crownbeach.com; 1-/2-bedroom villas NZ$525/700, honeymoon villa NZ$760)* has individual, thatched-roof, deluxe villas scattered around a sandy property beside a lovely beach. Prices are for two people per

bedroom and two kids under 12 years are free – extra children/adults cost NZ$50/75 each. The Cabana Bar & Grill is among the villas, close to the beach (see Places to Eat later).

Manuia Beach Hotel *(☎ 22461, fax 22464;* **w** *www.manuia.co.ck; garden doubles/triples NZ$335/435, beachfront NZ $494/594)* has 20 units set on a sandy beachside property. Units are well set up but have no kitchen. No kids under 12 years are allowed. The Manuia's island-style beachside bar is open to nonguests and has an island night on Saturday (see Entertainment).

Sunhaven Beach Bungalows *(☎ 28465, fax 28464;* **w** *www.ck/sunhaven; beachfront studios NZ$180, garden/beachfront bungalows NZ$215/240)* has four newish bungalows in a quiet garden with a swimming pool *and* a beach. Interiors are spotlessly clean. No kids under 13 years allowed.

South Coast

There's only one top-end accommodation option on Rarotonga's quiet south coast, but it's a beauty.

Takitumu Villas *(☎ 24682, fax 24683;* **w** *www.takitumuvillas.co.ck; bungalows from NZ$375)* has 10 luxury thatched-roof units right on the beach, facing an excellent snorkelling area. The units are fully self-contained and have spa pools and air-con. There's a discount for longer stays.

Muri Beach/East Coast

Five of Rarotonga's top-end places to stay are in the Muri Beach area, several of them right on the beach itself.

Shangri-La *(☎ 22779, fax 22775;* **w** *www .shangri-la.co.ck; garden/partial lagoon-view cottages NZ$250/300)* is on the beach, and has its own swimming pool as well. Cottages have air-con, TV and even Jacuzzis. Early-bird/self-servicing specials are from NZ$165/195 per night. Owner Elliot Smith is the author of the *Cook Islands Companion*.

Pacific Resort *(☎ 20427, fax 21427;* **w** *www.pacificresort.co.ck; 1-/2-bedroom garden units NZ$300/360, beachfront units NZ$550, 2-bedroom garden/lagoon/beachfront villas NZ$655/850/1150)*, right on Muri Beach, is definitely one of Rarotonga's most attractive resorts. The 64 self-contained units all have kitchens (some have just microwave ovens), sitting rooms and private verandas.

All guests have free use of the watersports equipment (kayaks, windsurfers, snorkelling gear etc). The resort's intimate Barefoot Bar, right on the beach, has a lovely view, and there's also the open-air Sandals Restaurant. Prices listed are for one or two people; a third costs NZ$50/70 in the units/villas. Kids under 12 years are free (sharing a room with their parents).

Manea Beach (☎ 25320, 23488, fax 25420; W www.manea.co.ck; bungalows NZ$250, villa NZ$400) is down a quiet side road. Five one-bedroom, spotlessly clean bungalows and one three-bedroom villa are jumbled together on this property. There are limited self-catering facilities in each unit.

Sokala Villas (☎ 29200, fax 21222; W www.sokala.com; villas NZ$480-690) offers an assortment of self-contained, one-bedroom timber villas right on the beach. Five villas have their own private swimming pool. All are elegant and excellently appointed. This place is especially popular with couples and honeymooners; children under 12 years are not accepted. With the early-bird discount, prices are between NZ$330 and NZ$470.

Avana Marina Condos (☎ 20836, fax 22991; e avanaco@oyster.net.ck; condos NZ$350), right on Muri Lagoon, overlooking Avana Harbour with a view across to Motutapu, has six spacious condos. Each has a pool, its own jetty, and dinghies and kayaks are free. The view's great and you can swim off this rocky beach, but *watch the current through the passage*! Children are made very welcome. Five of the units have two bedrooms and one has three.

Large Resorts

Rarotonga has only two really big resorts – the Rarotongan Beach Resort and the Edgewater Resort. Their 'rack rates' – the prices you'll pay if you walk in off the street – are high, but most of their business comes from airlines' and travel agents' package holidays, which make the room rates cheaper. Even if you can't afford to stay here, you might want to make use of their restaurants and bars.

Rarotongan Beach Resort (☎ 25800, fax 25799; W www.rarotongan.co.ck; garden/ beachfront rooms NZ$360/475, suites NZ$780-1525), in the southwest corner of the island, is a vibrantly painted, 156-room place with everything you'd expect in a modern resort:

swimming pool, plenty of complimentary beach and lagoon activities, tennis courts, a beachfront bar (see Entertainment later), two restaurants (see Places to Eat later), souvenir shops and huts, a travel-information desk, vehicle rental, a business centre and a kids club (available for nonguests too; NZ$20 per session).

Children stay free and extra adults cost NZ$75 each.

The resort beach has kayaks, snorkelling gear, volleyball and so on. An activities list at the front desk describes the various events being held each day. Nonguests are welcome to the restaurant and bar, dive centre, spa therapy centre and kids club, but are not allowed to use the other facilities.

Edgewater Resort (☎ 25435, fax 25475; W www.edgewater.co.ck; garden/superior/ beachfront/beachfront deluxe rooms NZ$240/ 280/375/415, VIP/honeymoon suites NZ$550), a concrete jungle on the beachfront at 'Aro-rangi, on the western side of the island, has over 180 rooms (if that sounds crowded to you, you're right), making it the biggest resort in the Cook Islands. The rooms are quite adequate, with the three categories differing mainly in their views (garden, partial beach view or beachfront) and furnishings. All have air-con, TV and in-house movies, and tea-and-coffee-making facilities (but no kitchens). The prices listed are for one or two people; a third person costs NZ$80. Children under 12 years are free.

The usual resort facilities are here: swimming pool, tennis courts, vehicle hire, and travel-information desk. On the resort grounds, and open to nonguests, is the poolside Mal's Bar (see Entertainment later) and the Edgewater Brasserie restaurant (see Places to Eat).

PLACES TO EAT

The widest choice of eating places is found in Avarua (see the listing earlier in this chapter), but there's also a scattering of places right around the island.

Restaurants

Restaurants tend to be scattered at distances around the island, with more on the western than on the eastern side. Since you'll probably have to travel at least some distance to get to any of them, and most of them are quite small, reservations are a good idea. These are listed in an anticlockwise direction around the island. They're all on the main road (Ara Tapu) unless stated otherwise.

Near Avarua East of town, within walking distance, **Club Raro** (☎ 22415; breakfast NZ$5.50-18, lunch & dinner mains NZ$20-30) is an option for poolside eating (and drinking – see Entertainment later) for nonguests as well as guests. When it's raining, dining (and drinking) moves inside. Island nights (NZ$35) are held on Monday.

'Arorangi/West Coast The west coast has a remarkable number of restaurants.

Kikau Hut (☎ 26860; mains NZ$17-22) is an attractive, airy restaurant specialising in European cuisine. It's a relaxed, fun spot for a meal. Hotel transfers cost NZ$5; minimum two people. Reservations are recommended.

Oasis Village (☎ 23743; mains from NZ$22) has a small, open-air Italian restaurant, Da Carlo's – bookings are preferred.

Alberto's Steakhouse & Bar (☎ 23597; mains NZ$15-35; open 6pm-9pm Mon-Sat) specialises in steak and curries, but also has fine seafood, pasta and other European dishes.

Hopsing's Chinese Restaurant (☎ 20367; mains NZ$13-26), between the Edgewater Resort and the Rarotongan Sunset, does some good seafood meals in addition to Chinese recipes. Takeaways are available (from 6.30pm).

Spaghetti House (☎ 25441; mains NZ$12-33) serves good pastas (meat or vegetarian), plus pizza, meat dishes and seafood. It also does takeaways.

Edgewater Resort (☎ 25435; breakfast NZ$8-20, all-day menu NZ$8-20, dinner mains NZ$17-35) serves meals at either the Edgewater Brasserie or the poolside Mal's Bar. The brasserie is huge and characterless but it hosts one of Rarotonga's most professional island nights, on Tuesdays and Saturdays (with/without dinner NZ$49/15). There's live entertainment every night except Friday, when there's a steak dinner followed by a nightlife tour.

Tumunu Bar & Restaurant (☎ 20501; mains NZ$20-25, desserts NZ$7) is a bizarrely decorated restaurant/bar with friendly (if slightly eccentric) staff. Seafood and steaks are the speciality here; try the big seafood platter (NZ$60 for two). It also has vegetarian dishes, children's meals and nightly specials. There's a roast-pork dinner on Sunday.

Windjammer Restaurant (☎ 23950; mains NZ$20-29, desserts NZ$9) has decor that is a bit soulless, but some say the food is among the best on Rarotonga. The Windjammer, beside Crown Beach Resort, is a great place to spoil yourself. Reservations are essential.

Cabana Bar & Grill (☎ 23953; breakfast NZ$12, lunch NZ$6-12, dinner mains NZ$25) at Crown Beach Resort, is open-walled and tropical, and serves food all day.

Manuia Sand Bar (☎ 22461; lunch NZ$6-14, dinner mains NZ$17-31, all-day menu NZ$7-11), at Manuia Beach Hotel, has delightful island decor and a sand floor. It specialises in seafood. Light meals are served all day. Saturday's island night costs NZ$42/10 with/without dinner.

Crusoe's Restaurant & Bar (☎ 21546; mains NZ$18-27), beside the pool at Castaway Beach Villas, specialises in local flavours, particularly on Sunday's 'island feast' nights (NZ$20).

Kaena Restaurant (☎ 25433; vegetarian & light meals NZ$9-13, mains NZ$18-32), 50m north of the Rarotongan Beach Resort, specialises in steak and seafood dinners. The Kaena looks rather plain from the outside but it's attractive inside. Reservations are recommended.

Rarotongan Beach Resort (☎ 25800; breakfast NZ$7-20, all-day menu NZ$8-25, dinner NZ$29) has two restaurants – the Treetops Verandah Restaurant for nightly buffet dinners and (overpriced) breakfasts, and a poolside/beachside bar for all-day dining. There's live music every night and an island-night umukai and show on Wednesday and Saturday (NZ$45 for meal and show). The resort's Sunday brunch (11am to 3pm; NZ$19) features a choir (at 1pm) and dancers.

South Coast Rarotonga's south coast is fairly quiet, but there are a few dining options.

Vaima Restaurant & Bar (☎ 26123; mains NZ$18-27) has a reputation as one of the best restaurants on the island. The island decor is beautiful and the food is well prepared and inexpensive. Hotel transfers can be arranged.

Local boy, Rarotonga

DALLAS STRIBLEY

Scooter travel, Rarotonga

PAUL DYMOND

Local children, Rarotonga

JEAN-BERNARD CARILLET

PETER HENDRIE

Aitutaki Lagoon

DALLAS STRIBLEY

Boat trip, Aitutaki Lagoon

JOHN BANAGAN

Snorkelling, Aitutaki Lagoon

MANFRED GOTTSCHALK

Akitua, a *motu* (lagoon islet) on Aitutaki Lagoon

Palm Grove (☎ 20002; breakfast NZ$3-9, dinner mains NZ$16) is a small restaurant serving breakfast and dinner. It's mostly used by Palm Grove's guests, but others are equally welcome.

Saltwater Cafe (☎ 20020) is a beachy café where satisfied patrons leave their graffitied praises on the ceiling. Our tip: wrap your jowls around a 'brilliant burger' and wash it down with a fruit smoothie. Wednesday is 'Wok Thai' night, and on Sunday the café runs hot.

Moana Sands Hotel (☎ 27189; mains from NZ$23) has, attached, the pleasant, new Pawpaw Patch restaurant.

Maire Nui Gardens & Café (☎ 22796; breakfast NZ$4-11, lunch NZ$12-14, hot drinks NZ$4-7, fruit smoothies NZ$5, cakes NZ$3.50-5) is a small café with seats overlooking a wonderful lush garden and pond. There's a NZ$3 entry fee for looking around the garden – well worth the price if you have time for a relaxing look around.

Muri Beach/East Coast The Muri Beach area has some fine restaurants.

Ambala Garden & Café (☎ 26486; meals NZ$10-12, cakes & muffins NZ$3-5; open 9am-3pm Thur-Sat), high above Muri Beach, serves delicious, if pricey, breakfasts, lunches and snacks in a peaceful garden setting. You're welcome to wander through the garden after your meal. Ambala would rather not share its sense of tranquillity with kids under 11 years (but we took ours along anyway). Reservations are a good idea for lunch.

Sails (☎ 27349; lunch NZ$7-22, dinner mains NZ$18-30, desserts NZ$8), at the Rarotonga Sailing Club, has an excellent view over Muri Lagoon, especially lovely when there's a full moon rising. The service can be half-hearted but the food is tasty. Reservations are recommended.

Pacific Resort (☎ 20427; buffet breakfast NZ$12, light lunch NZ$4-16, heavy lunch NZ$12-25, all-day snacks NZ$4-11, dinner around NZ$33) has an à-la-carte menu with steaks and seafood most nights, but it also has theme nights, including an island-night buffet (with a pretty lame show), a carvery night and a weekly barbecue – each NZ$40. Breakfast and dinner are served in the open-walled Sandals Restaurant. Lunch (and dinner if you like) is served in the beachfront Barefoot Bar, with both outdoor and indoor tables.

Flame Tree (☎ 25123; mains NZ$18-29; open from 6.30pm daily), near the end of Muri Beach, was once known as Rarotonga's best restaurant. It's facing stiff competition these days, but with delicious food, an elegant atmosphere and artistic decor, it still does well. Reservations are recommended.

Island Buffets

You'll get a good island-style buffet at any of the island nights at the big resorts, where they present dancing and entertainment in addition to the food (see the boxed text 'Island Nights', later in this chapter, for a list of who's dancing where). If you just want to eat, a couple of the more modest places to stay have excellent island buffets, cheaper than the island nights.

In 'Arorangi, **Backpackers International Hostel** (☎ 21847; guests/nonguests NZ$20/25) has an island buffet at 7pm on Saturday that is enormously popular; book by 4pm Friday.

Piri's Hostel & Cottage (☎ 20309; lunch or dinner with show NZ$45), on the island's south coast, does an umukai every Sunday. You help Piri Puruto III prepare the umu, learn how it's done, then dig in after the show (see Entertainment later).

Cafés & Fast Food

As well as fine cafés, there are a few places where you can get basic, cheap, fast food; they all have tables so you can dine there or take the food away. They are listed here anticlockwise around the island, and are all on the Ara Tapu unless stated otherwise.

Near Avarua These places are close enough to Avarua to be worth popping out to for a snack.

Just Burgers (☎ 22778; burgers NZ$2.50-10), on the main road in Pue, 1.6km east of Avarua, makes inexpensive American-style hamburgers, french fries, milk shakes and the like.

Airport Cafe (Rarotongan international airport; toasted sandwiches NZ$3.50, meals NZ$8, coffee NZ$2.50) is a good option if you're at the airport and badly need a meal.

'Arorangi/West Coast The west coast has the following places.

Priscilla's Takeaways (☎ 28072; snacks NZ$2-5) is a great, friendly spot to grab some quick munchies. Cook Islands food, such as *ika mata* (raw fish in coconut sauce) and *rukau* (taro leaves), share the shop with more traditional fast food, such as hotdogs and fish and chips.

Moko Cafe (☎ 27632; *breakfast & brunch NZ$7-10, paninis NZ$9, cakes & muffins NZ$3*), a funky new place, seems destined to become a travellers' favourite. Moko has good food and good coffee, plus a cheerful island decor and lots of toys to amuse the kiddies while you enjoy your Penang curry.

The Flamboyant Place (☎ 23958), in the shopping centre opposite Dive Rarotonga, has simple, tasty, inexpensive takeaways and hot meals.

Bunny's Diner (☎ 22718; *burgers NZ$5-6, fish & chips NZ$8*) sells basic breakfasts, burgers and sandwiches.

Cafe Maohi (☎ 20012; *snacks NZ$3.50-15*), attached to Kavera Central, is a small grocery store/Internet café selling tasty burgers and other similar takeaway fare.

South Coast Options on the south coast include the following places.

Eat Inn-Take Out (☎ 27730; *beside Wigmores Superstore*) is an open-air café serving hearty takeaway fare such as burgers and fish and chips. A nice option for a simple meal, or a cold beer, on the south coast.

Fruits of Rarotonga (☎ 21509; *light breakfasts NZ$3-5, jams & chutneys from NZ$3.60*), in Tikioki, is a popular little place selling reasonably priced home-made island-fruit products such as jams, chutneys and relishes. It also serves morning and afternoon teas.

From here back towards Muri Beach is perhaps the best snorkelling spot on the island, and the owners have developed a reputation as the loveliest bunch of people you could possibly ask to mind your bags. It's developed into quite a little travellers' hangout. The owners have assembled all the information you might want on Rarotonga; have a muffin and coffee after your swim and browse through a folder of Rarotongan restaurant menus while you plan your evening.

Muri Beach/East Coast A cluster of small **takeaway shops** along the main road in Muri Beach serve burgers and fast food of reasonable standard.

That's Pasta (☎ 22232; *dishes NZ$9-15*) has fresh-cooked pasta and delicious sauces that are a fine option for lunch. You can buy uncooked pasta and sauce (one serving from about NZ$5) to cook at home.

Blue Rock Cyber Cafe (☎ 23531) has the best toasted sandwiches on the island (NZ$2.50), hot drinks (NZ$1 to NZ$1.50) and magnificent smoothies (NZ$1.50 to NZ$3).

Self-Catering

See the Avarua section earlier for the big supermarkets and open-air market in that town.

Wigmore's Superstore (☎ 20206) is the only serious grocery store on the south coast. There's a good selection of foods, good prices, and a wide variety of produce fresh from Wigmore's farm.

Many small **shops** are dotted around the island. They are convenient and are open longer hours than the supermarkets, but like convenience stores in any country, their prices are usually higher than the supermarkets.

ENTERTAINMENT
Bars

Friday night is Rarotonga's big party night. Most of the bars and nightclubs are in Avarua (see the listings earlier in this chapter), but there are also a few possibilities around the island.

An establishment touted as a 'restaurant/bar' is usually a restaurant rather than bar – there's often no-one at the bar at all.

Resort bars are open to nonguests (with prices like they charge, they'll take anyone's money) but can be remarkably quiet some nights. It's not unusual to see them all but deserted by 8pm, unless the resort has put on an island-night performance. Even then the place might be completely empty an hour after the last bum has stopped wiggling.

Sports clubs around the island often have dances on. Check the classified advertisements in the *Cook Islands News* for details.

The following places, all on the Ara Tapu unless stated otherwise, are listed anticlockwise around the island.

Near Avarua Most of these places are within a (long) winding walk of Avarua.

Island Nights

Some say that Cook Islands dancing is the best in Polynesia; superior even to the better-known dancing of Tahiti. There are plenty of chances to see it at the island-night performances that are held virtually every night of the week.

The prices hotels quote for their island nights include buffet island meals. If you turn up after the buffet and only want to watch the show, you'll normally pay only a NZ$5 to NZ$10 cover charge. The show usually starts about 8.30pm (but can vary from 7pm to 11pm), and afterwards there's usually a live band.

At the time of writing, the following places were putting on island nights (prices are with/without dinner; some places don't allow nondiners to watch the show, ie, prices are for 'dinner and show', but if you come along and buy a few drinks they'll usually let you watch).

Monday
Club Raro (☎ 22415, near Avarua) NZ$35 (dinner & show)

Tuesday
Edgewater Resort (☎ 25435, 'Arorangi) NZ$49/15

Wednesday
Rarotongan Beach Resort (☎ 25800, 'Arorangi) NZ$45/20

Thursday
Staircase Restaurant & Bar (☎ 21254, Avarua) NZ$25/5

Friday
Banana Court Bar (☎ 29061, Avarua) NZ$3 (seasonal), **Pacific Resort** (☎ 20427, Muri Beach) NZ$50 (dinner & show)

Saturday
Edgewater Resort (☎ 25435, 'Arorangi) NZ$49/15, **Rarotongan Beach Resort** (☎ 25800, 'Arorangi) NZ$45/20, **Manuia Beach Hotel** (☎ 22461, 'Arorangi) NZ$42 (dinner & show)

Some resorts also hold barbecues and buffets, which may include live entertainment. Sunday, when most other restaurants are closed, is the big day for hotel barbecues and brunches.

The Tourist Authority office hands out a free printout with up-to-date information on most of the island nights around Rarotonga. (They list accredited ones only.) The quality of the performances vary, so if you're a fussy audience member, you'd better ask around. At the time of writing, the Edgewater Resort's was the most professional island night, but we thought the Staircase's was the most fun.

Club Raro (☎ 22415) has a poolside bar available to nonguests. Happy hour (NZ$1 off all drinks) is from 5pm to 6pm, daily.

The **Cook Islands Game Fishing Club** (☎ 21419) has cheap beers, friendly conversation (with the obligatory fishy tales) and a pool table – it's no wonder this place is popular on Friday and Saturday nights.

Nu Bar (☎ 26140), near the airport, is very popular with the locals on party nights (Friday and Saturday). If you're looking for somewhere to have a *quiet* drink, you're in the wrong place.

RSA Club (☎ 20590) is opposite the airport. The Returned Servicemen's Association has a casual bar with cheap beers. Locals come here to play pool and darts, and visitors are always welcome (it's a bet-

ter option than sitting around the airport to pass the time after you've checked in). Monday night is a big backpackers' event.

Rarotonga Golf Club (☎ 20621) has a bar open for well-behaved visitors from 8am weekdays.

'Arorangi/West Coast A few restaurants on Rarotonga's west coast have bars.

Alberto's Steakhouse & Bar (☎ 23597) is primarily a restaurant, but is not a bad spot for a quiet beer before dinner.

Hopsing's Chinese Restaurant (☎ 20367) has a bar with a particularly well-stocked top shelf. The Rotary Club meets here weekly.

Edgewater Resort (☎ 25435), west of the Ara Tapu, has a restaurant/bar with live entertainment of one kind or another every night except Friday. The island nights here, Tuesday and Saturday, are reputed to be Rarotonga's most professional (with/without dinner NZ$49/15).

Tumunu Bar & Restaurant *(☎ 20501)*, with a ceiling reminiscent of your average teenage boy's bedroom, is a friendly, offbeat place. There's usually a few friendly regulars propping up the bar in addition to the diners.

Cabana Bar & Grill *(☎ 23953)*, at Crown Beach Resort, is an open-air, pleasant spot to enjoy a beer while the sun goes down.

Manuia Sand Bar *(☎ 22461)*, at Manuia Beach Hotel, is the only bar on Rarotonga with a sand floor. It's a lovely spot for a sunset beer. There's live music on Wednesday (NZ$32 with dinner) and an island-night performance on Saturday (with/without dinner NZ$42/10). Happy hour is 4pm to 6pm daily.

Crusoe's Restaurant & Bar *(☎ 21546)*, at Castaway Beach Villas, has a well-stocked bar and vows never to close while a guest is still drinking.

Rarotongan Beach Resort *(☎ 25800)* has a lovely, tropical-style poolside/beachside bar with a great view of the sunset – this is one of Rarotonga's most elegant bars. There's live entertainment every night in the restaurant. The island-night performances (with dinner NZ$45) on Wednesday and Saturday are superb (and therefore *packed* with people – book ahead). The Raro Fun Bus Nite Life Tour (with/without dinner NZ$45/25) leaves from here on Friday night on a pub crawl around the island.

South Coast The **Vaima Restaurant & Bar** *(☎ 26123)* has a cosy little bar attached to the restaurant – the only bar on the quiet south coast.

Muri Beach/East Coast Surprisingly, Muri Beach, the backpacker capital of Rarotonga, has no cheap bars.

Sails *(☎ 27349)* is at the Rarotonga Sailing Club. This restaurant/bar has a wonderful terrace with a view out to the lagoon and the *motu* offshore.

Barefoot Bar *(☎ 20427)*, at Pacific Resort, is attractive and has a lovely view of the lagoon, and tables both indoors and out on the terrace. The bar here is never particularly full, except during dinner.

Videos

There are innumerable video-hire shops around Rarotonga. Some hire video players, and even the TV to go with it. Check the yellow pages in the Telephone Directory.

Piri Puruto III

Last but not least is Piri of **Piri's Hostel & Cottage** *(☎ 20309)* – see Places to Stay – who zips up coconut trees, demonstrates traditional firemaking and gives a generally entertaining and informative show. His one-hour performance costs NZ$13, and it's worth it. He also does a barbecued-fish dinner (NZ$15) and an 'early bird' coconut breakfast show (NZ$19) on various days of the week. Ring for a schedule, or pick up his pamphlet.

On Sunday Piri puts on a delicious *umukai* feast, cooked in an underground oven in the traditional Cook Islands Maori way. You can participate in the preparation and learn how it's done, then have a light lunch, see Piri's show and go for a swim while you wait for the feast to emerge. The cost is NZ$45; transport can be arranged. Children are half-price for all of Piri's activities.

Aitutaki Atoll

pop 1800 • area 18.3 sq km

Aitutaki, with its huge lagoon, is one of the most beautiful islands in the Pacific. It's the Cooks' second-most populated island, although in area it only ranks sixth. It's also the second-most popular island in terms of tourist visits. The hook-shaped island nestles in a huge triangular lagoon, 12km across its base and 15km from top to bottom. The outer reef of the lagoon is dotted with beautiful *motu* (lagoon islets) and they are one of Aitutaki's major attractions.

Aitutaki is also historically interesting, with a number of marae (ancient religious meeting grounds) that can still be visited today. The island is historically significant – it was the first foothold in the Cooks for the London Missionary Society (LMS). Only after converting Aitutaki's population did it move on to Rarotonga.

Aitutaki has some of the best island-night performances in the Cook Islands.

History
Various legends tell of early Polynesian settlers arriving at Aitutaki by canoe. The first settler was Ru, who according to various traditions came from either 'Avaiki (now called Ra'iatea, near Tahiti, in modern-day French Polynesia), or from Tubuaki (also in French Polynesia).

Wherever Ru's homeland was, it had become overcrowded, so Ru, his four wives, four brothers and their wives, and a crew of 20 royal maidens sailed off in search of new land, eventually reaching Aitutaki.

Ru went to the highest point on Aitutaki, the top of Maungapu, and surveyed the island. He divided the land into 20 sections, one for each of the 20 royal maidens, and completely forgot about his brothers! They left the island in anger – they had come all that way to settle new land, and yet Ru allotted them nothing. They continued over the ocean and eventually wound up in Aotearoa (New Zealand).

The original name of the island was Ararau 'Enua O Ru Ki Te Moana, meaning 'Ru in Search of Land over the Sea'. Later the name was changed to Aitutaki – *a'i tutaki* means 'to keep the fire going' – but the old name is still used in legends and chants.

Highlights

- Taking a cruise on Aitutaki's huge turquoise lagoon
- Climbing to the top of Maungapu for superb views of the entire island
- Watching an island-night dance performance – they're even more enthusiastic than those on Rarotonga – followed by a disco
- Enjoying the magnificent snorkelling, sand bars and coral ridges within Aitutaki's lagoon
- Spending a Sunday at O'otu Beach – kayaking around the *motu* (lagoon islets), then relaxing with an afternoon beer
- Taking a circle-island tour of Aitutaki, visiting villages along the way

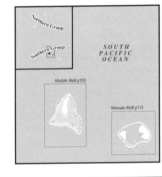

Other canoes followed Ru's party, coming from Tonga, Samoa and various islands in French Polynesia, landing at different places on Aitutaki. Each new group of people had to be accepted by one of the 20 maidens or their descendants in order to have a space on the island to settle.

The island's European discoverer was Captain William Bligh, on board the *Bounty*, on 11 April 1789. The famous mutiny took place just 17 days later as the ship was en route to Tonga.

In 1821 the missionary John Williams visited Aitutaki briefly and left behind Papeiha and Vahapata, converts from Ru's

Dogs & Pigs

There are no dogs at all on Aitutaki and nobody is allowed to bring them to the island. There haven't been any for quite a few years and there are numerous stories as to what happened to them. The most interesting is that during a 19th-century leprosy outbreak, dogs somehow copped the blame for carrying the disease, and were all hunted down. Another story is that a dog mauled the child of an *ariki* (high chief) who then banned all dogs. Whatever the reason, it's a relief not to have to swerve around them on your motorbike. And Aitutaki does have some healthy looking stray cats!

There are, however, plenty of pigs – that most popular of Pacific domestic animals. South Sea pigs have learnt to make coconuts a major part of their diet, and well-kept pigs also have papaya and taro mash. They're tasty pigs, although their flesh is even fatter than normal. There are even some pigs, kept on one of the *motu* (lagoon islets), that have learnt to dig up and break open *pahua* clam shells, which are an Aitutakian delicacy.

old homeland, Ra'iatea, to begin the work of bringing Christianity to the Cooks. Williams returned two years later to find that Papeiha had made remarkable progress. As a result, he was moved on to greater challenges on Rarotonga.

Later European visitors included Charles Darwin on the famous voyage of the *Beagle* in 1835. The first European missionary took up residence in 1839, and the 1850s saw Aitutaki become a favourite port of call for whaling ships scouring the Pacific. During WWII Aitutaki went through great upheaval when a huge American contingent moved in to build the island's two long runways, which until 1974 were larger than Rarotonga's airport runway.

Orientation

You can make a tour of Aitutaki in just a few hours. The road runs near the coast most of the way, and passes through several pleasant villages. Arutanga, about halfway down the west coast, is the island's main settlement; it runs north into Amuri and south into Nikaupara. On the east coast are other villages, much smaller and quieter – Tautu, Vaipae and Vaipeka. The numerous *motu* around the edge of Aitutaki's lagoon are unpopulated.

Information

The island's **information office** (☎ 31767; **e** *retire-tourism@aitutaki.net.ck*) is located next to the Orongo Centre.

The New Zealand Department of Lands & Survey's 1:25,000 topographical map of Aitutaki, widely available on both Rarotonga and Aitutaki, shows the island's roads and trails and the coral formations in the lagoon. *What's On* and *Jason's*, two free tourist publications, contain maps of both Rarotonga and Aitutaki, with items of interest to visitors (hotels, restaurants, sights etc) clearly marked. You'll find these maps, and others, at the information office.

Westpac (☎ 31714) has a **branch** (open 9.30am-3pm Mon & Thur) in the Administration Centre, and the **ANZ Bank agent** (☎ 31418) is next door to Fletcher's Bar & Grill in Arutanga. Both banks give cash advances on credit cards and change foreign currencies (cash and travellers cheques). The Aitutaki Pearl Beach Resort gives cash advances on credit cards, for a fee, but only to its guests.

The **post office** (☎ 31470) is at the Administration Centre at the intersection of the two main roads in Arutanga (the coast road and the road leading down to the wharf). Aitutaki issues its own special postage stamps that are not available on Rarotonga. The post office closes for an hour at lunch time.

The **Telecom office** (☎ 31680, fax 31683) is also in the Administration Centre. Here you can send and receive faxes, or buy a Kiaorana card to use in the **public phone** (☎ 31684; accessible 24hr) outside.

Ask at your hotel if you should boil the water before drinking it. At some places, the water comes from underground and should be boiled first; at others it may come from a special rainwater tank.

If you need medical attention, go up to the **hospital** (☎ 31002; open 24hr) behind Arutanga. There's a **police office** behind the Orongo Centre near the wharf. It is staffed infrequently.

The **Air Rarotonga office** (☎ 31888; **e** *airraro@aitutaki.net.ck*) is on the main

AITUTAKI ATOLL

AITUTAKI ATOLL

PLACES TO STAY
6 Paradise Cove
8 Are Tamanu; Matriki Adventures
9 Vaikoa Units
11 Josie's Beach Lodge; Ranginui's Retreat
12 Aitutaki Pearl Beach Resort
14 Pacific Resort
16 Sunny Beach Lodge
20 Tom's Beach Cottage
21 Rino's Beach Bungalows & Rentals
22 Josie's Lodge
34 Aitutaki Lodges
35 Gina's Garden Lodges
37 Maina Sunset Motel

PLACES TO EAT
7 Tauono's
28 Orongo Centre; Blue Nun Cafe; Information Office; Shops; Public Toilet; Police Office
36 Café Tupuna

OTHER
1 Ministry of Marine Resources
2 Golf Club
3 Four-Ways Store
4 Coconut Crusher Bar
5 United Rentals Express
10 Aitutaki Handcrafts
13 Samade
15 Fletcher's Bar & Grill; ANZ Bank Agent
17 Aitutaki Scuba
18 The Heineken Store
19 Swiss Rentals
23 Air Rarotonga
24 Maina Traders Superstore
25 Aitutaki Game Fishing Club
26 Roman Catholic Church
27 Administration Centre; Post Office; Telecom; Westpac Bank
29 CICC
30 Mormon Church
31 Hospital
32 Neibaa's Store
33 Anitonia's Handicrafts; Vaipae Wharf Petrol Station
38 Marae Tokangarangi
39 Marae Te Poaki O Rae

Black Rocks
14
15
16
17
18
Amuri
19
Sports Field
20
21
22
Sports Field
23
24
25
26
27
Wharf
28
29
Arutanga
Sports Field
30
0   500m

See Enlargement

1
2
3
5
4
6
7
8
9
Maungapu (124m)
10
Vaipeka
Airstrip
Jetty
13
11
O'otu Beach
12
Akitua
'Angarei
Ee
Mangere
Arutanga Passage
32
Arutanga
31
33
Vaipae Wharf
Vaipae
34
Nikaupara
36
35
37
Tautu
Tautu Wharf
38
39
Te Koutu Pt
Papau
Tavaerua Iti
Tavaerua Nui
To Manuae Atoll (101km)
To Rarotonga (259km)
Coral Ridges
Coral Ridges
Akaiami
Muritapua
Maina
Moturakau
Tekopua
Rapota
Tapuaeta'i (One Foot Island)
Motukitiu
0   1   2km
0   0.5   1mi

road in Arutanga. Public toilets are behind the Orongo Centre.

Beaches & Snorkelling

Beaches on most parts of the main island are beautiful but not that good for swimming because the water is so shallow. From the roadside opposite Fletcher's Bar & Grill you can walk all the way to the outer reef on a natural coral causeway that starts 50m from the shore – at low tide it's not more than knee-deep all the way.

There are interesting coral rock pools just inside the outer reef and places where you can snorkel. A little to the north of where this causeway meets the outer reef is the Tonga Ruta passage, where you can fish. The branches of the passage are very narrow – some are only 30cm wide – but they are over 15m deep and full of fish. This is one of the main passages through which the lagoon drains, so the outgoing current is very strong as the tide ebbs – be extremely careful.

If you continue around the corner beyond the black rocks on the beach, to the north of the Pacific Resort, there's a slightly better beach, with water about 1.5m deep and some interesting snorkelling. Beware of stonefish in this area, however.

The snorkelling is pretty good along this same stretch of coast all the way up to the airport, even though the water is not deep. The reef here is close in, and the coral formations support an abundance of life.

Snorkelling is also good near O'otu Beach (see that section later) and in the channel separating Akitua *motu* from the main island, especially at the outer end of the channel, towards the reef, and at the lagoon end, around the far tip of the *motu*. Lots of local children come to this channel to swim.

Anywhere there's a jetty – beside the wharf in Arutanga, or around the eastern side of the island – there's water deep enough to swim in, and you're likely to find lots of friendly local children doing just that. The best swimming, snorkelling and beaches are found out on the lagoon *motu*. See Lagoon Cruises, following, for how to get to them.

You may notice a substantial amount of dead, white coral. This is the legacy of recent, slightly warmer than usual temperatures

Coconut Crabs

Unfortunately for the large, blue-grey coconut crab (*unga*), its flesh is delicious. The crab has been eaten to near extinction on many Pacific islands, but is still common on some of the Cook Islands.

Coconut crabs are slow growers: they can take 20 years to reach their mature weight of 2kg or more, and they live to a ripe old age. They live close to the water and come out at night to feed on the flesh of coconuts. How they crack open the coconuts is something of a mystery. Some people believe that they simply use their enormous claws to crack them open, but others claim they scale the palm trees and snip off a few coconuts, which split open when they hit the ground.

in the lagoon. Sadly, global warming (see Ecology & Environment in the Facts about the Cook Islands chapter), boosted by periodic El Niños, will cause this to happen more and more often in the future. Aitutaki's coral will probably recover from this one-off 'coral bleaching' event, but as global warming worsens, the periods of increased temperatures will last longer and eventually the coral will not have time to recover.

Lagoon Cruises

Several operators offer trips on the lagoon and to the *motu* around it. Ask around, and at your hotel, about who is doing the cruises during your stay.

Always check exactly what is included in a cruise. Some go to only one island, others go to many; most are full-day cruises and include transport to and from your accommodation, snorkelling gear and a barbecued-fish lunch on the *motu*. If you can, it's worth bringing your own snorkelling gear – the boats sometimes don't have quite enough to go around.

Check whether there's a roof on the boat, unless you don't mind getting sunburnt (some boats have a substantial roof; others have just a small shelter). Prices are about NZ$50 to NZ$55 for a full day, including lunch. Cruises operate every day except Sunday, when the whole island takes a day off.

Cheaper options are the boats that do 'drop-offs' (ie, they drop you off on the *motu*, then come back and pick you up later). Take your own food.

Check out the following cruise operators.

Bishop's Lagoon Cruises (☎ 31009, e bishop cruz@aitutaki.net.ck) NZ$55 per person. Bishop's has three smallish boats, all with roofs. You visit several different dive spots, but you don't spend long at each one.

Kit Cat (☎ 31418, e mango@aitutaki.net.ck) NZ$55. Kit Cat has two boats: a 30ft catamaran (with a roof and a bar) and a smaller launch (with roof). The trips offer a good compromise between travelling comfort and snorkelling time.

Maina Sunset Motel (☎ 31511) NZ$55. Maina has two boats – both with roofs.

Matriki Adventures (☎ 31564, e matriki@aitu taki.net.ck) NZ$25. Matriki offers drop-offs only (boats are without roofs). There's a trimaran available for sailing or fishing trips just outside the reef (NZ$40).

Paradise Islands Cruises (☎ 31248, e titiaitonga@ aitutaki.net.ck) Aitutaki Pearl Beach Resort. NZ$50. Cruises are on the 34ft Polynesian-style catamaran, the *Titi Ai Tonga* (which has a roof and bar). If you're after a stately cruise with great food and plenty of room, this is the one for you.

Teking (☎ 31582) NZ$35 half-day. Drop-offs only, travelling on a roofless boat.

A peaceful alternative to the motorised boats of the lagoon-cruise operators is a tour on a poled outrigger canoe. **Tauono's** (☎/fax 31562) takes people out to the reef for snorkelling, swimming, fishing and reef-walking. The trip takes four hours and costs NZ$40/70 for one/two people.

Diving

On Aitutaki, diving outside the lagoon is an attraction. The visibility is great, and features include drop-offs, multilevels, wall dives, deep dives and cave dives. The drop-off at the edge of the reef is as much as 200m in places, and divers have seen everything up to, and including, whale sharks, humpback whales and an operating submarine!

The only professional diving operator on the island, affiliated with PADI and NAUI, is Neil Mitchell at **Aitutaki Scuba** (☎ 31103, fax 31310; e scuba@aitutaki.net.ck). Diving trips with/without gear hire cost NZ$90/80.

Discounts are available for multiple dives. If you're not a certified diver you can pay NZ$35 and go along just to snorkel. Diving certification courses cost NZ$550 for a minimum four-day course, and 'Experience Scuba' dives inside the lagoon, with no previous diving experience required, cost NZ$75. If you're really concerned about dive safety, you might find the Aitutaki operation a bit relaxed for your liking.

Other Water Sports

If you fancy tootling around the lagoon yourself, there are a handful of places where you can rent boats or kayaks. A kayak of your own is the *best* way to see the lagoon *motu*! The pub **Samade** (☎ 31526), directly opposite the Aitutaki Pearl Beach Resort, rents kayaks (one hour/half-day/full day NZ$10/15/20). Samade also does meals and drinks (see Places to Eat, and Entertainment, later).

A kayak trip on the lagoon followed by lunch and a beer on the beach is a great way to spend Sunday afternoon on Aitutaki – apart from Samade, the island is as quiet as a (church) mouse. **Ranginui's Retreat** (☎ 31657), between Samade and the resort, rents small inflatable dinghies called reef-runners (two hours/half-day/full day NZ$35/50/80), with see-through bottoms in which you can watch the marine life. **Matriki Adventures** (☎ 31564) rents dinghies for NZ$40 per day.

Fishing

You can go big-game fishing for marlin, tuna, wahoo and *ma'i ma'i* outside the reef, or hunt smaller reef fish inside the lagoon. There are several operators on the island – you'll see them advertised in pamphlets around the places to stay, or on signs on the side of the road. Most of them operate daily except Sunday. All prices include fishing gear. If you're heading outside the reef, *please* ask whether the operators take life jackets.

Aitutaki Sea Charters (☎ 31695) Big-game fishing trips (four to five hours) outside the reef cost NZ$110 per person

Barry Anderson (☎ 31492) Full-day trips inside and outside the lagoon are NZ$150/180 for one/two people

Clive Baxter (☎ 31025) Big-game fishing trips (four to five hours) outside the reef are NZ$105 per person

Matriki Adventures (☎ 31564) Tours just outside the reef are NZ$40 per person

Tauono's (☎/fax 31562) Reef-fishing trips are NZ$40/70 for one/two people

Exploring

If you've got wheels, or even if you're on foot, an exploration of Aitutaki's back roads can be enormously rewarding. Roads on the island are very well signposted, and it's a pretty small island so you'd have to work hard to get lost for long. Cars, little 100cc motorbikes, and mountain bikes can be hired from a number of places on the island.

Golf

To arrange club hire (NZ$10) and play a round (green fees NZ$20) on the Aitutaki Golf Course, phone **Ned Neale** (☎ 31188) or **Putangi Mose** (☎ 31508).

Arutanga

Arutanga is a pleasant, sleepy little South Seas town. There are a number of trade stores and a weathered old Cook Islands Christian Church (CICC) picturesquely situated by the playing fields next to the harbour. Built in 1828 the church is the oldest in the Cooks, and also one of the most beautiful, with carved wood painted red, yellow, green and white all around the ceiling, darker-coloured woodcarvings over the doorways, simple stained-glass windows, and an anchor placed on the ceiling with the inscription 'Ebera 6:19' (Hebrews 6:19). A colourful mural over the altar shows angels announcing 'Tapu, Tapu, Tapu' (Holy, Holy, Holy).

The church also has some of the best acoustics in the Cooks, wonderful for enjoying the spirited hymn singing. In the church yard there's a double-sided monument to the LMS's pioneering Reverend John Williams and to Papeiha, the Polynesian preacher who Williams left here in 1821.

The harbour is quiet, although there are often a few visiting yachts moored offshore. Larger ships have to be unloaded by barges outside the lagoon. You can get an excellent view of the island's whole western coastline from the end of the jetty.

The Orongo Centre, beside the harbour, was built as a banana-packing plant to handle the island's major export crop. It now contains the Blue Nun Cafe and some small crafts and clothing shops. The building occupies the site of the Orongo Marae, one of the island's most important marae; the large stones on the southern side of the building are part of this marae.

Marae

Aitutaki has a number of marae, in various states of overgrowth. If you're a marae aficionado, you'll notice the ones here are notable for the large size of the stones.

The main road along the east coast goes right through a big marae at the turn-off to the Aitutaki Lodges; the stones are along both sides of the road. The huge banyan tree arching over the road here is a memorable sight.

On the inland road between Nikaupara and Tautu, the sign saying 'Marae' will direct you to some of the most historically significant marae on the island. (However, only one of them, Te Poaki O Rae, was cleared at the time of writing). You might want to ask if the marae have been cleared before you go out to look for them.

Tokangarangi, hidden by bush, just off the inland road to your right, is a marae built by Temuna Korero, who came from 'Avaiki on the canoe *Ua-Tuau-Au*.

Further south are two very large marae, one on either side of the track. The one on your left (east), **Te Poaki O Rae** (The Stone of Rae), covers about 1.6 hectares. It has several groupings of stones, but the tallest one, at 2.8m, is attributed to Rae, who brought it from a more ancient marae elsewhere on the island. The line of stones on your right as you enter the marae area was where watchmen used to stand to guard the marae.

From the marae the road continues south to the coast, but it quickly deteriorates into a water-logged, muddy little track, buzzing with ravenous mosquitoes and travelled only by mad Lonely Planet authors in search of lost religious villages (which we didn't find anyway).

Maungapu

Maungapu, at just 124m, is the highest point on the island. It's an easy 30-minute hike to the top, from where there's a superb view of the island and the entire lagoon. The route to the top takes off from opposite the Paradise Cove motel and is marked by a sign on the road. It starts off gently and gets steeper as you near the top.

O'otu Beach

At O'otu you can share the Aitutaki Pearl Beach Resort's great view and excellent snorkelling without shelling out NZ$1000 a night for the privilege. **Samade** (☎ 31526) is the centre of attention here – a great open-air bar with kayak hire, food and, of course, beer (even on Sunday!). See Places to Eat, and Entertainment, later for more details. Nearby is **Ranginui's Retreat** (☎ 31657), which has reef-runners for hire.

The only sensibly priced accommodation options in the area are Ranginui's Retreat and Josie's Beach Lodge (see Places to Stay, later).

Snorkelling in this area is magnificent, or you can just watch the prolific sea life from the bridge to the resort.

Aitutaki Lagoon

Aitutaki's lagoon is one of the wonders of the Cook Islands. It is large, colourful and full of sea life, although fortunately not sharks. The snorkelling is spectacular. The lagoon is dotted with sandbars, coral ridges and 21 *motu*, many of which have their own stories.

Maina This island, in the southwest corner of the lagoon, offers some of Aitutaki's best snorkelling; on the coral formations near its shore and around the large powder-white sandbars just to the north and east. It is also the nesting place of the red-tailed tropicbird, which inspired Cook Islanders from as far away as 'Atiu to come seeking its red tail feathers to use in ceremonial headdresses. If you're here at the right time of year you may get to see them nesting on the island; their nesting season ends around December when they fly off to other lands.

Akaiami This is the *motu* where the old flying boats used to land to refuel. You can still see the wharf on the lagoon side of Akaiami. There are some thatched houses near the wharf, used for short camping trips to the *motu* by its traditional owners.

Eastern Motu From Akaiami southwards, the eastern *motu* are interesting to explore, but the snorkelling is not so good because there is little coral. It's an easy trip by kayak from O'otu Beach to any of these *motu*, and chances are you'll have them to yourself. If

Aitutaki Gets a Mountain

According to legend, Aitutaki was once just a low atoll. The inhabitants decided that they needed a mountain for their island, so they went off across the sea in search of one. Coming to Rarotonga, they spotted Raemaru, the mountain behind the village of 'Arorangi, and thought that it would be perfect. However, it was rather large for Aitutaki, so they decided they'd take just the top off and bring that home.

Late at night, they sneaked up the sides of Raemaru and encircled it, thrust their spears in until they had severed the top from the bottom, and took off with it. They held it aloft with their spears as they set off for Aitutaki in their canoes, spread out in the sea all around the mountain top.

When morning came, the 'Arorangi villagers looked up and noticed something was wrong. They set off in hot pursuit of the Aitutakians to reclaim their mountain. But the fierce Aitutakian warriors beat the Rarotongans back, using only their single free hands while still holding the mountain aloft between them with their spears in their other hands. After bringing the mountain top to Aitutaki, they placed it on the northern part of the island.

Back on Rarotonga, Raemaru today has a distinctly cut-off, flat-topped appearance.

you visit during the wet season (December to April), bring mosquito repellent.

Tapuaeta'i Aitutaki's most famous *motu*, certainly the one most visited by tourists, is Tapuaeta'i, or One Foot Island, with its lovely white stretch of beach. The brilliant, pale-turquoise colour of the water off this beach is truly amazing. The channel between One Foot Island and its neighbour, Tekopua, is very shallow and the pure white sand of the lagoon causes the water to gleam. There's no coral in the lagoon, so the snorkelling is not so good, although the clear water compensates for this. The Tapuaeta'i 'post office' (purely for the benefit of tourists – no-one actually lives here) will stamp your passport if you like. All the lagoon-cruise boats spend some time here, which is strange because it's not actually

Tapuaeta'i (One Foot Island)

The name Tapuaeta'i means not 'One Foot', but 'One Footprint'. There are several versions of how this *motu* got its name. One legend tells of how a father and son, fleeing warriors from the main island, sought refuge on Tapuaeta'i. Upon reaching the *motu's* shore, the father picked his son up, ran across the beach, and hid the child in a tree. When the warriors arrived they killed the father, but, having seen only one set of footprints leading away from his canoe, did not realise the man's son was there. The son returned to Aitutaki and told the story of how the single set of footprints had saved his life.

In another legend, a seafarer from Tonga was crossing the seas with his sister. She died, but he wanted to bury her on land, not throw her to the sharks, so he kept her body in the canoe until he sighted land. He entered Aitutaki's lagoon and landed on Tapuaeta'i, hoping to bury his sister on the *motu*. As he disembarked from the canoe, however, some fierce Aitutakians emerged from the bush and he jumped back into the canoe and sailed away, still bearing his sister's body and leaving only a single footprint in the sand.

---

that flash. Still, it's a very pretty island and there's a bar, which is nice after a day on the lagoon.

Moturakau & Rapota 'Tree Island' (Moturakau) is where the reality-TV show *Shipwrecked I* was filmed. There's little left now to show that those ground-breaking competitors ever lived (and bitched and moaned) here, but what is left of their hut remains.

If you were a fan of the show, it's worth checking the island out. It's amusing to wonder how the camera operators kept the dozens of lagoon-cruising vessels out of shot to support that 'miles from civilisation' feeling.

Nearby, Rapota was the site of a leper colony in the 19th century (when Aitutaki's dog population was chosen as a scapegoat for the disease).

An unfortunate pair of islands indeed – Rapota with its lepers, and Moturakau with reality TV.

Tauono's

Tauono's (*☎/fax 31562*) is operated by a couple renowned for their friendliness: Tauono, a local, and Sonja, his Austrian-Canadian wife. Tauono and Sonja give free garden tours – German, French, English and Maori are spoken.

Tauono conducts reef tours in an outrigger canoe (see Lagoon Cruises, earlier). He used to rent out a second canoe for DIY reef tours, but a coconut tree fell on the canoe!

A wide variety of organic fruits, vegetables and herbs can be picked to order from the lush garden; Tauono's also sells deep-sea and reef fish, European-style cakes, coffee and herbal teas.

Ministry of Marine Resources

Near the airport, the Ministry of Marine Resources (*☎ 31406; admission NZ$2*) is worth at least a quick visit. Several species of giant clams – the huge ones with wavy lips – are being raised in tanks here, and in a farm in the lagoon, for introduction into the lagoon. Baby sea turtles are also raised here.

Organised Tours

Island Tours (*☎ 31379; e islands@aitutaki .net.ck*), at Are Tamanu, has distinctive buses that mostly carry day trippers on organised tours, but you can join in too for this enthusiastically delivered introduction to the island. If there are enough people (minimum of four), Island Tours will do a historical tour (three hours; NZ$25). Two-hour circle-island tours cost NZ$18 and take place Monday through to Saturday.

Chloe & Nane's (*☎ 31248*) offers village and marae tours, and a bus service to church on Sunday. Circle-island tours cost NZ$30 and take place from Monday to Saturday.

Places to Stay – Budget

Paradise Cove (*☎ 31218, fax 31293; e mtl@ aitutaki.net.ck; house singles/doubles NZ$25/ 35, hut singles/doubles NZ$35/50, bungalows NZ$190*) is on a beautiful stretch of beach with fine, white sand and good snorkelling. Accommodation options are (dark) rooms in a large house, with shared kitchen, bathroom and lounge; or thatched-roof, free-standing huts and bungalows right on the beach. Huts are pretty basic; bungalows have their own fridge, bathroom and cooking facilities.

Vaikoa Units (π/fax 31145; singles/ doubles/triples NZ$40/75/80) has six self-contained motel-type units, each with a kitchen and bathroom. It's on a lovely stretch of white beach that's good for swimming and snorkelling. Stays of a week or more are discounted.

Tom's Beach Cottage (π 31051, fax 31409; e papatoms@aitutaki.net.ck; singles NZ$32-35, doubles/triples NZ$50/58, bungalow singles/doubles/triples NZ$86/94/104) is a friendly, relaxed place right on the beach, though it's too shallow for swimming. There are shared cooking facilities, a big common room and plenty of space out the back. All the rooms are in the main house except for one bungalow, which is out the back. Guests can rent bicycles (NZ$5 per day) and rattly old scooters (NZ$15).

Josie's Lodge (π 31111, fax 31518; singles/doubles/triples NZ$20/36/50) has six smallish bedrooms, plus one larger family room. All the rooms have canopy mosquito nets over the beds and lots of lace curtains for aesthetic appeal. You can do your own cooking or have meals prepared. Josie expects her guests to behave themselves – no drinking allowed. She also runs Josie's Beach Lodge.

Josie's Beach Lodge (π 31659; O'otu Beach; singles/doubles/triples NZ$20/38/50) is on a fantastic beach, and Samade is nearby, but you're a long way from town.

Matriki Adventures (π 31564; e matriki@aitutaki.net.ck; singles/doubles NZ$30/ 45) has one self-contained beach hut with limited cooking facilities, and an outside shower and toilet.

Places to Stay – Mid-Range

Gina's Garden Lodges (π/fax 31058; e queen@aitutaki.net.ck; Tautu; singles/ doubles/triples NZ$75/120/150), with four self-contained lodges in a peaceful garden setting, is run by one of Aitutaki's ariki (high chiefs), Manarangi Tutai Ariki (also known as 'Queenie'). The lodges accommodate up to four adults, or three adults and two kids. Scooter hire and ute (truck) hire is available.

Tom's Beach Cottage (π 31051, fax 31409; e papatoms@aitutaki.net.ck; singles/ doubles/triples NZ$86/94/104) has a private, self-contained, one-bedroom 'honeymoon' unit.

Renting a House

There are a few top-end houses to rent on Aitutaki, and some cheaper ones, too.

Rino's Beach Bungalows (π 31197, fax 31559; e rinos@aitutaki.net.ck; houses per week NZ$200, apartments per night NZ$200-300) has a couple of big, cheap, older houses in town, plus three brand-new, self-contained apartments 150m north of Fletcher's Bar & Grill.

The Heineken Store (Maki Trading; π 31003, fax 31249; house per night NZ$100) has a big two-bedroom house across from the store. It sleeps up to six people.

John Tini (π 23090; e tini@oyster.net.ck; villa NZ$180), a clean, new beach villa, is on a private section of land 800m north of Fletcher's Bar & Grill.

Check the **Jetsave Travel website** (w www .jetsave.co.ck) for other houses to rent on Aitutaki.

Sunny Beach Lodge (π/fax 31446; e sunny beach@aitutaki.net.ck; singles/doubles/triples NZ$75/85/95) has a row of five self-contained studio units. It's on the beach side of the road, opposite Aitutaki Scuba.

Rino's Beach Bungalows (π 31197, fax 31559; e rinos@aitutaki.net.ck; doubles NZ$111-221) has four self-contained studio units (which sleep six people), two beachfront rooms (five people), and two deluxe beachfront rooms (two people) with great views. Across the road, beside Rino's Rentals, is a three-bedroom house (see the boxed text 'Renting a House').

Places to Stay – Top End

Pacific Resort (π 31720, fax 31719; w www .pacificresort.com; singles & doubles from NZ$615, plus third person NZ$75) is a 30-room resort about 2km north of the centre of Arutanga. Rooms sleep up to three, and prices for doubles range from NZ$615 to well over NZ$1000. All the usual resort facilities are available – see the website for details.

Maina Sunset Motel (π 31511, fax 31611; w www.soltel.co.ck; Nikaupara; studio units NZ$160, units with kitchen NZ$195), a lagoonside motel about 1km south of Arutanga, has eight studio units and four one-bedroom units facing a courtyard. The prices listed are for doubles; extra children/adults cost another NZ$20/30. Kids under 12 years aren't allowed.

The beach here is muddy and shallow – no good for swimming – but there's a small swimming pool, and. There's also a restaurant and bar, and, for guests, snorkel-gear hire (NZ$5 per day) and motorbike hire (NZ$25 per day). Maina operates lagoon cruises (NZ$55 per person, including lunch).

Are Tamanu (☎ 31810, fax 31816; W www.aretamanu.com; doubles NZ$365-410) has 12 individual, thatched-roof luxury units set around a small garden area. Each unit has a king-size bed, air-con and fan, and full cooking and bathroom facilities. A pool looks right out onto the beach, with a private bar only metres away. Bicycles and kayaks are free. No kids under 12 years accepted.

Aitutaki Lodges (☎ 31334, fax 31333; W www.ck/aitutakilodges; Vaipae; 1-/2-/3-person chalets NZ$238/248/321 plus per extra child NZ$46), on the east coast of the island, has six A-frame chalets, each with a large veranda facing the lagoon. The view, of the lagoon and the motu stretching away in the distance, is unsurpassed on the island. The only drawbacks are that the beach here is muddy and unsuitable for swimming, and you're about 3.5km from town (a lazy one-hour walk each way). Motorcycle hire is NZ$30 per day (or walk up the road to Vaipae Wharf where the rate is NZ$20). You can cook for yourself or arrange for cooked meals; there's an open-air bar and dining room under a thatched roof.

Ranginui's Retreat (☎ 31657, fax 31658; e ranginui@aitutaki.net.ck; O'otu Beach; units NZ$120) has self-contained units that sit in fairly ordinary grounds, but the view from the deck across the channel and out to the lagoon is fantastic!

Aitutaki Pearl Beach Resort (☎ 31201, fax 31202; W www.aitutakipearlbeach.com; rooms NZ$335, bungalows NZ$595-1195), at the far end of the airstrip, is on Akitua motu, which is joined to the main island by a footbridge. It has all the mod cons, including two restaurant/bars (see Places to Eat, later), a swimming pool and many activities on offer. Meal plans are expensive: NZ$115 (all meals) per day. The resort's major drawback, apart from the price, is its considerable isolation from the rest of the island. Scooters (NZ$20/35 for four hours/one day) and cars (NZ$70/96 for six hours/one day) are available (if you're here for more than a couple of days, get into Arutanga and rent cheaper wheels there).

Places to Eat

Cafés, Bars & Restaurants A breezy open-air café/bar, the **Blue Nun Cafe** (☎ 31604; Orongo Centre; burgers NZ$4-7, mains NZ$9-14) has a view of the lagoon and the wharf, and sells basic foods such as curries, burgers and fish dishes. At night it transforms into a popular little bar, with 'island nights' on Wednesday and Saturday (see Entertainment, later). Food is served from 9am to 9pm Monday to Saturday.

Samade (☎ 31526; O'otu Beach; lunch NZ$7-9, dinner NZ$13-20), with tables both under the thatched-roof hut and out on the white sand, is a great spot for lunch or dinner. Sunday's lunch (NZ$15) is an umukai (traditional Polynesian food cooked in an underground oven). Tuesday's dinner is followed by an island-night dance performance (see Entertainment, later). Transport is available.

Pacific Resort (☎ 31720; mains NZ$24-36) serves up some of the best food (and wine) on the island – try the seafood!

Coconut Crusher Bar (☎ 31283; dinner NZ$13-26), on the northern side of the island, is a true island-style place, with a thatched-roof, open-air dining room, island decor, and live music most nights of the week. There's almost always a cheap meal (around NZ$12 to NZ$15) on the menu. Thursday's island-night buffet and floor show is NZ$25 (see Entertainment, later). Free transport is provided for diners.

Café Tupuna (☎ 31678; Tautu; brunch NZ$8-10, dinner mains NZ$20-24), way out in the middle of the island, is a veritable gourmet's delight. There's great coffee and great food, and staff can arrange transport if you give them enough notice.

There are two restaurant/bars at the **Aitutaki Pearl Beach Resort** (☎ 31201; breakfast NZ$10, lunch NZ$15-20 plus extras NZ$7, dinner mains NZ$25-35) – they're pricey, but good spots to spoil yourself. Nonresort guests are welcome, and free pickup is available. Breakfast is eaten in the indoors restaurant, Are Kai Kai, and lunch is eaten in the lagoonside, open-air Ru's Beach Bar. Dinner switches between the two venues, depending on the weather. Lavish buffets and island-style floor shows are put on three times a week (NZ$60 for dinner and show; the show alone is free) – Saturday night is a barbecue dinner, Monday is an *umukai* and Wednesday is seafood.

Maina Sunset Motel *(☎ 31511; Nikaupara; breakfast NZ$8-12, dinner NZ$18, dessert NZ$7)*, tucked away at the southern end of the island, has a restaurant that is a good option for a quiet lagoonside dinner.

Fletcher's Bar & Grill *(☎ 31950; mains NZ$18-30, desserts NZ$8, children's menu NZ$6)* serves some pretty ordinary meals, but the setting is pleasant. There's an island-night performance on Friday (see Entertainment, later).

Tauono's *(☎ 31562; lunch NZ$16, cakes NZ$5)* uses all-fresh ingredients in the garden – their delicious but pricey! If you're self-catering on Aitutaki, you won't find better fresh ingredients than here. Lunch is served from 12pm to 2pm, cakes from 3pm to 5pm.

Self-Catering The shops have the usual Cook Islands selection of tins and a very limited selection of fresh fruits and vegetables. The choice is more restricted than on Rarotonga and prices are much higher. It's worth bringing some supplies with you, particularly if you plan to cook for yourself.

Maina Traders Superstore *(☎ 31055)* is the biggest shop on the island. **The Heineken Store** *(Maki Trading; ☎ 31003)* also has a good selection.

Only the **Four-Ways Store** *(☎ 31492)*, near the airstrip, and **Neibaa's Store** *(☎ 31655)* in Vaipae are open on Sunday.

Tauono's *(☎ 31562)* offers a wide variety of organic fruits, vegetables and herbs from its garden (all fresh-picked when you come), plus deep-sea and reef fish. For more details, see the separate section earlier.

Entertainment

Aitutaki's handful of bars seem to take it in turns to put on an island night – Tuesday at Samade, Wednesday night at the Blue Nun, Thursday at Crusher's, Friday at Fletcher's and Saturday back at the Blue Nun. An island-night performance at these bars is invariably a great social event – the locals come along to watch in greater numbers than travellers, and invariably there's 'modern' (ie, 1970s onwards) music and dance afterwards.

Beers cost from NZ$2 for a glass from the tap and from NZ$3 for a can. None of these places have a cover charge. Most of them will come and pick you up from your accommodation if you ring and arrange it beforehand.

Fletcher's Bar & Grill *(☎ 31950)* has inside and open-air seating. There's an island-night performance on Friday (NZ$30 with dinner; the show alone is free), usually with a dance following that. Missing dinner would be no tragedy, but dining in does increase your chances of getting a good view of the show.

Coconut Crusher Bar *(☎ 31283)*, on the northern part of the island, features cheapish dinners and live music several nights, with an excellent, intimate island-night performance on Thursday nights (NZ$25 with dinner; free without); reservations are essential.

Samade *(☎ 31526; O'otu Beach)* has an island night on Tuesday, with the floor show starting at 8pm, followed by dancing until late (NZ$25 for meal and show; entrance is free for the show alone, 'as long as you buy a few drinks'). The tables out on the sand are a long way from the show. Sunday afternoons are particularly popular here, with kayak hire, traditional food and a magnificent beach making it *the* place to be. Beers, spirits and smoothies cost NZ$3.50.

Blue Nun Cafe *(☎ 31604; Orongo Centre)* has a big night on Saturday, when an island-night dance show, at 9pm, follows the barbecue buffet. There's another island night on Wednesday, and cheap beer (NZ$2.50 per can) on Tuesday and Thursday.

Aitutaki Game Fishing Club *(☎ 31379)*, at the foot of the wharf in Arutanga, is a simple place to enjoy a cheap beer, a friendly and relaxed atmosphere, and a beautiful view of the sunset.

There are two restaurant/bars at the **Aitutaki Pearl Beach Resort** *(☎ 31201)*. Island dance nights on Saturday, Monday and Wednesday are held at either Are Kai Kai restaurant or the open-air Ru's Beach Bar. It costs NZ$60 for dinner and show; the show alone is free. Ru's, beside the lagoon, is a nice place for a cold beer on any afternoon of the week.

AITUTAKI ATOLL

Pacific Resort (☎ 31720) has casual bar service beside its swimming pool and waterfall complex.

Shopping

Aitutakian crafts include pandanus purses, bags, mats and hats, white *rito* (bleached pandanus leaf) church hats, shell-and-*rito* fans, shell jewellery, wooden drums, ukuleles, *kikau* (palm leaf) brooms, and colourful *pareu* (sarongs) and T-shirts.

Aitutaki Handcrafts (☎ 31127) is near the airstrip. The talented Phillip Low carves traditional drums (from NZ$35), Tangaroa figures (NZ$30 to NZ$130) and ukuleles (NZ$250). In the small showroom attached to his house he also sells local weaving, and *rito* hats from the Northern Cooks (NZ$120).

Anitonia's Handicrafts (☎ 31207; Vaipae) sells *pareu* (NZ$8 to NZ$14), wooden drums (NZ$25 to NZ$35) and other handicrafts.

Tauono's (☎/fax 31562), a garden/café, sells a few handicrafts. See the separate section earlier.

Island crafts and souvenirs are available at a handful of little shops in the Orongo Centre, which is by the wharf in Arutanga. There are some pretty awful souvenirs available at Samade (☎ 31526; O'otu Beach), but perhaps if you have a few beers some of the T-shirts may start to look a little more attractive.

Getting There & Away

Air Aitutaki's large airstrip was built by US forces during WWII. It's the only airport in the Cooks with a two-way runway, and relative to the size of the planes that land here, it's enormous; you could fly Boeing 737s into Aitutaki.

Air Rarotonga (☎ 31888 in Arutanga, ☎ 31347 at the airport) operates three flights a day to Aitutaki, including day tours (see Organised Tours, later) from Monday to Saturday. Regular fares are NZ$184 each way (NZ$154 if you buy on Rarotonga instead of from overseas). Super Saver fares (you must take the last flight of the day from Rarotonga to Aitutaki and the first flight of the day from Aitutaki to Rarotonga) are much cheaper – NZ$123 one way, NZ$246 return.

All the Rarotonga-based travel agents offer package deals for flights, transfers and accommodation on Aitutaki. If you buy on Rarotonga, these packages work out to be cheaper than booking ahead from overseas. (However, if you wait until you're on Rarotonga to book, you do risk missing the flights and/or accommodation that you want.) Day tours are another option; see Organised Tours, later.

The Coral Route

Aitutaki had a pioneering role in Pacific aviation as a stopping point in Tasman Empire Air Line's (TEAL) 'Coral Route'. Back in the 1950s TEAL, the predecessor to Air New Zealand, flew across the Pacific on an Auckland–Suva (Fiji)–Apia (Samoa)–Aitutaki–Pape'ete (Tahiti) route. Most of the journey was in four-engined Solent flying boats.

The stop at Aitutaki was purely to refuel, carried out on the uninhabited *motu* of Akaiami. It took over two hours, so passengers had a chance to take a swim in the lagoon. The old Solents carried their 60-odd passengers in some degree of luxury. Food was actually cooked on the aircraft, in contrast to today's reheated airline meals. At that time, the fortnightly flight into Pape'ete was the only direct air link between Tahiti and the rest of the world, and the aircraft's arrival there was a major event.

Usually the trips were uneventful, but on one occasion a malfunction at Aitutaki required offloading the passengers while the aircraft limped on to Tahiti on three engines. It was a week before it arrived back to collect the passengers – who by that time had begun to really enjoy their enforced stay on hotel-less Aitutaki.

On another occasion, the aircraft was forced to return to Aitutaki when the Tahiti lagoon turned out to be full of logs. The trip to Tahiti was attempted twice more before the lagoon was clear enough for a landing. One of the TEAL flying boats is now on display at the Museum of Transport & Technology (MOTAT) in Auckland, New Zealand.

See the Getting Around chapter for more information about Air Rarotonga's flights, contact details, Super Saver conditions, and multi-island deals, as well as travel-agent packages.

Boat See the Getting Around chapter for information on interisland cargo ship services between Rarotonga and Aitutaki. Often a stop on Aitutaki is included in trips between Rarotonga and the Northern Group islands. The narrow reef passage is too hazardous for large ships to enter, so they are loaded and unloaded outside the reef by barge.

Aitutaki, a popular yachting destination, is an official port of entry for the Cook Islands.

Organised Tours Day trips from Rarotonga to Aitutaki are offered by **Air Rarotonga** (☎ 31888 in Arutanga, ☎ 22888 on Rarotonga), departing from Rarotonga international airport. Trips (adult/child NZ$397/ 195) include an island tour, lagoon cruise (on Paradise Islands' *Titi Ai Tonga*) with snorkelling gear provided, lunch on the lagoon, and plenty of time for swimming, snorkelling and soaking up the sun. Children under two are free. Bookings can be made directly with Air Rarotonga or through travel agents on Rarotonga. Flights depart at 8am and return at 6.30pm, Monday to Saturday.

Getting Around
To/From the Airport Connecting with all arriving and departing flights is **Island Tours** (☎ 31379); the cost is NZ$8 (each way) between Arutanga township and the airport. The two resorts and some hotels provide airport transport for their guests.

Car, Motorcycle & Bicycle Hire Several places on the island rent motorbikes (100cc scooters), cars and bicycles. (Ask at your hotel to see if they rent them; several hotels do.) A lot of places give discounts for longer periods (a week or more). You can get a driving licence at the police station behind the Orongo Centre.

John Tini (☎ 23090) Amuri. Motorbikes are NZ$20 per day.
Matriki Adventures (☎ 31564) Amuri. Motorbikes are NZ$20 per day, dinghies are NZ$40.

Ranginui's Retreat (☎ 31657) O'otu Beach. Motorbikes cost NZ$15/20 per half-day/full day, inflatable dinghies are NZ$35/50/80 for two hours/half-day/full day, and scootcars are NZ$35/50/80.
Rino's Beach Bungalows & Rentals (☎ 31197) Arutanga. Bicycles are NZ$5 per day, motorbikes are between NZ$20 and NZ$25, and Jeeps are between NZ$70 and NZ$85.
Swiss Rentals (☎ 31600) Amuri. Bicycles cost NZ$5 per day and motorbikes NZ$20.
United Rentals Express (☎ 31161) Amuri. Bicycles are NZ$7 per day, motorbikes NZ$20, and there's one car for NZ$50.
Vaipae Wharf Petrol Station (☎ 31489) Vaipae. Motorbikes are NZ$20 per day and 4WDs are between NZ$60 and NZ$70.

Manuae Atoll

pop 0 • area 6.2 sq km
Collectively known as Manuae, these two tiny unpopulated islets, Manuae and Te Au O Tu, belong to the people of Aitutaki, 101km away. Manuae Atoll is protected as a marine reserve.

Manuae is an island whose discovery, and therefore traditional ownership, is disputed. Aitutakians say it was first discovered by the great Polynesian explorer Ruatapu, a contemporary of Tangi'ia. From Ra'iatea

MANUAE ATOLL

Mataara

Turakino Passage · Landing

Te Au O Tu

Turakino

Manuae

Turakino Passage

Arekai · Ruakau

Arikirauru

Nanupoto

To Aitutaki Atoll (101km)

SOUTH PACIFIC OCEAN

0 · 1 · 2km
0 · 0.5 · 1mi

AITUTAKI ATOLL

(the Society Islands), Ruatapu sailed to Rarotonga, Tonga and back to the Southern Cooks and Manuae. He sailed on to Aitutaki to become one of that island's greatest chiefs, but he sent two sons back to Manuae to settle there. ('Atiuans say that the island had already been settled at that point, by two 'Atiuan brothers and their Aitutakian wives.)

Manuae has the notable honour of being the first of the modern-day Cook Islands to be seen by James Cook. He sped past in 1773, naming it Hervey Island (the name he eventually applied to the entire group). But in 1777, on his third and final voyage, Captain Cook stopped and spoke with the inhabitants via a Tahitian interpreter, Omai.

Whether it had been settled by 'Atiuans or Aitutakians originally, in 1777 Omai was told that Manuae was part of the 'Atiuan realm of influence – its people, like those of Ma'uke and Mitiaro, subservient to an 'Atiuan *ariki*. The people of Aitutaki had close family ties with Manuae, however, and travelled there often to gather coconuts.

In 1823 the missionary John Williams visited the island and found about 60 inhabitants. However, soon afterwards, a group of Aitutakians gathering coconuts on Manuae were killed by the locals, and the resulting punitive raid all but wiped out Manuae – there were only a dozen or so people left in the late 1820s, and European missionaries transplanted those to Aitutaki.

Later, a series of Europeans made temporary homes here. The best-known was the fertile William Marsters, who in 1863 was moved to Palmerston Atoll with his three wives (see that atoll's chapter).

Manuae was a penal settlement for a period of time in the 1890s and early 1900s, where prisoners were sent to cut copra before the construction of the Rarotonga jail. Since then it has been uninhabited except for occasional coconut-harvesting visitors from Aitutaki, and fishermen.

There's an airstrip on Manuae, visible as you fly over en route from Aitutaki to 'Atiu, but it hasn't been used for many years.

'Atiu, Ma'uke & Mitiaro

'Atiu, Ma'uke and Mitiaro are often referred to by the collective name Nga Pu Toru, 'The Three Roots'. The three islands are in close proximity – it takes only 10 minutes to fly from one to another – and they can easily be visited as a group.

The islands have been closely tied historically – over the centuries there has been a lot of travel between the three (mostly instances of 'Atiu invading the other two) – and they are also very similar geographically. They're characterised by a narrow lagoon, *makatea* (raised, fossilised coral reef) around the edges and a higher interior.

For the traveller, these islands offer an easy introduction to a far more traditional Polynesia than you'll find on Rarotonga or Aitutaki. No traveller who trades another few days on Rarotonga for some time on 'Atiu, Ma'uke or Mitiaro will regret the decision.

'Atiu

pop 611 • area 26.9 sq km

The third-largest of the Cook Islands, 'Atiu is noted for its *makatea*. Unlike all the other islands in the Cooks, including Mangaia with its similar geography, the villages on 'Atiu are not on the coast. The five villages – Areora, Ngatiarua, Te'enui, Mapumai and Tengatangi – are all close together in the hilly centre of the island.

Prior to the introduction of Christianity, the people lived spread out around the lowlands, where taro is grown. When the missionaries persuaded the people to come upland and move the original settlements together, they effectively created a single village. The island's administration centre and the Cook Islands Christian Church (CICC) form the centre, and the villages radiate out from this centre on five roads, like the five arms of a starfish.

'Atiu has an enormous amount to offer visitors – there are some fine beaches, magnificent scenery, excellent walks, ancient marae (pre-European religious meeting grounds) and the *makatea* is riddled with limestone caves, some of which were used as ancient burial sites. Of all three islands in

Highlights

- Descending to the home of the *kopeka* ('Atiu swiftlet) birds in Anatakitaki on 'Atiu
- Drinking home-brewed beer and discussing island politics in a traditional *tumunu* (bush-beer drinking session) on 'Atiu
- Watching the creation of intricate textile arts at the Atiu Fibre Arts Studio
- Attending a service at Ma'uke's Divided Church, where a line down the centre separates the villages
- Swimming in the freshwater, underground pools of Ma'uke and Mitiaro's *makatea* caves
- Watching the beautiful *vaka* (outrigger canoes) heading out to fish on Ma'uke or Mitiaro
- Renting a motorbike and exploring backcountry roads on all three islands

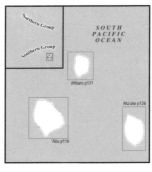

this chapter, 'Atiu is the best set up for tourism, but that's not saying much – 'touristy' the island is not! Most visitors stay for only a couple of days, but that really isn't long enough. Unlike Rarotonga, however, 'Atiu is not a place for easy lazing around – you have to get out and do things; burn some energy.

History

'Atiu's traditional name is 'Enua Manu', which can be translated to 'Land of Birds' or 'Land of Insects' – so-named, one legend

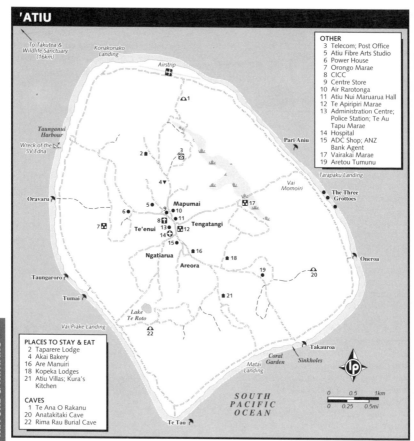

'ATIU

OTHER
3 Telecom; Post Office
5 Atiu Fibre Arts Studio
6 Power House
7 Orongo Marae
8 CICC
9 Centre Store
10 Air Rarotonga
11 Atiu Nui Maruarua Hall
12 Te Apiripiri Marae
13 Administration Centre;
   Police Station; Te Au
   Tapu Marae
14 Hospital
15 ADC Shop; ANZ
   Bank Agent
17 Vairakai Marae
19 Aretou Tumunu

To Takutea &
Wildlife Sanctuary
(16km)

Konakonako
Landing

Airstrip

Taunganui
Harbour

Wreck of the
SV Edna

Pari Aniu

Tarapaku Landing

Vai
Momoiri

Oravaru

The Three
Grottoes

Mapumai

Te'enui

Tengatangi

Ngatiarua

Areora

Oneroa

Taungaroro

Tumai

Lake
Te Roto

Vai Piake Landing

Takauroa

Coral
Garden

Sinkholes

Matai
Landing

SOUTH
PACIFIC
OCEAN

0   0.5   1km
0   0.25   0.5mi

Te Tau

PLACES TO STAY & EAT
2 Taparere Lodge
4 Akai Bakery
16 Are Manuiri
18 Kopeka Lodges
21 Atiu Villas; Kura's
   Kitchen

CAVES
1 Te Ana O Rakanu
20 Anatakitaki Cave
22 Rima Rau Burial Cave

'ATIU, MA'UKE & MITIARO

relates, because nothing but birds and insects lived here when it was first discovered. Numerous legends tell of early settlers arriving by canoe and of visits by legendary Polynesian navigators from Raiatea and Tahiti (in the Society Islands) and Samoa.

'Atiu has had a colourful and bloody history – the 'Atiuans were the greatest warriors of the Cook Islands and specialised in creating havoc on all their neighbouring islands.

In the early 18th century 'Atiu was controlled by seven different *mataiapo* (chiefs), who warred almost constantly among each other. After a momentous battle, three of these *mataiapo* were elevated to the rank of *ariki* (high chiefs) while the others became *ta'unga atua* (priests). This marked the start of 'Atiu's ascendancy in the region, as the three *ariki* extended their power over the neighbouring islands of Manuae, Ma'uke and Mitiaro. They also attacked Rarotonga and Mangaia, although they weren't successful in bringing those two islands under their control.

The European discovery of 'Atiu is credited to James Cook on 3 April 1777. Cook sent three of his boats ashore to try to procure supplies. His men spent a long day being feted (and pickpocketed) by the 'Atiuans, but effectively came back empty handed. At one point, when a large oven was being prepared, Cook's Tahitian hitchhiker, Omai, became convinced that it was intended for himself and his companions and asked the 'Atiuans if they were preparing to eat them – the 'Atiuans expressed shock at the mere thought of such an idea. However, tales that came to light subsequently, of the 'Atiuans' eating habits regarding the natives of Ma'uke and Mitiaro, makes you wonder about their ingenuousness. Omai bought the story anyway (lovely bloke – but no rocket scientist).

With his men safely back on board, Cook sailed away and managed to find the necessary provisions on the neighbouring island of Takutea, where he left 'a hatchet and some nails to the full value of what we took from the island'.

The Reverend John Williams turned up on 19 July 1823, searching for Rarotonga, an island he kept hearing of while crossing Polynesia. Williams carried on board an *ariki* from Aitutaki, who told the leading 'Atiuan chief, Rongomatane Ngaka'ara Ariki, that Aitutaki had already converted to Christianity and that many of the gods there had been destroyed. Rongomatane took the mission party to his personal marae and challenged them to eat the sugar cane from a sacred grove. When the missionaries ate the cane and did not drop dead on the spot Rongomatane became an instant convert, ordered all the idols on the island burnt and told his people to come and listen to the missionaries' teachings.

Rongomatane told Williams that he ruled two other islands close by – Ma'uke and Mitiaro – and that he would like the people on those islands to receive the Gospel as well. He accompanied Williams' ship to these two islands, converting the inhabitants with great speed. There was good reason behind Ma'uke and Mitiaro's rapid acquiescence to Rongomatane's wishes. He was, at the time, the paramount *ariki* of all three islands and had led war parties to both Ma'uke and Mitiaro when the locals needed reminding who was boss. On one vengeful attack on Ma'uke alone Rongomatane's party had killed hundreds, and set up 'Atiuans as chiefs of the island. It's hardly surprising, then, that Ma'ukeans embraced Christianity with such alacrity!

After Williams' successful visit to Nga Pu Toru he still hadn't found Rarotonga, the island he was looking for in the first place. Luckily, 'Atiu had invaded Rarotonga in the past and Rongomatane knew exactly in

No Dancing in Cyclone Season

Up until 1990, dances on 'Atiu had an interesting twist between 1 January and 31 March, a hold over from the 'blue laws' days (when religious laws controlled Cook Islands life). The original London Missionary Society (LMS) missionaries who founded the Cook Islands Christian Church (CICC) managed to convince the people of 'Atiu that if they held dances during the cyclone season, it could cause a cyclone to strike the island! Right up until the 1990s the CICC was still opposed to dances being held at that time. The Roman Catholics, however, had no such compunctions so their dances usually managed to go on regardless.

These days, although no-one is willing to admit to believing in such silly superstitions, there are still very few dances held from January to March.

which direction it lay; he easily directed Williams towards it. Taking the ship to Oravaru beach on 'Atiu's western shore, they lined up the stern of the ship with a big rock in the lagoon, Williams took a compass reading and sailed off in a beeline to find Rarotonga without trouble.

The missionaries subsequently made occasional visits to 'Atiu from Tahiti but in 1836 the Tahitian convert Papeiha was sent back from Rarotonga and started the serious work of bringing Christianity to the island.

Gospel Day is still celebrated on 'Atiu on 19 July every year, often with *nuku* (traditional plays) acting out the drama of how the gospel came to 'Atiu.

Geography & Geology

The island is rather like a very low-brimmed hat with a flat outer rim. This flat outer rim is the *makatea*, a region of sharp, tortured rock formations densely covered in tropical greenery. The *makatea* starts off around 5m in height at the coast and gradually slopes up to around 20m at its inner edge. There's a circular band of swamp at this inner edge that's now extensively used for taro cultivation, where water running off the hills has eroded the edge of the *makatea*. Inland from the swamp the land slopes up to the forested inner plateau – the original

'ATIU, MA'UKE & MITIARO

volcanic core – where coffee and other crops are grown.

'Atiu's geology is fascinating (if you're into that kind of thing). The island rose out of the sea as a volcano cone around 11 million years ago. The cone was worn down to a shoal, then upheaval raised the shoal to form a flat-topped island. Further eons produced a wide coral reef around the island but then, about 100,000 years ago, further upheaval pushed the island another 20m out of the sea. The coral reef became a coastal plain of jagged, fossilised coral formations, stretching back about 1km from the new coastline to the older central hills. In the past 100,000 years a new coral reef has grown up around most of the island, but this is only 100m wide.

Culture

'Atiu has three *ariki* titles: Rongomatane, Ngamaru and Parua. The 'palaces' of Queen Ada (Rongomatane Ada Ariki) and King Henry (Ngamaru Henry Ariki) are two of the nicest houses in town. (The present holder of the Parua *ariki* title lives offshore – not a popular move.) 'Atiuans are fiercely proud of their heritage; when they talk of 'Atiu's historical dominance of nearby islands, Ma'uke and Mitiaro, you suspect they still consider those islands their fiefdom. Traditions such as *tutaka* (community inspections) and *tumunu* (bush-beer drinking sessions) are stronger here than on other Cook Islands.

Traditional crafts still practised on 'Atiu include *tapa* (bark cloth) – 'Atiu's *tapa* flowers are very popular on Rarotonga. There's very little for sale here, however; see Shopping for more information.

Information

The Administration Centre, housing the **island secretary** *(☎ 33269, fax 33369)*, and the CICC form the centre of the island. The **police station** *(☎ 33120)* is in the Administration Centre.

The **'Atiu Tourism Society** *(☎ 33031; w www.atiutourism.com)* is a good source of information about the island. The **'Atiu Island** website *(w www.atiu.info)* is another good source.

Cash advances on credit cards (Visa, MasterCard or Bankcard) are available from the **ADC Shop** *(☎ 33028; Areora)*.

Travellers cheques (NZ dollars only) can be cashed at the **Centre Store** *(☎ 33773; Te'enui)*.

The **post** and **Telecom offices** *(☎ 33680, fax 33683; open 8am-midday & 1pm-4pm Mon-Fri, if you're lucky)* are in the same building, in Mapumai village. You can make international and interisland phone calls, and send and receive faxes.

Tap water on 'Atiu is probably OK to drink, but if you'd rather not risk a few days with an upset stomach, boil it or buy it bottled. The **hospital** *(☎ 33664, 33064)* is staffed from 8am to 3pm, Monday to Friday; 24 hours if there's an inpatient staying. Electricity on 'Atiu operates 24 hours a day.

What to Bring Two important items to bring with you to 'Atiu are a torch (flashlight) and mosquito repellent. The places to stay or cave-tour guides will lend you a torch for cave exploring but one of your own is a handy backup.

Leave your fancy restaurant clothes behind on Rarotonga. If you'll be poking around in caves or on the *makatea* you'll need things like old T-shirts, torn shorts and worn-out running shoes. The big exception is if you plan to go to a dance or to church. Gowns and suits are not needed, but women must wear a dress or skirt and sleeves (and a hat, if you have one) to church, and men must wear long pants.

Standards of modesty on 'Atiu, as on all the outer islands, are more conservative than on Aitutaki or Rarotonga. You'll earn some disapproving glances going without a shirt or wearing very-short shorts or swimming gear in town.

Books If you want more information on 'Atiu there are some interesting books available. *Atiu through European Eyes* is a collection of references to 'Atiu from books and reports. *Atiu, an Island Community* is a study of 'Atiu's current conditions and customs, written by 'Atiuans. *Atiu Nui Maruarua* is a bilingual collection of legends about 'Atiu, told in 'Atiuan Maori and English. All of these books are published by the University of the South Pacific (USP) and are available at USP's Rarotonga Centre in Avarua; you'll find some of them at the **Centre Store** on 'Atiu. The information about 'Atiu and 'Atiuans in chapter four of

Ronald Syme's *The Lagoon is Lonely Now* is amusing.

Caves

The *makatea* is riddled with limestone caves, complete with stalactites and stalagmites. You'll stumble across many small caves in any ramble through the *makatea* so take a torch (flashlight). A good, strong walking stick is a great help when walking in the sharp *makatea*, so bring one along, cut yourself one or ask your guide to cut you one.

Tours of the various caves on 'Atiu typically take two to three hours and cost NZ$15 to NZ$20 per person. You must go with a guide, partly because the caves can be difficult to find but also because the caves are on family land and permission must be obtained before you enter. Many of the caves were used for burials. The place where you're staying can help you to arrange a guide.

Te Ana O Rakanui is an easy walk off the road. The landowners require visitors to go with a guide: **Aue Rakanui** (☎ 33256) – see Organised Tours, later. The cave is extensive, with numerous entrances and exits, and it is very easy to get confused. You have a choice between trusting Aue, or panicking. Just to calm your nerves, the bones of 'Atiu's 'fourth *ariki*', Rakanui Ariki, and his family are plainly visible.

In the southeast of the island is **Anatakitaki**, also called 'Cave of the Kopekas'. *Kopeka* are tiny birds, very much like swifts, which live in huge numbers inside the cave. When they come out to hunt insects they are never seen landing; only in the cave do they rest. Inside the pitch-dark cave they make a continuous chattering, clicking noise which they use to find their way around, like bats. Some of the chambers in this extensive cavern are very large. **Atiu Tours** (☎/fax 33041) lead tours of the cave, including a longish walk across the *makatea* from the plateau road; see Organised Tours, later.

In the southwest the **Rima Rau** burial cave is a smaller cave reached by a vertical pothole. There are many bones to be seen in this cave and nearby there's a very deep sinkhole with a deep, cold pool at the bottom. No-one was leading tours to Rima Rau cave at the time of writing, but ask at the

place you're staying in case the situation has changed.

Lake Te Roto is noted for its eels, a popular island delicacy. On the western side of the lake, a cave leads right through the *makatea* to the sea. You can wade through it for a considerable distance if the water in the lake is low enough. Try **Tura Koronoe** (☎ 33012) for tours to Lake Te Roto.

Warning Take great care when you are walking across the *makatea* – the fossilised coral is really, *really* sharp. If you slipped and fell you'd be in big trouble. Wear good shoes, too; if you stub your toe while wearing sandals you'll probably cut it right off.

Beaches & Coast

'Atiu is not great for swimming – the surrounding lagoon is rarely more than 50m wide and the water is generally too shallow for more than wading and gentle splashing around. You can swim or snorkel at 'Atiu's 'Olympic Swimming Pool', aka **Taunganui Harbour**, where the fish are abundant and the water is clear and deep. (You can usually see the unpopulated island of Takutea from here.)

There are, however, countless beautiful, sandy strips all along the coast. You can easily find one for yourself and when you tire of sunbathing just slip into the water for a cool dip. Some of them are easily reached but to get to others a little pushing through the bush is required, although the coastal road is rarely more than 100m from the coast. Thatch-roofed shelters have been erected near several beaches including Taungaroro, Matai and Takauroa.

Oravaru Beach on the west coast is where Cook's party made its historic landing. There's a large rock in the water just off the beach, which the chief Rongomatane used in directing John Williams to Rarotonga. Farther south is the longer sweep of **Taungaroro Beach**, backed by high cliffs and sloping fairly steeply into the water. South again is **Tumai Beach** and there are plenty of others.

On the northeast coast there's a 1km-long stretch where there is very little fringing reef and the sea crashes directly onto the cliffs. At the end of the road there's a rarely used emergency boat landing, **Tarapaku**, and a pleasant stretch of beach. More beaches, and three lovely seaside **grottoes**, are south between Tarapaku Landing and Oneroa beach. The grottoes can only be visited when the sea is calm on the east side of the island. You can swim in two of them.

The southeast coast takes the brunt of the prevailing trade winds and the sea, washing fiercely over the reef, is often unsafe for swimming. There are, however, a series of picturesque little beaches including **Matai Landing** and **Oneroa**. Oneroa is the best beach for finding beautiful shells; a surprising number of old shoes are also washed up!

South of Oneroa is the turn-off to **Takauroa Beach**. If you walk about 100m back along the rugged cliff face there are some sinkholes deep enough for good snorkelling. They are only safe at low tide or when the sea is calm.

At low tide, the lagoon from Takauroa Beach to Matai Landing drains out through the sinkholes and tropical fish become trapped in a spot known as the **Coral Garden**, which becomes a fascinating natural aquarium. The Coral Garden can be reached by walking along the reef from Takauroa beach, but only at low tide, when there are no waves washing over the reef; at other times it is dangerous and not as interesting to visit anyway without the trapped fish.

The most popular beaches on the island are Matai Landing and Taungaroro, because of their beauty and ease of access.

Vairakai Marae & Vai Momoiri

The steep road between Tengatangi village and Tarapaku Landing is worth taking, as it passes through all different kinds of vegetation including plantations, taro patches, *makatea* and littoral forest. The road passes the impressive 37m-long wall of the **Vairakai Marae**, built out of 47 large limestone

Tumunu – Bush-Beer Drinking Sessions

Don't miss the opportunity to attend a *tumunu* (bush-beer drinking session) while you're on 'Atiu. It's a direct descendant of the old kava ceremony of premissionary times. Drinking kava, a non-alcoholic narcotic prepared from the root of the pepper plant *Piper methysticum*, was a communal activity with strict ceremony involved. In several Pacific countries – Vanuatu, Fiji, Tonga and Samoa – kava is still popular today, but in the Cook Islands the missionaries managed to totally stamp it out (to the point where the plant is quite rare now).

When kava drinking was banned, the *tumunu* appeared as its replacement – men would retreat to hidden places in the bush to drink home-brewed 'orange beer' following much the same ceremony as when they drank kava. The *tumunu* itself is the hollowed-out coconut-tree stump which was traditionally used as a container for brewing the beer.

Tumunu are still held regularly on 'Atiu, although the container is likely to be plastic these days. There are eight separate *tumunu* locations on 'Atiu, all of which are a short distance from the main village. They are fairly safe to visit – even when drunk, people tend to behave well at a *tumunu*. Although an invitation is required to join in, just walking past will usually secure you a shouted invite.

The staff at the place where you're staying can arrange a trip to a *tumunu* if you'd rather go with company (not a bad idea sometimes). Traditionally the *tumunu* is for men only, but some *tumunu* do welcome women, and for tourists the rules relax somewhat anyway, and any visitor, male or female, is welcome.

Like the old kava tradition, there's quite a ceremony to a *tumunu* gathering. The barman sits behind the *tumunu* and ladles the beer into a coconut-shell cup. Each drinker swallows the drink in a single gulp and returns the empty cup to the barman who fills it for the next in line. You can pass if you want to but by the end of the evening everybody is decidedly unsteady on their feet – including, sometimes, the barman who is supposed to keep everyone in line! At some point in the evening the barman calls the school to order by tapping on the side of the *tumunu* with the empty cup and someone will say a short prayer. Visitors are then welcomed and asked to say a few words about themselves. Guitars and ukuleles are usually around to provide music and accompaniment to song.

As a visitor to the *tumunu* you should bring a donation for the next brew – NZ$5 per visit is OK; NZ$10 is enough for a week if you're going to keep coming back to that particular *tumunu*.

slabs, six of which are cut with curious projections on their top edges. It also passes **Vai Momoiri**, a deep canyon filled with brown water and connected by a short tunnel to a second, similar sinkhole. At the beach end of the road is a thatched shelter that's good for a little sit down out of the sun.

Other Marae

'Atiu has a number of interesting marae remains. One of the best known is **Orongo Marae**, near Oravaru beach. You must have a guide to visit this marae because it's difficult to find and it's on private land. The marae was cleared in 2001, but the jungle grows very fast around here – ask around to see if the marae is still clear and ask at the place you're staying about a guide.

Te Apiripiri Marae where Papeiha is said to have first preached the Gospel in 1823 is behind Rongomatane Ada Ariki's palace, the house opposite the Administration Centre. There's little left of the marae apart from some stalactites or stalagmites lying on the ground beside the road to Tengatangi but a stone commemorating Papeiha's sermon marks the spot.

Te Au Tapu, a marae still used for investiture ceremonies, is between the Administration Centre and the palace of Ngamaru Henry Ariki. You cannot access the marae but it's clearly visible from the road.

Coffee Plantations

Coffee has been grown on 'Atiu for over a century now, but its development has been somewhat erratic. The plant was introduced to 'Atiu by early 19th-century traders and missionaries. By the beginning of the 20th century almost 50 tonnes of coffee was being exported each year. Production and export declined after that, however, and by the 1940s coffee was produced only for local consumption.

There was a resurgence in the 1950s when a few growers once again began working the old coffee plantations and the government established nurseries and two small farms. Green coffee beans were exported for several decades, but, once again, production went into decline and by 1980 the industry had dwindled to the point where coffee was again only picked for local consumption.

In 1983, German-born Juergen Manske-Eimke moved to 'Atiu, imported modern machinery and equipment, set up a coffee factory, and the Atiu Coffee Growers Association was formed. The 'Atiu coffee business is now rebounding; about eight tonnes of roasted coffee is now exported each year, grown on plantations totalling about 22 hectares (54 acres). The supermarkets, resorts and restaurants of Rarotonga alone consume more than half of 'Atiu's production – the rest is exported to New Zealand (NZ), Tahiti and the USA.

There are two brands of coffee sold from 'Atiu: Juergen's **Atiu Island Coffee** (☎ 33031; W www.adc.co.ck/coffee/), and **Atiu Coffee** (☎ 33088). Of the two, Atiu Island Coffee is the much larger operation and is machine roasted; Atiu Coffee is hand roasted. We're not going to buy into the fraught argument of which is best – you'll have to buy them both and decide for yourself. You can buy either brand of coffee, ground or whole beans, from the Centre Store and Atiu Villas for about NZ$12. (Both brands are also available on Rarotonga – try Foodland or the CITC Supermarket, which even serves Atiu Coffee in its car park café.) You can also order Atiu Island Coffee via Juergen's website.

If you're a coffee fiend, there's a tour available: talk to Juergen Manske-Eimke of **Atiu Island Coffee** (☎/fax 33031); see Organised Tours, later.

Atiu Fibre Arts Studio

The Atiu Fibre Arts Studio (☎ 33031, fax 33032; W www.adc.co.ck; Te'enui; admission free) specialises in *tivaevae* (appliqué works), the colourful patterned bedspreads which are among the most famous handicrafts of the Cook Islands.

Tivaevae are ceremonial cloths normally made only for home use. The cost for a machine-sewn double to queen-size *tivaevae* is about NZ$600 to NZ$1100; a hand-sewn one, requiring countless hours to make, costs NZ$1500 and up. You can buy one on the spot or custom order it in the pattern and colours you want. *Tivaevae* are available in traditional or contemporary patterns, or a mix of the two.

The studio also produces a variety of other textile arts using appliqué techniques similar to those used in making *tivaevae*

Tutaka

Four times a year, a committee goes around to inspect all the houses on 'Atiu for their condition and cleanliness. This *tutaka* is done in many of the Cook Islands, but on 'Atiu it's a big occasion, with the local ladies bringing out all their best handicrafts to proudly put on display in their homes. The major *tutaka* of the year is just before Christmas. It's easy to spot the inspection committee going around, since they're all in uniform, and if you ask permission you can join them. The *tutaka* inspection is held on a Wednesday and Thursday, and that same Friday there's a big ball with prizes handed out for the village that wins the competition.

Some years ago, 'Atiu's imaginative menfolk adopted the *tutaka* tradition and extended it to cover the *tumunu* (bush-beer drinking gatherings; see the boxed text earlier). Essentially this meant travelling from *tumunu* to *tumunu*, sampling the beer and rating each gathering according to quality of the beer, food, singing and even the hut itself. Anywhere else they'd call it a pub crawl – but here they called it a *tutaka tumunu*.

quilting, plus fabric painting and hand-dyed fabrics. All products of the studio are exhibited in its gallery, workshop and café building.

Andrea Eimke, the operator of the studio who originally hailed from Germany, can tell you everything you want to know about local arts and crafts. Andrea is interested in promoting cultural exchange, inviting artists and craftspeople to come and share their skills with the studio and learn 'Atiuan crafts. For visiting artists she can help to arrange accommodation and craftmaking facilities.

Other Attractions

The old, island-style CICC in the centre of the village has walls over 1m thick. If you're staying in town, you'll hear the bell summoning CICC members to church at 4am four mornings each week. If you're a light sleeper and know you won't be getting back to sleep anyway, you might as well join them.

'Atiu has a surprising number of **tennis courts**. In the 1990s the five villages got into a tennis-court-building competition, each attempting to build a better one than the next! There are now nine tennis courts on the island, although they're used more for volleyball, netball and soccer practise than for tennis.

Fishing

Catching fish can be a serious business on 'Atiu. Not only is it an important source of income, but a man who promises his family that he'll catch fish but comes home, as all fishermen must sometimes do, empty handed, is *'akama* (shamed) in front of his family.

However, fishing is also fun…fishing, with a long bamboo rod and line, off the edge of the reef, is a popular way to pass the time, but it's on nights when the moon is dark and the *maroro* (flying fish) are spawning, that the fun really starts. 'Atiuan fishermen don a miner's helmet with a bright spotlight, grab a large butterfly net in one hand and take to their boats to scare *maroro* up with the light and snatch them out of the air with the net. The air is thick with flying fish and the howls and laughter of the fishermen. Now tell me that isn't fun!

If you didn't bring fishing gear, you can buy most of what you need from the **Centre Store** (☎ 33773; Te'enui), or there's a tour available (see Organised Tours). Ask around about ciguatera (a form of fish poisoning – see Health in the Facts for the Visitor chapter) before you go indiscriminately eating any reef fish you catch.

Organised Tours

Atiu Tours (☎/fax 33041; e atiutours@ihug .co.nz) is run by Marshall Humphreys who offers a very personal 3½-hour circle-island tour (NZ$40) visiting marae, historical spots, beaches and other points of interest. Home-made muffins (very nice) and coffee are supplied. The younger Humphreys lead an excellent 2½-hour *makatea*-and-cave tour to Anatakitaki cave (NZ$20). Take good shoes for picking your way across the *makatea*, and togs (bathers) if you fancy a subterranean, candle-lit swim.

George Mateariki (☎ 33047) runs two- to three-hour ecological/bird-watching tours (NZ$20). George oversaw the release of the endangered *kakerori* (see Fauna in the Facts about the Cook Islands chapter) here from

'ATIU, MA'UKE & MITIARO

Rarotonga, and will gladly share tales of the species' success on 'Atiu.

Papa Moe *(☎ 33013)* will introduce you to the hidden joys of reef fishing – stand near the edge of the reef with a rod and line, and wonder what Tangaroa, the god of the sea, will deliver today. Papa Moe supplies all the gear and you get to keep some of the fish (NZ$25).

TK Fishing & Coastal Tour *(☎ 33040; e captain@vilatours.co.ck)* offers a coastal tour that circumnavigates the island by boat, which includes a running commentary (if you get him on an off day, some of it might even be true). You visit shipwrecks, Captain Cook's Passage and more. The two-/three-hour tours cost NZ$50/100.

Aue Rakanui *(☎ 33256)* leads you to his family's cave, Te Ana O Rakanui, and (with a little prompting) will tell you the story of his ancestor, Rakanui Ariki (NZ$20). This is a story you won't read or hear anywhere else! BYO wheels.

Juergen Manske-Eimke *(☎ 33031; w www .adc.co.ck/coffee/)* offers a tour of a coffee plantation and factory (NZ$15). A minimum of two participants is required.

Paiere Mokoroa *(☎ 33034; Taparere Lodge)*, a retired historian, was a leading contributor to *Atiu, an Island Community* (see Books under Information, earlier) and can talk the hind leg off an 'Atiuan dog with his tales of ancient times. Paiere's tours of historical sites of interest (two hours going on four) cost NZ$26/5 for adults/children.

Places to Stay

Bookings for all places to stay can be made at Rarotongan travel agencies (see Information in the Rarotonga chapter).

Are Manuiri *(☎ 33031, fax 33032; w www.adc.co.ck; Areora; share rooms per person NZ$30, singles & doubles NZ$60, triples NZ$75)*, a pleasant three-bedroom house, right in the centre of Areora village, has a shared kitchen, living room and thatched veranda. The managers, Andrea Eimke and Juergen Manske-Eimke, will ensure that you're well looked after. More so than the other accommodation places, Are Manuiri makes you feel an integral part of village life. No kids under 10.

Atiu Villas *(☎ 33777, fax 33775; w www .atiu.info/atiuvillas/; standard bungalow* singles/doubles/triples NZ$100/110/120, family bungalows NZ$110/120/125)* is about 1km out of Areora. Roger and Kura Malcolm offer four delightful, individual A-frame chalets making maximum use of local materials. Each chalet has a single and double bed and a mezzanine area where another one or two people could sleep. There's also one larger family unit sleeping up to six people. Each unit comes with a kitchen, and fridge and cupboard full of food (at the end of your stay you're simply billed for what you've used). Beside a lawn tennis court is Kura's Kitchen (see Places to Eat, and Entertainment, following).

Taparere Lodge *(☎/fax 33034; shared rooms NZ$35, twins & doubles NZ$78 plus per extra person NZ$20)* is a single lodge housing two self-contained units that can sleep three or four. The grounds are lovely, and the hosts, Nga and Paiere Mokoroa, are very accommodating. Booking can be a problem – keep trying the number listed here, use a Rarotongan travel agency, or email **Atiu Tours** *(☎/fax 33041; e atiutours@ ihug.co.nz)*. If you don't want to share a room with others, let them know in advance.

Kopeka Lodges *(☎ 33283, fax 33284; singles/doubles NZ$95/115)*, modern and private, comprises three self-contained lodges on a quiet property south of town.

Mata Arai has a **house** *(☎ 33088)* to rent for NZ$150 per week (minimum two-week stay).

Places to Eat

Kura's Kitchen *(☎ 33777; Atiu Villas; dinner NZ$25; open for dinner from 7pm Mon-Sat)* provides evening meals for motel guests and casual diners. Book before 3pm; if there are no guests dining they don't open.

If you're in town more than a couple of days, you'll probably be looking after some, if not most, of your own meals. If you're staying at **Atiu Villas** your cupboards will be stocked for you. Otherwise, 'Atiu has two grocery stores: **ADC Shop** *(☎ 33028; Areora)* and the slightly larger **Centre Store** *(☎ 33773; Te'enui)*.

Akai Bakery *(☎ 33207; Mapumai)* sells freshly baked bread at about midday. It's closed Saturday, but they start baking again when the Seventh-Day Adventist Sabbath ends at dusk on Saturday afternoon – so at

11pm there's bread available and usually a small crowd of midnight bread fanciers there to buy it.

Atiu Tours *(☎/fax 33041)* can sometimes supply fresh fruit and vegies.

Maroro, an 'Atiuan delicacy, are caught at night and can be bought from trucks on the street the following morning (listen for the honking horn) for about NZ$1 per fish.

Entertainment

Kura's Kitchen *(☎ 33777; Atiu Villas)*, a thatched, open-air, pavilion bar, holds dances on some Saturday nights – usually when there are visitors on the island. The dances feature a rousing local band and occasional floor shows.

Atiu Nui Maruarua Hall is opposite the CICC. Dances are held on most Friday nights (but see the boxed text 'No Dancing in Cyclone Season', earlier). If there's a fundraiser on, you'll pay NZ$2 for live entertainment; otherwise it's just a straight disco.

See the boxed text 'Tumunu – Bush-Beer Drinking Sessions' earlier, to read about where most 'Atiuan men go to drink.

Shopping

Apart from the **Atiu Fibre Arts Studio** *(☎ 33031)* – see separate section, earlier – there's no one place to buy crafts on 'Atiu. Many people sell from their homes though; ask around if you're interested in buying. Sometimes you'll see women working in one of the community halls, and you're welcome to stop and watch, although their crafts probably won't be for sale.

If you follow the sound of tapping hammers you'll find women making *tapa*, or bark cloth. 'Atiu's *tapa* flowers are sold on Rarotonga and you might find some for sale (NZ$3 to NZ$10) here either at the **Centre Store** *(☎ 33773; Te'enui)*, **Maara Ngaroi** *(☎ 33274)* or **Maara Marama** *(☎ 33211)*.

Punua Tauraa *(☎ 33203; Te'enui)* sells magnificent ukuleles from his house just north of the Centre Store (a sign pointing the way to the Atiu Fibre Arts Studio stands in his front lawn). A hand-crafted ukulele will cost you from NZ$200.

Ngere Tariu *(☎ 33011, 33014; Te'enui)*, living right across the road from Punua's house, is a skilled carver who carves mostly Tangaroa figures (from NZ$15) for the

Rarotongan market. You're welcome to pop in Monday to Friday between midday and 6pm.

Aue Rakanui *(☎ 33256)*, the cave tour guide, carves *toki* (axes; NZ$15 to NZ$100) and weaves *'inaki* (eel nets).

'Atiu coffee (either of the two brands; see Coffee Plantations, earlier) is a popular souvenir.

Getting There & Away

Air 'Atiu is well served for air transport: **Air Rarotonga** *(in town ☎ 33888, airport ☎ 33201;* **w** *www.airraro.com)* flies between Rarotonga and 'Atiu Monday to Saturday. It costs NZ$330 return (NZ$237 if you buy your ticket on Rarotonga instead of overseas). Weekly Aitutaki–'Atiu flights cost NZ$330 return (NZ$237 on Rarotonga). Many flights continue on from 'Atiu to Mitiaro and Ma'uke (there are no direct flights between 'Atiu and Ma'uke); since these flights take only 10 minutes each, it's easy to visit all three islands.

Rarotongan travel agencies organise flight/accommodation packages, either to 'Atiu alone or as part of a multi-island tour, that turn out to be cheaper than buying everything yourself (if you buy the package on Rarotonga). See the Getting Around chapter for more information about travel-agency packages, and Air Rarotonga's flights, multi-island deals and contact details.

The 'Atiu office of **Air Rarotonga** *(open 7am-3pm Mon-Fri)* is in Mapumai (they stay open later if there's a late flight).

Boat Interisland cargo ships sail to 'Atiu; see the Getting Around chapter for details.

The all-weather harbour at Taunganui is too small to take ships, so passengers and freight are unloaded onto aluminium boats while the ship stands offshore. 'Boat day' is an island event and worth witnessing if you happen to be here at that time.

Getting Around

'Atiu is great for walking but you'll need wheels if you want to see much of the island. All the places to stay can rent you a motorcycle (NZ$25 per day), either through **T & J Rentals** *(☎ 33271; Areora)* or one of their own (guests get preference if there's a shortage of motorbikes).

Takutea

Clearly visible from 'Atiu, the small sand cay of Takutea is only 6m above sea level at its highest point and has an area of just 1.2 sq km. It was named by one of 'Atiu's earliest settlers, the Rai'atean Mariri, who named it Taku Ku Tea (My White Squirrel-fish) after catching a white specimen of the usually red *ku* there. The island has also been called 'Enua-iti which simply means 'Small Land', and has always belonged to the people of 'Atiu. James Cook visited Takutea in 1777, shortly after he left 'Atiu, and paused to gather food for the livestock on his ship.

Takutea is 16km northwest of 'Atiu and coconut-collecting parties used to visit often from 'Atiu. Today Takutea is unpopulated and rarely visited, except by the occasional fisherman who seldom steps ashore and a yearly expedition from 'Atiu to gather coconuts.

Many seabirds, including frigates and tropicbirds nest on the island. To protect these breeding birds, Takutea was set up as a wildlife sanctuary in the 1950s by the 'Atiuan chiefs on behalf of the people of 'Atiu.

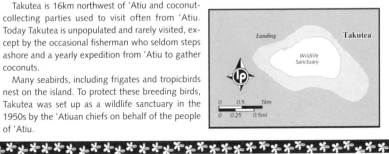

At the time of writing T & J Rentals didn't have any bicycles, but check anyway. You could also try **Atiu Tours** (☎ 33041).

Are Manuiri (☎ 33031; Areora) rents out a 4WD car for NZ$65 per day. **Clara George** (☎ 33255) runs a taxi service in her open-back pick-up (if it's raining, you'll have to fight over the single cabin seat).

All the places to stay will pick you up and drop you off at the airport, charging about NZ$12 return.

'Atiu's roads have been on the verge of an improvement project – sealing them from the airport as far south as Atiu Villas – for some time. Go to a *tumunu* if you want to hear an update on progress and any technical/political problems they're having.

Ma'uke

pop 440 • area 18.4 sq km
Of all the easily visited Southern Group islands, Ma'uke is probably the least visited, and for some travellers the island holds an appeal for that very reason. There's no reason for the lack of tourists – it's not a difficult destination: flights are regular and organised accommodation is on hand. Ma'uke can easily be combined with a visit to nearby 'Atiu and/or Mitiaro.

History

Ma'uke takes its name from its legendary founder 'Uke but there are several versions of what the name means. One story claims that it means 'Clean 'Uke'. This legend tells of Tangi'ia, one of the two famous mariners who settled Rarotonga, coming to ask 'Uke's aid in going to war against the Samoans. 'Uke replied, 'My hands are clean', ie, he did not want war. It is said that 'Uke came to Ma'uke in search of a peaceful place to live, and he wanted to continue to live in peace. Prior to this exchange, Ma'uke had been known as 'Akatoka-manava, which means 'My Heart is at Rest, at Peace'. These were the first words uttered by 'Uke when he arrived from Ra'iatea, landing at Arapaea on the eastern coast in the huge canoe *Paipaimoana*, which carried a large group of settlers. Ma'uke is still referred to as 'Akatokamanava in song, dance, legend and in formal address.

'Uke had two daughters, renowned for their exceptional beauty, and when the two famous Rarotongan settlers, Tangi'ia and Karika, came seeking these girls for marriage, they went to live on Rarotonga. 'Uke's four sons also went to other islands, so that 'Uke became a common ancestor for all the islands of the southern group.

Prior to the arrival of Christianity, Ma'uke was dominated by the island of 'Atiu. The 'Atiuans would descend on

MA'UKE

PLACES TO STAY	
3 Cove Lodge	
6 Tiare Cottages	

OTHER	
1 Hospital	
2 Sports Field	
4 Air Rarotonga	
5 Administration Centre;	
Marae O Rongo; Ma'uke	
Market; Hard Court	
8 Tura's Bar	
9 Puarakura Marae; Aretoa	
Store; Ariki Store	
10 The Divided Church (CICC)	
11 Telecom; Post Office	

13 Paepae'a Marae	
17 Marae Rangimanuka	
19 Kea's Grave	

CAVES	
7 Kopupooki	
(Stomach Rock)	
12 Vai Tango	
14 Vai Ou	
15 Vai Moraro	
16 Vai Tunamea	
18 Vai Moti	
20 Motuanga Cave	
21 Vai Ma'u	
22 Vai Tukume	

murderous, cannibal raids under any number of perceived justifications. 'Atiu's premier chief in the early 19th century, the *ariki* Rongomatane, led many attacks on Ma'uke, and was feared here as a ruthless taker of slaves and eater of men. In 1823, when the first European, the missionary John Williams, arrived on Ma'uke, it was Rongomatane who showed him the way and arrived with Williams. It's perhaps not surprising that the Ma'ukeans were converted to Christianity with an ease and speed that astonished the missionaries.

Despite Christian influence, Ma'uke still remained subject to 'Atiu. When the British Protectorate of the Cook Islands was declared in 1888, it was an 'Atiuan chief, Ngamaru Ariki, who gave permission on behalf of Ma'uke. NZ officially ended 'Atiuan rule in the early 1900s.

The relatively famous author, and local personality, Julian Dashwood (known as 'Rakau' on the island) lived for years on Ma'uke where he ran the island store (his old house, near the airport, will be pointed out to you as you pass by with any local). See Books in the Facts for the Visitor chapter for more information about Dashwood; his second book, *Today is Forever*, is largely about Ma'uke.

Geography & Geology

Like 'Atiu, Mangaia and Mitiaro, Ma'uke is a raised atoll with surrounding *makatea*. Inland from the *makatea*, which is densely forested with lush jungle-like growth, a band of swampland surrounds the fertile central land. The central area of the island is flat, rising little higher than the *makatea*; Ma'uke is barely 30m above sea level at its highest point. Like the other *makatea* islands, Ma'uke has numerous limestone caves.

Culture

Ma'uke's three *ariki* titles – Tararo, Teau and Samuela – are descended from three chiefs appointed by 'Atiuan conquerors in the 19th century (however, Ma'ukeans *really* don't like to be reminded of that!). One of the few 'palaces' in the outer Cooks that really looks the part stands opposite Ariki Store in the centre of the island. It was built for Tararo Jane Ariki in 1982, but Tararo politics interrupted construction and it stands impressive but unfinished.

The bell you hear at 6.30pm every night (10.30pm on Friday and Saturday) sounds the curfew for kids under 16 years.

Information

The **Administration Centre** is near the wharf. Here you'll find the mayor, **island secretary** (☎ 35141, fax 35142) and a 24-hour **Kiaorana-cardphone** (☎ 35155). The **police station** (☎ 35086) is between the Administration Centre and the wharf.

The **Telecom** and **post office** (open 8am-12pm & 1pm-3pm Mon-Fri) are in Ngatiarua village, in the centre of the island. There's a 24-hour **Kiaorana-cardphone** (☎ 35685) outside.

The **hospital** (☎ 35664) is staffed from 8am to midday and 1pm to 4pm Monday to

Friday. The **doctor** (☎ 35123) lives in the house just north of the hospital.

There's an ANZ agent, **Wendy's Store** (☎ 35102), northeast across the playing fields from the Divided Church in Areora, which can change US dollars. Electricity operates on Ma'uke from 5am to midnight.

What to Bring If you'll be doing any walking on the island, you'll need mosquito repellent, and if you'll be doing any walking across the *makatea*, be sure to bring some sturdy shoes. Old ones are best because they'll take a beating from the razor-sharp *makatea*. Don't try to walk across the *makatea* in sandals or thongs (Jandals; flip-flops) – the rocks are liable to shift suddenly (with a sound strangely reminiscent of crockery shifting in the sink) and they really are sharp – you could easily cut yourself very badly.

You may want to bring some snack food with you – the small village shops are considerably more expensive than those on Rarotonga.

Since the power goes off at midnight, bring a torch (flashlight). A good torch is also necessary for getting the most out of the caves.

Caves
Like 'Atiu and Mangaia, Ma'uke has *makatea* riddled with limestone caves, many filled with cool water that are wonderful for swimming. The walk through the *makatea* to the caves – lush jungle, with coconut palms and shade trees, pandanus, mosses, ferns and tropical greenery in wild profusion – is as much of an attraction as the caves themselves. The shade, and the swim at the end, is welcome on a hot day.

The easiest cave to reach, and one of the larger ones on the island for swimming, is **Vai Tango**, just a short walk from Ngatiarua village. The crystal blue pool may look smallish, but scuba divers have found that it extends more than 100m back and 50m across under the earth. The pool is often full of children on Saturday and after school, but at other times you may get it all to yourself.

Other interesting caves in the north part of the island, just a short walk south and east off the coastal road (which you leave at the lopsided 'Oneunga' sign), are **Vai Ou**, **Vai Moraro** and **Vai Tunamea**. You follow

The Divided Church

In 1882 Ma'uke's CICC was built by two villages, Areora and Ngatiarua. When the outside was complete, however, the two villages could not agree on how the inside should be fitted out. Eventually the argument became so acrimonious that the only solution was to build a wall down the middle and let each village have its own church within a church.

A new pastor managed to convince his congregations that this was not in the spirit of neighbourly Christianity and the wall was removed, but the interior of the two 'ends' of the church are still constructed and decorated in different styles and each village has its own entrance. Inside, the church is 90° offset from the usual layout, with the pulpit at the centre of one long wall. The two villages each sit at their own end and they take turns singing the hymns! There's a dividing line down the middle of the pulpit and the minister is traditionally expected to straddle the line while preaching.

Outside, one of the church's two entrances has three crosses representing Ma'uke's three *ariki* (high chiefs). The other gate has two pointy knobs that apparently represent missionary John William's wife's hairdo (that must have been some 'do!). Inside, the 12 pillars that support the roof of the church represent the 12 apostles. One of them is decidedly crooked – Judas, perhaps?

Today, Ma'uke's population is nearly half CICC, and nearly half Roman Catholic, with the rest made up of a few families of Seventh-Day Adventists and one family of Mormons (there's plenty of room for visitors in the Mormon church).

an ancient coral pathway about 15 (careful) minutes through lush tropical bush leading first to Vai Ou, worth climbing down into for a swim. The tracks turns hard left here – another four minutes and you'll find Vai Moraro down on your right. Also known as the 'Crawling Cave' – you have to crawl down through a slit in the rock-face to get inside – it opens up into a big cave. The pools are small, although deep, and they taste slightly salty. Be especially careful walking around inside Vai Moraro, as the rocks are wet and very slippery. About three minutes further east is Vai Tunamea, a deep, deep hole with a pool at the bottom. You could climb down into it – but we decided cowardice was the better part of valour in this case.

Motuanga Cave – also known as the 'Cave of 100 Rooms' (doesn't that sound like a bad horror movie?) – is Ma'uke's best known cave. Motuanga is entered on land but extends out towards the sea and under the reef. In some of the last rooms people have reached, the waves can be heard crashing above you.

There is nobody around today who has reached all of Motuanga's 100 rooms; the rocks are slowly closing in and nowadays you can only get into eight of them, even with scuba gear. There is a legend of one man, Timeni Oariki, who did swim through all of them, finally emerging out into the sea – where he was eaten by sharks! Motuanga and nearby **Vai Moti** – a great place to swim according to Ma'uke's school kids – can only be found with the help of a guide. (The track is OK, but the small roads leading to it are a veritable maze!)

Steep-sided **Vai Tukume** is hidden beside a midden of discarded cans and broken bottles more treacherous to cross than any jagged *makatea*, but the cave is easy enough to find.

Vai Ma'u, looking like the gateway to the Underworld, is found after an uneasy walk through dark jungle where gnarly old trees twist through the *makatea*. Crabs the size of your hand, scuttling across the path, finish off this Tim Burton–esque nightmare. The path leads straight there from behind a small old quarry on the side of the road.

Beaches

A road runs right around the coast of Ma'uke, a distance of 18km. The fringing reef platform is narrow but **Teoneroa Beach** is fairly good as is the beach at **Arapaea Landing** on the eastern side of the island. The beaches on the southern side of the island, like **Anaokae**, are pleasantly secluded. Other beaches, such as **Anaraura** and **Teoneroa**, have picnic areas with thatched shelters providing welcome shade on a hot day. **One'unga**, on the east side, is also a nice little beach for a picnic. All around the island the waves have beaten the shoreline cliffs into overhanging formations.

Heading south from Tiare Cottages, the first turn-off towards the sea leads you to **Kopupooki Beach** (Stomach Rock). The name comes from a cave situated to your left as you face out to sea – go just past the last outcrop of rock that you see from the beach and you come to this very cute little cave, full of fish and good for swimming and snorkelling. You can only reach it at low tide; at other times, the pounding waves make it too dangerous. Except for the harbour, this is probably the only place deep enough for a good salty swim, since the reef all around the island is quite shallow. Many more little caves and beaches are dotted around the island.

Marae

Like all the other Cook Islands, Ma'uke has many marae, or ancient religious meeting grounds.

Puarakura Marae is a modern marae, built in the 1980s for the Ariki Teau and still used today for ceremonial functions. There's a triangular area enclosed within a rectangle within another larger rectangle, with seats for the *ariki*, the *mataiapo* and the *rangatira* (nobility).

Near Ma'uke's reservoir is **Marae Rangimanuka**, the marae of 'Uke, Ma'uke's famous ancestor and namesake. It's completely overgrown but if you stumble about in there you'll find an old stone seat where 'Uke's rear may once have rested.

Near the harbour, the ancient **Marae O Rongo** was once huge but all you see today are a few large stones and a coral platform. This was the marae of Rongo, the Polynesian god that was later associated with the Holy Spirit when people struggled to fit Christianity into the local pantheon: Tangaroa the Father; Tane the Son; Rongo the Holy Spirit. The marae is behind the Administration Centre; the little road going along the left (inland) side of the building leads right to it.

Paepae'a, built in 1997 for Samuela Ariki, is an impressive marae on the road north from Ngatiarua to the airstrip.

Organised Tours

There are a couple of people taking travellers on tours of Ma'uke's marae, caves and interesting spots. Tautara and Kura at Tiare Cottages should be able to set you up

Vaka (outrigger canoe), south coast of Aitutaki Atoll

Limestone caves near Anatakitaki (Cave of the Kopekas), 'Atiu

Outside a local church, 'Atiu

Palm trees, Mangaia

Makatea (fossilised coral reef), south coast of Mangaia

with someone, or you could try **Clem Vainetutai** (☎ 35014) or **Pi Tua** (☎ 35083). Prices vary according to where you want to go and what you want to see but NZ$20 to NZ$25 is usual.

Places to Stay

Tiare Cottages (☎ 35083, fax 35102; singles/ doubles NZ$30/45) is right on the coast, near Kimiangatau village and Kopupooki Beach. It has several simple cottages with cement-and-pandanus walls, and sometimes-thatched roofs. Each cottage has a fridge, and nearby there's an open-air kitchen/dining area, toilets and (cold) showers.

The owners, Tautara and Kura Purea, will meet you with *ei* (necklaces) at the airport. Generally, you do your own cooking, but Kura will put on some meals (breakfast NZ$6.50, dinner NZ$12.50). Island or cave tours (NZ$20), fishing trips (NZ$75) and other activities can be arranged. Check your bill carefully.

Cove Lodge (☎ 35664, 35048; house per week NZ$50), a long-term rental house, near the hospital, is operated by Aunty Tini. The lodge sleeps up to six people.

There are other **long-term houses** available too for about the same price. Ask around.

Places to Eat

If you're staying at **Tiare Cottages** you can get a few home-cooked dinners each week for an extra NZ$12.50 per meal. Otherwise, it'll be self-catering. Bring a can opener.

There are four grocery stores, all selling a magnificent variety of canned NZ beef and all open, approximately, from 8am to 4pm Monday to Friday and until midday on Saturday: adjacent **Aretoa Store** (☎ 35111; Makatea) and **Ariki Store** (☎ 35103; Makatea) are across the road from the imposing, crumbling Tararo Ariki palace. **Wendy's Store** (☎ 35102; Areora), northeast across the playing fields from the Divided Church, is also open some Saturday evenings and 'sometimes' on Sunday.

On Friday morning, starting at about 8.30am, you can buy fresh produce at the **Ma'uke market**, near the wharf. You can also buy burgers (NZ$4) and hot meals (NZ$15).

Entertainment

Tura's Bar (☎ 35023) is down a little road that heads off the main road opposite Ma'uke College. There's only one 'pub' on Ma'uke and this is it. Open most Friday nights, it's a great place to dance and sing with the locals.

Another entertainment option is watching the volleyball and soccer games on the **hard court** near the wharf.

Kea's Grave

One of Ma'uke's beaches, Anaiti, has a special history. Up on the cliff above the sea is a mound of grey coral stones – the grave of Kea.

Kea's husband, Paikea, was out fishing one day in his canoe when a terrible storm blew him out to sea. Kea believed her husband was dead, and she cried and cried on that cliff overlooking the sea until she died of grief, and the people buried her there.

Paikea had not died at sea, however. He was blown over 100km by the storm, eventually reaching the island of Mangaia. He was almost killed there by the locals but escaped and sailed to Rarotonga. From there he departed for Aotearoa (NZ) and never returned to the Cooks again.

There are a few versions of how Paikea got to NZ: on the *Takitumu* canoe (which is known to have stopped at Rarotonga on its way from the Society Islands to NZ), on the *Horouta* canoe (which visited Rarotonga from NZ to get kumara), or, most famously, on the back of a whale. However he travelled, Paikea ended his voyage at Whangara, on the East Coast of NZ's North Island. A carved meeting house there bears a carving of Paikea, on the apex of the rooftop, sitting atop a whale.

So Paikea found fame after being washed out to sea. Immortalised in legend and sculpture, he is today a revered ancestor of NZ Maori tribes both on the East Coast and in the South Island. But poor Kea remains in her grave here on a cliff on Ma'uke, where she died of grief for her lost love.

If you want to pay your respects, look for two large stones beside the coastal road, on the seaward side. Walk towards the sea here, keeping just right of the small beach. Kea's grave is on a small headland.

'ATIU, MA'UKE & MITIARO

Getting There & Away

Air Flying five times a week between Raro-tonga and Ma'uke is **Air Rarotonga** *(Kimi-angatau ☎ 35888, airport ☎ 35120;* w *www .airraro.com)*. The cost is NZ$368 return (NZ$255 if you buy the tickets on Raro-tonga instead of from overseas).

A visit to Ma'uke can easily be combined with 'Atiu and Mitiaro; stopping at more than one island brings the fare down to just NZ$124 per sector on a multi-island pass.

Rarotongan travel agencies (see Informa-tion in the Rarotonga chapter) can organise package tours, including air fare and ac-commodation, that are cheaper than buying everything yourself (if you buy on Raro-tonga). See the Getting Around chapter for more information about travel-agency packages, and Air Rarotonga's flights, multi-island deals and contact details.

Boat See the Getting Around chapter for details on interisland cargo ship services among the Cook Islands. A visit to Ma'uke can often be combined with visits to some of the other Southern Group islands.

Getting Around

Tiare Cottages rents a rattly old motorbike (the famous *Night Rider* that one of Ma'uke's roads was named after!) for NZ$20 per day, and bicycles (NZ$8.50 per day) to guests and nonguests alike. Tiare also provides airport transfers (NZ$5 return).

Mitiaro

pop 236 • area 22.3 sq km

Mitiaro is not one of the Cooks' most phys-ically beautiful islands, but there are plenty of things you can do there to pass a pleasant few days. The people on the island are al-ways happy to see a new face, and if you stop to talk to them they are very friendly. They all live in one small village on the west side of the island. To see the sights of Mi-tiaro, especially the caves and the marae, you'll need a local person to guide you. This can be arranged at the place where you're staying.

History

Like Ma'uke the island of Mitiaro was sub-ject to repeated raids from 'Atiu, but unlike the Ma'ukeans the Mitiaroans did not hide in caves. They stoutly defended their fortress, Te Pare, protected by the sharp *makatea*, but were nevertheless overcome by the 'Atiuans. The small and declining population that lives on Mitiaro today is thought to be almost entirely descended from raiding 'Atiuan warriors. The Rev-erend John Williams arrived on Mitiaro on 29 July 1823 accompanied by the 'Atiuan *ariki* Rongomatane, as he had been on Ma'uke, and the island was soon converted to Christianity, but 'Atiuan raids continued, even after the arrival of Christianity, into the 1840s.

Before Christianity came to Mitiaro, the people lived in inland villages – Taurangi, Atai, Auta, Mangarei and Takaue. As on Rarotonga, when the missionaries came, they moved the people out to live on the coast, where they built a village around the church. The old village sites are now the plantation areas where the food is grown.

Geography & Geology

Mitiaro is another island with a raised-coral, limestone outer plain, the *makatea*. Like Ma'uke, but to an even greater degree, the interior of the island is very flat – the *makatea* rises to a maximum of 9m above sea level, the interior foodlands to about 12m. Much of the interior of Mitiaro is swampland, just 1m above sea level. Two parts of this swamp are deep and permanent enough to be labelled as lakes: the pro-saically named Te Rotonui (Big Lake) and Te Rotoiti (Small Lake).

People, Economy & Culture

This is a small island. All the inhabitants of Mitiaro are related to one another in some way. As the local *va'ine* (ladies) complain: 'We'll *never* find a husband on this island! All the men here are our cousins!' In fact the people of Mitiaro, Ma'uke and 'Atiu are all in much the same situation – a great deal of intermarriage has taken place down through the years. Everybody on Mitiaro seems to have family on Ma'uke, 'Atiu, Rarotonga and even farther afield, and there's much visiting back and forth.

With everyone on Mitiaro being a rela-tive, it makes for a high degree of cooper-ation. There's not much money around, but agriculture and fishing produce abundant yields; there's a lot of sharing and everyone gets what they need.

There are very few unemployed young people on the island. Plantation work or fishing, in family-related businesses, is about all Mitiaro has to offer though. This is great for feeding the family but not for getting cash money, as all the fish and plantation produce is used here on the island and most of it gets traded back and forth among families. So while there's plenty of work for the young people to do and everyone on the island has plenty to eat, those who want to do anything other than plantation work, or fishing, or those who want to earn money somehow, must still leave the island eventually.

Although most people on Mitiaro now live in Western-style houses, they usually have outbuildings, made of traditional thatch, serving as cookhouses, fishing shacks and the like. A few people (very few) do still live in traditional thatch huts; it's an interesting sight to see an electricity meter hooked up to a hut made of sticks and pandanus!

Mitiaro has three *ariki* titles – To'u, Tetava and Te Ma'eu. Mitiaro, with Pukapuka and Mangaia, differs from other Cook Islands in that the central land court was never allowed to survey the island and officially allocate land. On Mitiaro, when land disputes arise, they are settled by the three *ariki*.

Information

The **Administration Centre**, near the wharf, houses the **post office**, **Telecom** (☎ 36680),

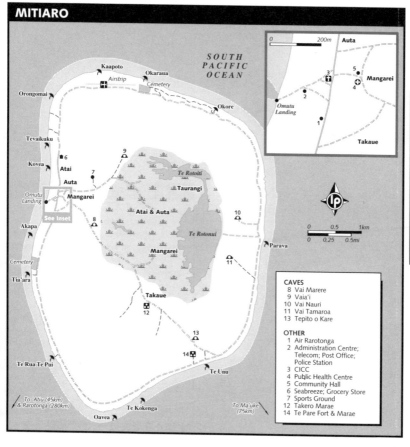

MITIARO

CAVES
8 Vai Marere
9 Vaia'i
10 Vai Nauri
11 Vai Tamaroa
13 Tepito o Kare

OTHER
1 Air Rarotonga
2 Administration Centre;
   Telecom; Post Office;
   Police Station
3 CICC
4 Public Health Centre
5 Community Hall
6 Seabreeze; Grocery Store
7 Sports Ground
12 Takero Marae
14 Te Pare Fort & Marae

'ATIU, MA'UKE & MITIARO

police station (☎ 36150, 36122), **island sec-retary** (☎ 36108, fax 36157) and the mayor. You'll (probably) find these offices open from 8am to 4pm Monday to Friday. There's no 24-hour public phone but when Telecom is open you can make toll calls or Kiaorana-cardphone calls there.

The small **public health centre** (☎ 36120, 36170, 36136; open 8am-4pm Mon-Fri) is east of the CICC beside the community hall. Emergency cases are sent by plane to Rarotonga.

Julian Aupuni (☎ 26260) is Mitiaro's tourism officer. Ask for him at the Admin-istration Centre. If you need to change money, change it before you come to Mitiaro. Electricity is available daily from 5am to midnight.

What to Bring As on Ma'uke (see Infor-mation under Ma'uke, earlier), bring sturdy walking shoes, a torch (flashlight), and some snack food. Be well prepared to ward off mosquitoes when you come to Mitiaro; a significant portion of the island is covered by either lake or soggy swampland, provid-ing an ideal breeding ground.

You might also want to bring sunglasses – the white surface of the crushed-coral roads on Mitiaro is extremely reflective and bright all around the island. (And staring at the white-washed CICC in direct sunlight won't do your eyes any good either.)

Beaches, Caves & Pools

Mitiaro has some fine little beaches and the reef at low tide is excellent for walking on all around the island. In common with the other islands with *makatea* Mitiaro also has a number of beautiful caves, with pools of fresh water that make great swimming holes. The *makatea* looks parched and dry; you would never guess that out there some-where are cool, clear pools, hidden under the ground. The water in the pools, as well as in the lakes and the swamp, rises and falls with the tide, riding on top of the salt-water lens beneath the island.

Just a 10-minute walk from the village on the Takaue road, **Vai Marere** is the only sul-phur pool in the Cook Islands. All you see from the road is a big hole in the ground but it opens up into a large cave with stalactites. The water is darker than in other pools, possibly due to the sulphur content. It's

refreshingly cool and the minerals make your skin and hair feel silky and soft after a dip.

Vai Nauri, on the eastern side of the is-land, is a large, brilliantly clear pool in a big cave. You can reach the water either by climbing down one side and wading in, or by going around to the other side and leap-ing off the 3m cliff, as the locals kids do (screaming as you leap is compulsory). When the kids aren't there, it's very peace-ful to sit in the cool cavern and listen to the water dripping down from the stalactites on the ceiling, falling like rain. When the kids are there you can cast any thoughts of peace out the window so you might as well join in the fun. There's a road right up to Vai Nauri.

Vai Tamaroa is another large pool, this one open to the sky. Tamaroa is about 15-minutes' walk across sharp *makatea* from the coast road; the start of the track is marked by a sign commemorating a 1980s Boys Brigade pro-ject. The trail across the *makatea* is faint, and a bit dangerous (this is *not* a walk for san-dals!), but you can get there without a guide if you take care to watch the path. All around Vai Tamaroa are cliffs about 10m high, and the more nimble locals love to jump down into the water. (Apparently, despite appear-ances, it's not impossible to climb back up the cliffs again, but we decided not to test that.) Mitiaro's women hold their *terevai* gatherings (see the boxed text) at both Vai Tamaroa and Vai Nauri.

Terevai

The women of Mitiaro have a grand old cus-tom known as *terevai*. On special occasions, such as when family visits over Christmas, a group of women get together and go to one of the island's pools (Vai Nauri and Vai Tamaroa are the two favourites). On the way there they sing the old bawdy songs of their ancestors – many of them action songs – with graphic movements accompanying the lyrics. The mood gets exuberantly racy and by the time the women have trekked out to the pool, everyone is in high spirits. Once at the pool Christianity reasserts itself, but only for a short while: a prayer, a hymn and a chant precede a wild, synchronised leap into the water. (At Vai Tamaroa, only the nimble make the leap, because it's a long hard climb back out.)

'ATIU, MA'UKE & MITIARO

Vaia'i, or Sandalwood Cave, named for the sweet-smelling trees that grow there, is in Mitiaro's north and also has a good freshwater swimming hole. However, people rarely go there nowadays because the track is difficult to find (it was destroyed by a cyclone a few years ago). You'll need a good guide – the path starts well but it's pure bush bashing by the end of it.

Tepito o Kare, in Mitiaro's southeast, is a cave too small for swimming, but with fresh water it's good for drinking. Fishermen used to stop by here to quench their thirst as they walked back inland from Te Unu Beach after fishing trips.

Marae & Fort

There are marae in the inland areas where the villages used to be, although many are now overgrown.

Takero Marae is on the inland road south of 'town', beneath an ancient chestnut tree on the western side of the road. This area is where the old Takaue village used to stand. Casting around among the undergrowth you might find the huge stone seat of the *ariki* and there are several old graves nearby.

In the southeast part of the island are the stone remains of ancient, well-built **Te Pare Fort**, built as a defence against 'Atiuan raids. Hidden and protected by the surrounding *makatea*, Te Pare's underground shelter was large enough for the people to congregate in during times of danger, while above was a lookout tower from which approaching canoes could be seen.

Footsteps could be easily heard on the loose stone pathway to the fort, and Te Pare's small marae ensured there was spiritual as well as physical protection. Despite all this, the fierce 'Atiuan warriors found the fort by standing on tall **Te Pooki Ikei** rock, nearby. They attacked, standing on their war clubs to protect their feet from the sharp *makatea*, and overpowered the defenders. The current three *ariki* of Mitiaro are descended from the foremost Mitiaro warriors, who were appointed by the 'Atiuan conquerors to represent the three *ariki* of 'Atiu.

To visit Te Pare fort and marae, you must first ask the permission of Po Tetava Ariki, the *ariki* to whom the marae belongs. His *tumu korero* (speaker), Mitiaro's tourism officer, **Julian Aupuni** (☎ 26260), will take you to the fort for NZ$20; there's an easy walking track across the *makatea*. A visit is well worthwhile.

Plantations

Back in the old days, people set up their villages where they grew their food. When houses were moved to the seaside village in the 1800s, families continued to use their old plantation areas. Nowadays there are roads across the *makatea* to the plantations and you can drive there, although many people still make the long trip on foot. The new visitor may wonder why they don't simply grow their produce closer to the village but there's a good reason for it: the old agricultural areas with their surrounding peat deposits are the most fertile spots on the island.

The CICC

The white-painted CICC – the third church that the London Missionary Society (LMS) built in the Cooks – with its blue trim, parquet ceiling decorated with black and white stars, and stained-glass windows is a fine sight and the singing on Sunday is, as usual, superb. Mitiaro also has a small Catholic church and an Assembly of God church.

Cemeteries

Many old cemeteries are dotted around the island. The cemetery on the north side of the island is the most interesting one. It has a few modern-style cement tombs, but also many older graves simply marked by an upright slab of coral. At almost every grave, both old and modern, some possessions of the deceased person are left at the headstone. Most of the graves have a plate, bowl, cup, glass, bottle and/or silverware sitting by the headstone, placed so that the spirit of the deceased can eat their meals on their own dinnerware.

Immediately after a death, the family brings food out to the grave and leaves it until it is gone. This continues for a month or two, until it is felt that the spirit has departed, however the plates and cutlery are left permanently. There is a very strong belief that the spirit continues to live on after death, and every effort is made to ensure that the spirit will not become angry with the living. Tin or enamel bowls and cups adorn older graves, while newer ones have more modern plates and cutlery. One grave has a whole box full of medicine bottles, some still containing the medicine; another has babies' bottles and (if this doesn't bring a tear to the eye, you're a heartless stone) one tiny baby's shoe.

Another cemetery, an easy walk south of town, also has supplies left for the departed, and with more recent graves, is more often cleared and mowed.

Lakes

Except in one spot, where a road leads right up to the shore of Te Rotonui, Mitiaro's lakes are hard to approach, and although the water is clear the lake bottoms are horribly muddy. If you approach the lakes by any other means than that one road, the ground becomes increasingly soggy and wallows more and more unsteadily under your feet the closer you get to the lake. Where the road arrives at Te Rotonui, though, the ground is firm – there's a boat landing and a pleasant picnic spot.

The local men often fish in the lakes for the prolific fish and Mitiaro's famous eels. The eels are caught at night by blinding them with a light and then whacking them with a bush knife. They can also be caught by baited hooks, or by hooking them around the body and hoisting them out of the water. There are plenty of eels in the lakes; 10 or more eels can easily be caught in a couple of hours. Milkfish, another renowned delicacy, are also plentiful in the lakes, due to a Japanese project stocking the lakes with fish brought from Aitutaki, Penrhyn and Hawaii.

Organised Tours

The only tours available on Mitiaro are run by the tourism officer **Julian Aupuni** (☎ 26260) to Te Pare in the south of the island (see Marae & Fort, earlier) for NZ$20.

Places to Stay & Eat

Seabreeze (☎ 36153, fax 36683; rooms per person NZ$65), operated by Mikara and Joe Herman, is a guesthouse on the outskirts of town with three rooms inside the main house and a self-contained unit out the back. Seabreeze also rents out bicycles (NZ$10 per day) and motorbikes (NZ$25). Rates include three hearty meals.

Nukuroa Beach Guesthouse (☎ 36106; adults/children NZ$82/44) is a pleasant local home with a few rooms for travellers. Mi'i O'Bryan, holder of the Te Ma'eu ariki title, will keep you fed and happy.

Limited food supplies are available a Mikara and Joe's **grocery store** but price are higher (and the selection smaller) tha on Rarotonga; you may want to bring som snacks with you.

Shopping

Mitiaro women make a variety of woven pandanus products for everyday use – floo mats, table mats, fans, handbags, basket and the like – while the artistic specialty o Mitiaro menfolk is carved wooden bowls However, there are no commercial outlet for these goods, and few people are actually very interested in selling their wares (quit a refreshing lack of commercialism actu ally!). Ask around in case the situation ha changed, but you're probably out of luck.

Getting There & Away

Air Mitiaro is served by **Air Rarotonga** (ir town ☎ 36888; [w] www.airraro.com) three times per week. The cost is NZ$368 returr (NZ$255 if you buy the tickets on Rarotonga instead of from overseas). Air Rarotonga's office is two houses south of the CICC.

A visit to Mitiaro can easily be combined with visits to Ma'uke and/or 'Atiu – each is only a 10-minute flight from Mitiaro, and i you visit more than one island, the cost per sector is reduced to NZ$124.

Rarotongan travel agencies (see Information in that island's chapter) can include Mitiaro in multi-island accommodation/flight packages that are cheaper than buying everything yourself (if you buy on Rarotonga). See the Getting Around chapter for more information about travel-agency packages, and Air Rarotonga's flights, multi-island deals and contact details.

Boat See the Getting Around chapter for details on interisland cargo ship services among the Cook Islands. Stops at Mitiaro are often made in conjunction with visits to 'Atiu and Ma'uke.

Getting Around

The people you're staying with will pick you up and drop you off. Motorbikes and bicycles can be rented from Seabreeze. Circumnavigating Mitiaro on foot takes about two hours if you don't stop to sniff the frangipani.

Mangaia

pop 780 • area 51.8 sq km

The second-largest of the Cook Islands, Mangaia is similar in size to Rarotonga, although its population is much smaller and has declined sharply in the last decade. The island is a geological oddity, very similar to 'Atiu. The central hills are surrounded by an outer rim of raised coral reef known as the *makatea*. The lagoon inside the fringing coral reef is very narrow and shallow.

Although Mangaia's geography is basically similar to 'Atiu's, it is much more dramatic. The *makatea* rises rapidly from the coast and in most places it drops as a sheer wall to the inner region. There are places where you can climb to the top of the cliff for impressive, uninterrupted views. The inner cliff of the *makatea* is such a major barrier that some of the cuttings through it are quite spectacular, the one through to Ivirua in particular.

All the streams and rivers running down from the central hills run into a dead end at the inner cliff of the *makatea*, filtering through it and emerging as small freshwater springs at or near the seashore. After heavy rains, streaks of Mangaia's red soil can be seen stretching from the *makatea* out into the sea from these water runoffs.

Scrub, ferns, vines, coconut palms and other trees grow on the *makatea*. Taro swamps are found around the inner edge of it where water collects between the hills and the coral flatlands, and in the central valleys, which are the most fertile part of the island and are planted with various crops.

Much of the island's hilly central area is planted with Caribbean pine trees, which prevent erosion. The trees, a New Zealand (NZ) aid project, were initially expected to become an important timber crop, but with the retrenchment of most of Mangaia's forestry staff following the 1996 economic crisis, the trees were left unpruned and unthinned. Now, it wouldn't be economical to harvest the trees.

Pineapples, which a few years ago were the island's principal export crop, are still grown, but not on the grand scale that they once were. After one year in the early 1990s when hundreds of boxes of pineapples

Highlights

- Wandering around the high, sheer inland cliffs and rich agricultural valleys
- Walking through the lush vegetation and cuttings in the *makatea*
- Climbing to the plateau of Rangimotia
- Exploring Te Rua Rere burial cave and other caves
- Canoeing across Lake Tiriara to explore the cave at the far end

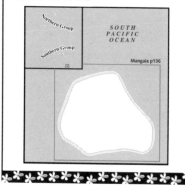

rotted on the wharf waiting for shipment, most farmers now raise pineapple only on a small scale for local consumption. Mangaian pineapples are still justly famous – big, sweet and juicy. Mangaian taro is also said to be some of the finest in the Cook Islands – you'll often see it for sale at Punanga Nui Market in Avarua on Rarotonga.

A crop that's taking off on Mangaia is *maire*, the sweet-smelling plant that is sent to Hawaii to be made into *lei* (necklaces).

History

The Mangaians have an unusual legend of their early history. Most Polynesian islands have some sort of legend about a great ancestor arriving on a fantastic canoe, but not the Mangaians. Nobody sailed from anywhere to become Mangaia's first settler. Rangi, Mokoaro and Akatauira, the three sons of the god Rongo, father of Mangaia, simply lifted the island up from the deep, becoming its first settlers and the ancestors of the Nga Ariki tribe.

The traditional name of the island was A'u A'u (literally 'Terraced' – named for the 'steps' of the *makatea*), short for A'u A'u Nui o Rongo ki te Au Marama (Big Terraced Land of Rongo in the World of Daylight). See the special section 'Cook Islands Myths & Legends' for how Rongo became Mangaia's premier deity.

The island's current name is comparatively new; it is short for a name bestowed by Tamaeu, an Aitutakian who arrived on Mangaia in 1775. Mangaia means 'Peace' or 'Temporal Power' – the name relates to 42 battles between the island's various groups and the peace that was finally established when one leader eventually achieved *mangaia*, or power, over the whole island.

Two years later, James Cook claimed the European discovery of Mangaia during his second Pacific voyage. He arrived on 29 March 1777, but the reception was not the friendliest and it was not possible to find a place to land, so Cook sailed north to a more friendly greeting at 'Atiu.

The reception was even less inviting when Reverend John Williams turned up on Mangaia in 1823. The pioneering missionary had left Aitutaki to search for Rarotonga. Coming first upon Mangaia, he attempted to set Polynesian missionaries ashore, but the Mangaians attacked them, so Williams dropped the idea and sailed off again. A couple of missionaries from Tahaa (in present-day French Polynesia) were landed in 1824, and although they were

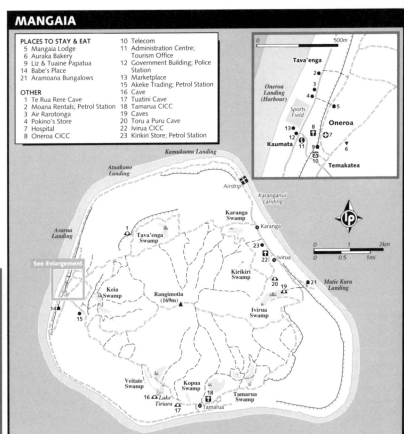

MANGAIA

PLACES TO STAY & EAT
5 Mangaia Lodge
6 Auraka Bakery
9 Liz & Tuaine Papatua
14 Babe's Place
21 Aramoana Bungalows

OTHER
1 Te Rua Rere Cave
2 Moana Rentals; Petrol Station
3 Air Rarotonga
4 Pokino's Store
7 Hospital
8 Oneroa CICC

10 Telecom
11 Administration Centre; Tourism Office
12 Government Building; Police Station
13 Marketplace
15 Akeke Trading; Petrol Station
16 Cave
17 Tuatini Cave
18 Tamarua CICC
19 Caves
20 Toru a Puru Cave
22 Ivirua CICC
23 Kirikiri Store; Petrol Station

fairly inept, their successor, the Rarotongan preacher Maretu (see Books in the Facts for the Visitor chapter) was successful. Maretu's book, *Cannibals & Converts* (widely available on Rarotonga), describes Mangaia's subsequent conversion to Christianity.

Traditionally, the Mangaians had a reputation for being a dour, ethnocentric lot – an attribute which perhaps helped to keep the aggressive 'Atiuans at bay. The warriors of 'Atiu wreaked havoc on Ma'uke and Mitiaro but never had much success over Mangaia.

In recent years Mangaia has suffered from a dramatic population decline. Since the mid-1970s the population of the island, stable for some time at around 2000, has fallen to almost a third of that.

Society

Mangaia has just one *ariki* (high chief), the queen Numangatini Nooroa Ariki, who lives in New Zealand (NZ). The island's six traditional districts are ruled by *kavana* (governors or district chiefs), while the 30-odd *kairanganuku* (subchiefs) are the people who actually own the land, not the *ariki*. A Mangaian saying sums it up: 'You are my king; you own nothing'.

Mangaians still identify strongly with whichever of the six districts their family came from. Whether it's sporting events or dance competitions, the people divide down district lines. Each district is also divided into tribal areas; as you walk through the inland *makatea* you'll often see short stone walls marking ancient tribal boundaries.

As a result of the Bible being preached here by Rarotongans, the Mangaian language is now almost identical to Rarotongan. It's believed that older Mangaians spoke a very different language – more similar to NZ Maori than to Rarotongan. Some differences do remain; the most common greeting in Mangaian is *tangi ke*, rather than the Rarotongan *kia orana*.

Orientation

Oneroa, Tamarua and Ivirua, the three main villages, are all on the coast, with Oneroa on the western side of the island, Ivirua on the eastern side and Tamarua on the southern side. Oneroa, the main village, has three parts: Tava'enga and Kaumata are on the northern and southern parts of the coast, respectively, and Temakatea is up above, reached by a road cut through the *makatea* cliff. The airstrip is on the northern side of the island.

Information

Mangaia's **tourism office** (☎ 34289, fax 34238) is in the Administration Centre at the bottom of the Temakatea road cutting. The director, Mataora 'Happy' Harry, is exceptionally friendly and a mine of information on Mangaian history. When the tourism office moves across the road, Mataora hopes to set up a small museum in this building.

Pokino's Store (☎ 34092) in Oneroa is the island's ANZ agent. You can get credit-card cash advances here, and cash NZ travellers cheques.

The **Telecom office** (☎ 34680, fax 34683) is in the upper part of Oneroa, in Temakatea, not far from the hospital. Here you can make long-distance telephone calls, and send and receive faxes. There's a 24-hour **public phone** (☎ 34000) you can use with your prepaid Kiaorana card.

At the time of writing, the post office was temporarily housed in the Telecom office. When the government building, opposite the Administration Centre, is complete, the post office will move back there.

Mangaia's **hospital** (☎ 34027) is open for consultations from 8am to 10am Monday to Friday, but there's someone there 24 hours for emergencies. There is electricity daily from 5am to midnight.

Churches & Marae

There are big, old, white Cook Islands Christian Churches (CICCs) in Oneroa, Ivirua and Tamarua, dating from the time of Maretu, the Rarotongan missionary. The Tamarua church, surrounded by a shady grove of ironwood trees, is especially beautiful – look for the woodcarving and the sennit-rope binding on the roof beams. In front of the Oneroa church an interesting monument lists ministers of the church, both *papa'a* (foreigners) and Maori, as well as Mangaians who have worked as missionaries abroad.

Mangaia has numerous premissionary marae (religious ceremonial grounds). There are 24 around the island, but you'll need a local expert to find them. Tuara George (see the Caves section) can take you. Many marae are remote, overgrown and disused. On Mangaia, marae are no longer used in modern ceremonies, as they are on some other Cook Islands. The tourism office (see Information earlier) will be able to tell you which marae are most accessible.

Rangimotia & Island Walks

Rangimotia (169m) is the highest point on the island. It's not really a peak, more of a high plateau. You know when you're at the top (there are two telephone masts), but you have to explore a few hundred metres in several directions to see the entire coast. From the Oneroa side of the island there's a dirt road right to the top. Other roads and tracks, less distinct, follow the ridges of Mangaia's rolling hills back towards the coast. From the summit the dirt road heads back down to the circle-island road about halfway between Ivirua and Tamarua.

If you turn right at the circle-island road you'll be heading towards Tamarua, the third village on the island. The road runs just inland from the *makatea* for most of the distance. Along this stretch the *makatea* is not edged with much of a cliff, but shortly after the trail climbs back onto the raised coral there is an impressive drop, and at a point shortly before Tamarua you can turn off the road for a great view over a **taro plantation**. From Tamarua the road runs close to the coast, with numerous paths down to the reef. Or you can take the shorter (but steeper) direct route back to Oneroa.

From Oneroa up to Rangimotia, down to Tamarua and back to Oneroa is a pleasant, but quite long, day's walk; over 25km in total.

There's no limit to the **walks** you can take in the interior of the island – an extensive network of firebreaks and rough dirt roads follow many of the ridges. However, it's not hard to get lost, so take care.

Several of the **cuttings** through the *makatea* cliffs are beautiful for short walks, with narrow roads winding between the high, grey *makatea* cliffs, hanging with vegetation. The cutting from Ivirua village heading inland to the taro swamp behind the village is probably the most beautiful on the island, with its steep walls draped with ferns and vines.

Caves

The *makatea* is riddled with caves, the largest and most spectacular of which is **Te**

Rua Rere. This burial cave was rediscovered in the 1930s by a local, Tuaratua George, and Robert Dean Frisbie (see the Books section in the Facts for the Visitor chapter). Te Rua Rere means 'jump' (possibly because people used to jump down into the cave opening).

You do have to climb down into the opening. The branches of a tree emerge at ground level and at the other end of this opening there's a fine view out from the *makatea* cliff. As you enter, the high, narrow cliffs seem to close overhead. At first, there are several small openings above you and a tree root winds down one through to floor level. Then you have to slither through a low, muddy opening, and the cave becomes much more enclosed. Be sure to bring a torch (flashlight) and insect repellent, as there are many mosquitoes near the cave entrance. The cave is not difficult to explore, but wear old clothes because you'll get quite dirty.

This is a very dramatic cave and most of the time it is very high, yet narrow. It holds many crystalline, glistening-white stalactites and stalagmites, but the most interesting feature, apart from the human skeletons, is simply how far it continues. There are no major side chambers but the main cavern continues on and on. Some people brave enough to keep exploring reckon that it continues for at least 2km. No-one, though, has ever reached the end.

Tuara George, whose family has been exploring this cave for decades, is the guide (see Organised Tours, later).

Mangaia has many other caves, and many people who can take you to see them. Each cave is on private land, so arrangements must be made with the appropriate landowner in order to visit (see Organised Tours for more information). All the accommodation owners (see Places to Stay) can arrange guides to different caves. The tourism office (see Information) also has details on cave trips.

Beaches & Lake Tiriara

Countless little beaches and bays dot the coastline, although they're not that good for swimming – the reef is very shallow and generally close to the coast. The only place where the water is deep enough is at the wharf at Avarua Landing near Oneroa.

Many locals swim at the wharf, afterwards going across the *makatea* about 100m to the left (south) to where a small freshwater spring gushes up from the *makatea* beside the seaside, with refreshing cool water and tiny fish. The spring is too small for swimming, but you can sit in the water to wash off the sea salt.

On the southwestern side of the island, Tuaati Beach is a tiny unmarked beach too shallow for swimming, but you can splash around and it's very attractive. There's also a sandy beach at Karanganui Landing on the northeastern side of the island, where again you can get wet, but it's too shallow for swimming.

Lake Tiriara, the only lake on the island, is surrounded by swamp and high reeds, but it's clearly visible from the inland road from Tamarua to Oneroa. The sheer cliffs of the *makatea* rise behind the lake on the opposite side from the road. At the base of the cliff a cave mouth is visible (the lake is connected, underwater, to the coast via this cave). **Clarke's Island Tours** (☎ 34303) – see Organised Tours – takes visitors across the lake and into the mouth of the cave by canoe.

Taro Plantations

Each of the huge, sodden valleys of Mangaia is almost filled with taro plantations. It's worth a trip inland to one of these plantations to see the impressive earthworks diverting water into various plots. (Take mosquito repellent.) The inner cliff of the *makatea* towers over one end of the valley, with tiny ancient tracks weaving down from the cliff to the crops. Each valley belongs to one of Mangaia's six traditional districts, corresponding to the areas where families lived before missionaries gathered them all together for convenient preaching.

Organised Tours

Clarke Mautairi of **Clarke's Island Tours** (☎ 34303 or Babe's Place ☎ 34092) offers a full-day island tour for NZ$50, and a tour of Lake Tiriara (and the cave) by canoe for NZ$30.

Island tours, by motorbike or truck, can be arranged through **Aramoana Bungalows** (☎ 34278) for NZ$50, and **Mangaia Lodge** (☎ 34324) for NZ$30. These tours are a good way to orient yourself soon after you arrive.

The Mangaian Kingfisher

If you're lucky, while you're on Mangaia you'll see a *tanga'eo* (Mangaian kingfisher), a bird endemic to Mangaia (ie, it's found nowhere but here). In the 1970s it was feared that the *tanga'eo* had become extinct, pushed out of its habitat by Indian mynahs, and its eggs plundered by rats. However, the *tanga'eo* survived, and its population is now estimated at 500.

Walk through Mangaia's native-forest interior and you've got a fairly good chance of spotting one of these small birds, recognisable by their relatively large beak, blue-and-white plumage and confident manner.

Tere Tauakume (☎ 34223) leads a fascinating three-hour tour (NZ$35) of several interconnected caves in the Ivirua area, telling stories of his ancestors as you walk. Highlights include the views of Ivirua's taro plantation from the *makatea* cliff, and Tere's theory of the origins of Polynesia, delivered in pitch-darkness in his booming voice, with the bones of his ancestors sitting nearby – who's arguing?

Tuara George leads a one-hour tour (NZ$20) that passes by a number of ancient human skeletons inside Mangaia's most impressive cave, Te Rua Rere. Ask about the tour at Babe's Place (see Places to Stay).

Ora Peraua (☎ 34280) leads tours of Toru a Puru burial cave (NZ$20).

Places to Stay

All the places to stay on Mangaia make some provision for guests' food, either cooking meals for you or allowing you to prepare your own. Most accommodation is in Oneroa, the island's principal village.

Mangaia Lodge (☎ 34324, fax 34239; *Oneroa; singles/doubles/triples NZ$25/40/60*) is in Temakatea, the upper section of Oneroa. This colonial-style lodge has three large bedrooms, a kitchen and a sunny, enclosed common terrace. There's a pretty basic separate toilet/shower block. You're welcomed at the airport with *ei* (traditional necklaces) and, back at the lodge, a prayer. The prices listed include breakfast; otherwise you do your own cooking (meals can be arranged by request; NZ$10). Group rates are available.

MANGAIA

Babe's Place (☎ 34092, fax 34078; Oneroa; singles/doubles/triples NZ$60/100/114), in the Kaumata section of Oneroa, beside the sea and near Tuaati Beach, has a large, modern two-bedroom house with shared dining area and a lounge. There are also four roomy motel-style units, subtly decorated – love those lurid pink bedspreads! Self-catering isn't really an option here as there are limited cooking facilities. Rates include airport transfers and three meals a day. Next door there's a bar open on Friday and Saturday nights for darts and dancing.

Mangaia Lodge and Babe's Place can be booked via the travel agents on Rarotonga (see that island's chapter).

Aramoana Bungalows (☎ 34278, fax 34279; w www.aramoana.com; Ivirua; tiny singles/doubles NZ$35/55, small bungalow singles/doubles NZ$60/80, medium bungalow singles/doubles/triples NZ$115/135/165) has several free-standing, one- or two-room cabins around large grounds near the sea, with a good beach just a short walk away. The owners can arrange activities such as island and cave tours, and reef fishing. It's a bit isolated here on the far side of the island; a motorbike (Aramoana's decrepit ones cost NZ$30 per day) is a necessity if you want to see much of Mangaia. Meals can be provided – breakfast and dinner costs around NZ$35 per person; lunch NZ$10. If you want to cook for yourself, let staff know from the outset. Kids under 12 years are half-price; kids under six years are free.

Liz & Tuaine Papatua (☎ 34164; Oneroa; room per person NZ$25, with meals NZ$35) rent a large bedroom in their home in the Temakatea section of Oneroa, near the hospital and overlooking the sea.

For groups of four or more people, there's also the option of staying at one of Oneroa's community halls. They each have fully equipped kitchens, showers and foam mattresses. The cost is about NZ$50 per night for the hall, whatever the size of the group. (Contact the tourism office for more details.)

Places to Eat

Aramoana Bungalows (☎ 34278; Ivirua) prepares meals for its guests, but casual diners are also welcome. Ring ahead to say you're coming.

Auraka Bakery (☎ 34281; Oneroa; meals NZ$8.50-15), a restaurant and bar, is unfortunately only open when there are plenty of travellers on the island.

Self-Catering If you're staying long you might want to bring some of your own food with you. There are several stores around, but their selections are rather limited, and you should have a good look at use-by dates on canned and packaged goods.

Pokino's Store (☎ 34092; Tava'enga) is the best-stocked shop on the island, but even its selection is limited. **Kirikiri Store** (☎ 34133), north of Ivirua, and **Akeke Trading** (☎ 34206), inland from Oneroa, have a reasonable range of foodstuffs.

Fresh vegetables are in particularly short supply at certain times of the year. There's a weekly Friday morning **market** (at 8am) beside the post office in Oneroa, where you can get whatever fruits and vegetables are around.

Fresh-baked bread (NZ$1/2 unsliced/sliced) is available at **Auraka Bakery** (☎ 34281) or at **Pokino's Store** several days a week.

Entertainment

Babe's Place (☎ 34092; Oneroa) offers the only regularly scheduled entertainment on the island, hosting a dance on Friday and Saturday nights – it's a good chance to mix with the locals. Friday night is a dance competition while Saturday is straight-out dancing. Shows are held here sometimes.

Aramoana Bungalows (☎ 34278; Ivirua) has a bar, but it's only open when there are lots of guests staying.

Auraka Bakery (☎ 34281; Oneroa), like Aramoana Bungalows, has a bar that is only open when there are lots of travellers on the island (ie, very rarely).

Shopping

Various arts and crafts are practised on Mangaia, but there are no crafts shops or other organised outlets. The tourism office (see Information, earlier) is one of the best places to find out about what's on offer, and tourism officer Mataora Harry often has some crafts for sale. You can buy traditional woven reef sandals for NZ$12, stone pounders for upwards of NZ$10, and Mangaia's famous carved-stone axes from NZ$200.

Pupu Ei

Almost everyone on Mangaia makes *pupu ei* (long necklaces of tiny white or yellow shells). The *pupu* shells come from tiny black land snails that can only be found after rainfall. Boiling the shells in caustic soda produces the yellow colour, but they can also be grilled to make them white, or dyed a variety of colours. They're then individually pierced with a needle and threaded to make the finished *ei*. It's a time-consuming business.

On Rarotonga, *pupu ei* from Mangaia fetch as much as NZ$90 a dozen, and they are even more expensive elsewhere in the Pacific, but you can get them for around NZ$60 a dozen on Mangaia. Ask almost any woman on the island where you can buy some.

The people who make arts and crafts welcome interested visitors to stop by and have a look. Ask at the tourism office where to find Glen Tuara, who makes calcite-stone taro pounders, and Tuaiva Mautairi, who carves Mangaian ceremonial adzes, drums, stone pounders, wooden fruit bowls and various other wood carvings. *Tivaevae* (appliqué works) are made on Mangaia, but they are generally not for sale.

Getting There & Away

Air Flights with **Air Rarotonga** (☎ 34888 in Tava'enga; W www.airraro.com) operate between Rarotonga and Mangaia four times a week. The cost is NZ$245 return (NZ$237 if you buy the tickets on Rarotonga rather than overseas).

Rarotonga-based travel agents (see that island's chapter) organise package tours, including air fare and accommodation, that are cheaper than buying everything yourself (if you buy on Rarotonga). See the Getting Around chapter for more information about package deals and Air Rarotonga's flights, multi-island passes, and contact details.

Boat Interisland cargo ships operate from Rarotonga to the other islands of the Cooks, including Mangaia. See the Getting Around chapter.

Getting Around

Moana Rentals (☎ 34307), in Tava'enga, north of Oneroa, rents new motorbikes for NZ$30 per day. **Aramoana Bungalows** (☎ 34278; Ivirua) rents much older motorbikes for the same price (who needs brakes?). You can get petrol at Moana Rentals, Akeke Trading (Oneroa) and Kirikiri Store (Ivirua).

Walking is fine, especially the route across the island via Rangimotia, but the distances are quite long and you can't count on getting a ride from a passing vehicle as there is so little traffic. One Lonely Planet author tested this by walking from Ivirua to Oneroa via Tamarua and saw not one vehicle going his way. (He reported that the walk takes about four hours.)

Palmerston Atoll

pop 52 • area 2.0 sq km

Palmerston is something of a Cook Islands oddity: it's far to the west of the rest of the Southern Group, and, unlike those islands it's an atoll, more like the Northern Group islands.

Palmerston's lagoon is 11km wide at its widest point, and 30-odd small islands dot the reef. Passages are shallow – at low tide the lagoon is completely closed off – and visiting ships have to anchor outside the reef.

With transport available every fortnight, Palmerston is now a real option for travellers, although it's not cheap. If you are a nature lover you'll enjoy the birdlife, coconut crabs, turtles, whales and dolphins on and around this isolated atoll. However, the people of Palmerston are even more fascinating!

History

Palmerston Atoll was populated infrequently in the distant past; it was known as Ava Rau (Many Passages) on other islands. When James Cook sighted Palmerston Atoll in 1774, it was unpopulated; he named the atoll after the first lord of the admiralty (always a good career move).

Cook didn't stop on that first occasion, but in 1777 when he passed by on his third voyage his ships did pause and boats came ashore to seek provisions. Palmerston has the singular honour in the Cook Islands of having had Captain Cook actually step ashore.

In 1850 the crew of the *Merchant of Tahiti* rescued four starving Europeans on the island. The castaways, having landed on an uninhabited, unclaimed island, had a legal right to claim it, but they traded that right to the *Merchant of Tahiti's* captain for their passage to Rarotonga. Palmerston's claim eventually made its way to a Scottish trader in Tahiti. He needed representatives on the island and found one in William Marsters, an Englishman living on Manuae Atoll, near Aitutaki. Marsters moved to Palmerston in 1863.

William Marsters became a living legend, an Old Testament–like figure who created and shaped an entire tribe. The present

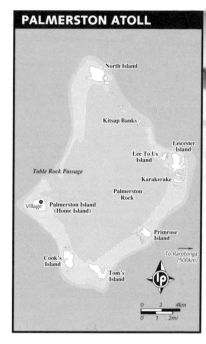

PALMERSTON ATOLL

North Island

Kitsap Banks

Leicester Island

Lee To Us Island

Table Rock Passage

Karakerake

Palmerston Rock

Village ● Palmerston Island (Home Island)

Primrose Island

Cook's Island

To Rarotonga (500km)

Tom's Island

0   2   4km
0   1   2mi

inhabitants of Palmerston Atoll are all Marsters, all descended from William and his three Maori wives. They populated not only Palmerston – to this day you'll find people with the surname Marsters all over the Cooks, and it's a common name on cemetery headstones. William Marsters died on 22 May 1899 at the age of 78 and is buried near his original homestead.

At one time the population of the atoll was as high as 150, but it has dropped steadily, with young people moving away to the bright lights of Rarotonga and Auckland, New Zealand (NZ). Communication with the mainland has improved dramatically with the acquisition of *Marsters Dream* (see Getting There & Away later in the chapter) and a phone/fax link arriving during 2001 and 2002.

Along with the construction of a new school in 2001, these factors help reduce Palmerston's sense of isolation, and it is hoped that the population will at least stabilise at its present 50-odd people.

Culture

Palmerston's small population are all descendants of William Marsters. This is the only place in the Cook Islands where English is the native tongue. However, it's a unique kind of English, with a distinct Gloucestershire burr (from Marsters' home town) and many 'borrowed' Maori words introduced, it is thought, by Marsters' wives.

Marsters divided his family into three families, descended from each of his wives. Careful rules were spelt out concerning the resources and land for each family and interfamily marriage. However, conflict between the three families is not uncommon. Palmerston's island council, unique in that its members are appointed and not elected, is chosen to represent the three families equally.

As well as the handful of Marsters on Palmerston itself, more than 2000 live on Rarotonga and in NZ. All consider Palmerston 'home'.

The atoll's small population earns its living primarily through fishing; many of the delicious tuna you'll find on restaurant tables in Avarua were caught in the deep waters off Palmerston.

Information

Palmerston's mayor and island secretary are based in Avarua, Rarotonga. This makes getting information about travel and accommodation fairly easy. At the time of writing the mayor is **George Marsters** (☎ 20893), who lives near Avatiu Harbour, and the island secretary is **Lydia Sjip-Marsters** (☎ 24005, fax 24006; e primrose@oyster.net.ck), near Arai-Te-Tonga.

You can contact people on Palmerston either by high-frequency radio (phone ☎ 020 to arrange this with Telecom) or by phoning the single public telephone on the island (☎ 37684). There is electricity from 6am to midday and 6pm to midnight (it's spaced out like that so that freezers, storing tuna for export, won't defrost).

Places to Stay

Palmerston has no organised accommodation for visitors, but the atoll has long had a tradition that the first person to greet an arriving yacht will welcome you into his or her home.

If you decide to visit on *Marsters Dream*, the mayor or island secretary (see Information) will be able to arrange homestay accommodation for about NZ$30 per day.

Getting There & Away

In late 2000 the people of Palmerston Atoll bought an ex-torpedo boat from the Swedish navy, which they fitted out for freight and passengers. Renamed *Marsters Dream*, the boat travels between Rarotonga and Palmerston twice a month, taking fish caught off Palmerston to the market at Avarua and bringing supplies back to Palmerston. *Marsters Dream* has made an enormous difference to Palmerston's population, making it much more a part of the mainstream.

You can arrange transport on the boat (NZ$300 return; 22 hours each way) with the mayor or island secretary (see Information). The boat stays at Palmerston for six days, quite long enough to visit every *motu* (lagoon islet) and meet every person on the atoll. Book early; there are only eight passenger berths available. The landing fee at Palmerston is US$5.

There are no flights to Palmerston, and the interisland freighter ships stop very infrequently.

Yachts are always welcomed at Palmerston, although the only mooring buoy at Palmerston is used by *Marsters Dream* whenever she's here. Anchoring is discouraged with a NZ$35 fee, as it damages the coral.

The Northern Group

The northern islands of the Cooks are scattered coral atolls, specks of land in a vast expanse of sea. They are all low-lying and from a ship cannot even be seen from more than 10km away. Severe cyclones have been known to send waves right across the islands.

History

The Northern Group atolls have the longest history of any of the Cook Islands. They were first discovered about 2000 years ago when Polynesian voyagers set out from Samoa and Tonga towards the unknown east. On the way to discover what are now called the Society Islands (French Polynesia), they found these tiny atolls.

The atolls were not settled until some centuries later. In fact, most were settled by explorers from the Southern Group islands, arriving almost a millennium after the atolls were first discovered.

Society

Although atolls such as these conjure up the romantic image of a Pacific island – complete with sandy beaches, clear and shallow lagoons, and swaying palm trees – in fact, life is hard on an atoll. Fish may be abundant in the lagoon, but atoll soil is only marginally fertile and the range of produce that can be grown is very limited. Fresh water is always a problem. Shallow wells are often the only source of drinking water and the supply is limited and often brackish.

Atoll life has another drawback apart from these natural ones, and that is sheer isolation. Today, people want economic opportunity, education for their children and contact with the outside world. On a tiny island where the only physical contact is a monthly trading ship, these things are clearly not available. Returning islanders and telephone connections have whetted appetites for the outside world, and the populations of many northern islands are declining rapidly.

Environment

The tiny, low-lying atolls of the Northern Group are most at risk from global warming (caused by the 'greenhouse effect'; see

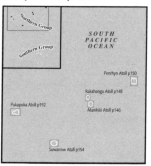

Ecology & Environment in the Facts about the Cook Islands chapter). On most atolls, the highest point above sea level is barely 5m, and the vast majority of crops and housing are on land only 1m or 2m high. Severe cyclones have already been known to wash right across these islands (most recently, on Manihiki in 1997; see History in the Manihiki Atoll section). Over the next century, sea levels will rise, and such storms may become more common and even more severe. At the same time, coral reefs, both a source of seafood and the best protection from heavy seas, are likely to be killed off by coral bleaching, and the atolls' freshwater supplies will be contaminated by the rising seas.

Within 100 years, according to even conservative predictions, the Northern Group atolls will probably be uninhabitable. The people of this ancient culture will be forced to find a new home.

Travel to the Northern Group

Once you start talking to travel agents about the Northern Group, you'll find yourself hearing over and over again lots of reasons *not* to go: 'The flights are very expensive. There's no accommodation. There's nothing to eat.' One travel agent told us that Manihiki 'isn't like Aitutaki, you know'. You start to wonder if they're hiding a secret military facility up there. The truth is, though, visiting the Northern Cooks really *is* hard work. Transport, accommodation, food – they all present difficulties.

If you're serious about visiting the Northern Group, talk to people who know the islands to find out what you can expect. Each outer island has a hostel in Avarua on Rarotonga (most of them are near the National Culture Centre) and the hostel caretakers are excellent sources of information regarding their home islands.

To arrange accommodation (which you have to do before you are allowed to buy a ticket) talk to a travel agent (for Manihiki, Penrhyn and Pukapuka; see Travel Agencies later) or contact the island councils (see each atoll's Information section in this chapter).

Don't allow yourself to be discouraged. If you talk to (Southern) Cook Islanders about the Northern Group they'll tell you that visiting these islands is a once-in-a-lifetime experience. In fact, many people from the Southern Cooks will sit on an uncomfortable, tossing cargo boat for almost a week to get there and still count themselves lucky for the opportunity.

Travel Agencies For more information about the three islands that planes fly to (Manihiki, Penrhyn and Pukapuka), contact **Air Rarotonga** (☎ 22888, fax 23288; **e** book ings@airraro.co.ck). Cook Islands Tours & Travel, Hugh Henry Travel & Tours, Jetsave Travel and Tipani Tours (see Travel Agencies in the Rarotonga chapter for contact details) can arrange flight and accommodation packages to these three islands. Such packages usually work out cheaper than buying the flights and accommodation separately.

For the other islands, talk to the two inter-island shipping companies, Mataroa Shipping and Taio Shipping (see the Boat section in the Getting Around chapter for contact details) as well as Cook Islands Tours & Travel, which can arrange transport and accommodation packages.

Accommodation Although only Manihiki and Penrhyn have established guesthouses

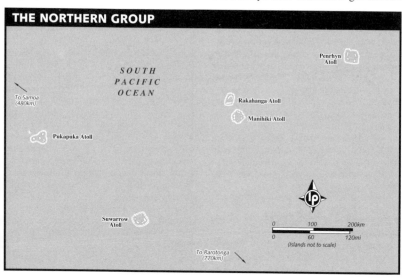

THE NORTHERN GROUP

SOUTH PACIFIC OCEAN

To Samoa (480km)

Penrhyn Atoll

Rakahanga Atoll

Manihiki Atoll

Pukapuka Atoll

Suwarrow Atoll

To Rarotonga (770km)

0   100   200km
0   60   120mi
(Islands not to scale)

for visitors, on any of the islands visitors are made welcome and some arrangement can always be made. Plan to pay your way, however, both in cash and with food or other supplies. (Food supplies are limited on the islands and the arrival of a ship is always a major occasion.)

You might be able to arrange accommodation through the island councils on some islands. Their phone and fax numbers are listed under Information in the individual atoll sections.

If accommodation phone or fax numbers don't work (not uncommon), try the island council or Telecom numbers, and ask them to pass the message on.

See Travel Agencies earlier for companies offering transport and accommodation packages.

Getting There & Away

Air You can fly to Manihiki and Penrhyn once a week, and Pukapuka occasionally. Flights take 3½ to four hours from Rarotonga and are quite expensive – it costs as much to fly to the Northern Group islands from Rarotonga as it does to fly to New Zealand (NZ), and can take even longer.

Bad weather, limited fuel supplies and too few bookings can sometimes cause the flights not to run. Take out travel insurance to cover unavoidable delays when you fly to the Northern Group islands.

Boat Apart from flying, the only regular way of getting to the Northern Group islands is on the interisland cargo ships. The ships unload and load at the islands by day, so if you're doing a circuit of the islands you'll only spend a few hours at most of them, overnighting just at Manihiki and Penrhyn. If you want to stay longer you either have to wait until the next ship comes by (remembering that voyages are often cancelled – so your one-month stay could become two months or longer), or, on the islands with airstrips, you could always take the boat one way and then fly out.

Manihiki Atoll

pop 660 • area 5.4 sq km
Manihiki is one of the most beautiful atolls in the South Pacific, perhaps even more

beautiful than Aitutaki. Nearly 40 islands, some of them little more than tiny specks of land, encircle the 4km-wide and totally enclosed lagoon of Manihiki. The main village is Tauhunu and there is a second village, Tukao. Manihiki has no safe anchorage for visiting ships; they have to stay offshore.

What Manihiki does have is pearls and pearl shells, especially the famous Manihiki black pearls, which are the economic mainstay of the atoll and a significant export for the Cook Islands. The abilities of the atoll's pearl divers are legendary – they can dive to great depths and stay submerged for minutes at a time. Such deep-sea free diving is uncommon these days, with modern technology now utilised to make the process simpler and safer.

History
According to legend, Manihiki and Rakahanga (then still joined together) were discovered when they were still underwater, by a Rarotongan named Huku. The landmass was fished up from the waves by the demigod Maui (see the special section 'Cook Islands Myths & Legends'), and when Huku and Maui fought for possession, the land was broken into two pieces – Rakahanga and Manihiki.

From the time of the victor, Huku (probably about AD 1500), until the 19th century,

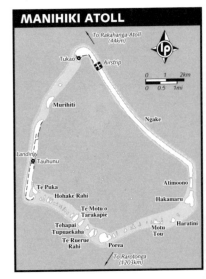

MANIHIKI ATOLL

To Rakahanga Atoll (44km)

Tukao • Airstrip

0   1   2km
0   0.5   1mi

Murihiti

Ngake

Landing • Tauhunu

Te Puka

Hohake Rahi

Te Motu o Tarakapie

Atimoono

Hakamaru

Tehapai
Tupuaekaha

Haratini

Motu
Tou

Te Ruerue
Rahi

Porea

To Rarotonga (1203km)

Manihiki and Rakahanga were populated by just one group of people. Most of the time, the population lived on Rakahanga, but would migrate en masse to feed on the fish of Manihiki's lagoon whenever supplies on Rakahanga were depleted. Many lives were lost on these interisland trips as canoes were blown off course.

Manihiki may have been sighted by the Spanish explorer Pedro Fernández de Quirós in 1606. However, de Quirós' sighting was somewhat ambiguous, so credit for the European discovery is normally given to Captain Patrickson of the US ship *Good Hope* in 1822. Patrickson and a successive stream of whalers and traders bestowed a series of forgettable names upon the island – Humphrey, Great Ganges, Liderous, Gland, Sarah Scott and Pescado. Fortunately, none of them stuck.

Christian missionaries came to Manihiki in 1849 and left two Polynesian missionary teachers behind. They also, unwittingly, left disease. The ensuing epidemic quickly convinced the islanders that they had not been behaving themselves and that they should embrace Christianity. In 1852 the missionaries convinced the people to divide themselves between Rakahanga and Manihiki and settle permanently. See the Rakahanga Atoll section for more about relations between the two islands.

The women of Manihiki were famous for their beauty, a reputation that continues to this day. In the late 19th century, however, that notion led to raids by Peruvian slavers and a variety of Pacific ne'er-do-wells. In 1869 'Bully Hayes' spirited off a number of islanders, supposedly for a visit to Rakahanga; in reality they ended up as plantation labourers in Fiji.

In 1889, when relations between the British and French in the Pacific were tense, the islanders fell out with their missionaries and invited the French from Tahiti to take over the island. A French warship duly turned up, but the missionaries speedily hoisted the Union Jack and the French opted for discretion rather than valour. Later that year the island was officially taken under the British wing.

In November 1997, Manihiki was struck full-on by Cyclone Martin. Winds were severe, and chest-high waves washed right over the low-lying atoll, completely submerging the land for a time. Both of the island's villages, Tauhunu and Tukao, were destroyed, and most of Manihiki's crops were lost. The population raced to save themselves by launching boats onto the protected lagoon, but even the lagoon was lashed by strong winds and high waves, and many boats were sunk, depositing whole families into the sea. Miraculously, considering the extent of the destruction, only 19 lives were lost.

In the aftermath of the cyclone, with not a single building standing, much of the population (hundreds of people) were evacuated to Rarotonga. They returned slowly, as buildings were replaced and foodstuffs recovered. The villages have since been completely rebuilt, at great cost. The NZ government paid for some of it, but the whole of the Cook Islands, plus expat communities in NZ, and other Pacific nations such as Fiji, Samoa and Niue, were involved in the fundraising. Both Tauhunu and Tukao now sport state-of-the-art cyclone shelters.

The pearl industry, even back then earning several million NZ dollars per year, was completely wiped out by the cyclone. It has recovered since, however, and now generates over NZ$18 million per year. In fact, these days, with the income from pearls, Manihikians are among the richest Cook Islanders. Many of the people working here are from the Southern Cooks, lured by the good money paid to pearl divers.

Literature

Manihikian literary giants are few and far between, but one Manihikian author, Kauraka Kauraka, published a number of books; see Books in the Facts for the Visitor chapter. Sadly, Kauraka passed away on Rarotonga in 1997; he is sorely missed. His grave is on Manihiki.

Information

Manihiki's brand-new **administration centre** (☎ 43054, fax 43683), rebuilt after Cyclone Martin, is at Tauhunu, as is the **island council** (☎ 43102). **Telecom** (☎ 43680, fax 43683) is in Tukao.

There's a **hospital** (☎ 43664) at Tauhunu and a **health office** (☎ 43364) at Tukao. Bring insect repellent; all those empty oyster shells make excellent breeding grounds for mosquitoes.

Manihiki's electricity was wiped out by Cyclone Martin in 1997, and it was 2½ years before the lights came back on. Now, generators raised high out of harm's way supply electricity from 6am to midday and 6pm to midnight.

Water shortages are common on Manihiki. Showers are usually restricted to a dip in the lagoon or a rinse with a bucket of cold water.

Things to See & Do
There are a surprising number of things to do on Manihiki. Visiting a pearl farm is a must – for NZ$30 you can do a guided tour, including watching the technical part of the job (seeding the oysters) and snorkelling down to check out the oysters underwater. You can also travel around the lagoon in a small boat, swimming, snorkelling, fishing and (if you've been successful) enjoying a barbecued-fish lunch.

Places to Stay & Eat
Manihiki Guesthouse (☎/fax 43307; Tauhunu village; adults/children NZ$82/45), a three-bedroom, modern guesthouse, offers accommodation with shared facilities. The friendly owners, Bernardino and Jane Kaina, offer tours, activities and great cooking. Rates include three meals and airport transfers.

Manihiki Lagoon Lookout (☎/fax 43331; Tukao village; adults/children NZ$70/35), perched on poles above the lagoon, is a unique place to stay. Rates include three meals.

Getting There & Away
Air Flights with **Air Rarotonga** (☎ 22888 on Rarotonga; W www.airraro.com) operate between Rarotonga and Manihiki once a week. The cost is NZ$1244 (return) for the 4-hour flight. Depending on demand, the flights may be routed through Pukapuka (1½ hours away) or Penrhyn (one hour).

Boat See the Boat section in the Getting Around chapter for details on travel by interisland cargo ship to Manihiki. You can get to Rakahanga by boat from here, but it's only recommended if you've got a few weeks to spare (it's not unusual for people to be stranded on Rakahanga during bad weather).

Rakahanga Atoll

pop 130 • area 4.1 sq km
Only 44km north of Manihiki, this rectangular atoll consists of two major islands and a host of *motu* (lagoon islets) almost completely enclosing a central lagoon about 4km long and 2km wide at its widest points.

Without the pearl wealth of Manihiki, the island of Rakahanga is conspicuously quieter and less energetic. Copra is the only export product, although the islanders grow breadfruit and *puraka* (a taro-like vegetable). The *rito* (bleached pandanus leaf) hats woven on Rakahanga are particularly fine. The population is concentrated in the village of Nivano, in the southwestern corner of the atoll.

History
Legends tell of a landmass being hauled up from under the sea by a fisherman, and being broken into two sections, the islands of Rakahanga and Manihiki, during a fight – see the special section 'Cook Islands Myths & Legends'. A Rarotongan, Huku, won that fight, and with his sister and

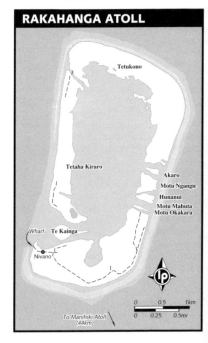

RAKAHANGA ATOLL

Tetukono

Tetaha Kiraro

Akaro
Motu Ngangie
Hunanui
Motu Mahuta
Motu Okakara

Wharf   Te Kainga

Te Kainga

Nivano

To Manihiki Atoll (44km)

0   0.5   1km
0   0.25   0.5mi

Lost en Route

Although missionaries tried from as early as 1852 to put an end to voyaging across the 44km between Rakahanga and Manihiki, people continue to shuttle back and forth, sometimes with harrowing results.

In June 1953, for example, nine islanders set out at night to sail from Manihiki to Rakahanga. Come dawn, they were lost – a squall had blown them off course and where they were, relative to the two islands, was a mystery. Fortunately, ancient Polynesian navigation skills had not been forgotten and the crew, with no modern instruments or charts, set sail for Pukapuka, 500km to the west. Five days later, in what was hailed as an extraordinary navigational feat, they arrived on Pukapuka.

In 1965 a small boat from Manihiki suffered engine failure midway between the islands and was swept away to the west by the steady 3- to 4-knot current that runs between the islands. Sixty-five days and almost 3500km later the crew landed at Erromango in Vanuatu. The book *The Man Who Refused to Die* by Barry Wynne recounts the tale of this extraordinary voyage and the persistence of Techu Makimare, the hero of the crew.

brother-in-law (and a certain amount of 'keeping it in the family') populated Rakahanga/Manihiki.

Of the two islands, people chose to live on Rakahanga because the larger islands and superior soils could support the cultivation of their crops. However, whenever Rakahanga's crops were depleted, or wiped out by storms, the entire population would move to Manihiki, where the lagoon yielded ample seafood to see the population through while Rakahanga's crops recovered. The journey between the two atolls was perilous, though, and many lives were lost making the crossing.

On 2 March 1606 the commander of the ships *Capitana* and *Almiranta*, Pedro Fernández de Quirós (who, as navigator to Mendaña, had already discovered Pukapuka 10 years earlier) sighted the island. He reported that the islanders were 'the most beautiful white and elegant people that were met during the voyage'. Furthermore, he continued, the women were exceptionally

beautiful and 'if properly dressed, would have advantages over our Spanish women'.

Such reports were no doubt the genesis for many romantic notions of the South Seas. De Quirós was not the only member of the expedition to be impressed. A Franciscan friar on the expedition named Rakahanga the island of Gente Hermosa (Beautiful People).

Over 200 years were to pass before the island was again visited by Western ships – first a Russian expedition in 1820, then a series of whalers and trading ships. In 1849 Polynesian missionaries arrived on Manihiki, an island still uninhabited most of the time, populated only temporarily by groups from Rakahanga. In 1852 the missionaries convinced the islanders to divide themselves permanently between the two atolls so that people would no longer be killed at sea while making the crossing.

The traditional link between Rakahanga and Manihiki was revived in 1997 when Cyclone Martin devastated crops on Manihiki. For some time afterwards, Manihiki was dependent on crops from Rakahanga (which had escaped the worst of the cyclone).

Rakahanga's communication with the outside world took a great leap forward in 2001, when a new Telecom link brought telephone communication with other Cook Islanders into many homes. (At the time, the entire Rakahanga phone book, only 30 numbers, was published in the bottom right-hand corner of one page of the *Cook Islands Herald*.)

Information

Rakahanga's **island council** (☎ 44036, fax 44035) is at Nivano, along with the **Telecom office** (☎ 44680, fax 44683) and **health office** (☎ 44664). There is electricity from 6am to midday and 6pm to midnight.

Getting There & Away

Rakahanga's airstrip is no longer used and has slowly been reclaimed by the jungle and the sea. The only way to get to Rakahanga is by boat. The quickest option is to fly to Manihiki (see that atoll's section earlier) and then take a small boat for the three-hour trip to Rakahanga. However, Manihiki–Rakahanga boats won't run when the weather's rough, so you run the risk of

THE NORTHERN GROUP

being stranded on Rakahanga until the weather clears. If during that time the weekly Rarotonga–Manihiki flight comes and goes, you'll just have to extend your stay for another week.

Penrhyn Atoll

pop 600 • area 9.8 sq km

Penrhyn, often still called by its traditional Maori name, Tongareva, is the northernmost of the Cook Islands and its lagoon is unlike most of the other atolls in the Cooks in that it is very wide and easily accessible. Not only is it accessible to ships, it also has plenty of sharks – mostly harmless blacktips. There are two main settlements: Omoka in the west and Te Tautua in the east. The lagoon is so large, 14km across, that from Omoka, Te Tautua isn't visible except for its church roof.

Penrhyn was famous throughout the Pacific at one time for its natural mother-of-pearl, which is still found to this day. More recently, Penrhyn has joined Manihiki in the lucrative business of pearl farming. Some interesting shell jewellery is produced on Penrhyn, and it's famous for its fine *rito* hats.

History

Polynesian legends relate that Penrhyn was fished up from the depths of the ocean by the god Vatea, in 'Avaiki. He used a fishhook baited with a star, but when that did not work he tore a piece of flesh from his thigh, baited the hook with it and promptly pulled up the island from the deep. He then hung the hook in the sky. The tale of an island fished out of the sea is a common legend in Polynesia, most often associated with the demigod Maui (see the special section 'Cook Islands Myths & Legends').

Penrhyn was discovered by settlers from the Samoan islands as they sailed towards Tahiti and the Society Islands. It's believed that the island's Maori name, Tongareva (Land Floating in the South), refers to the discovery of the island from Savai'i (Samoa) in the north. Various legends tell of explorers who visited on their way from Samoa to Tahiti or vice versa.

The atoll takes its European name from the British ship *Lady Penrhyn*, which

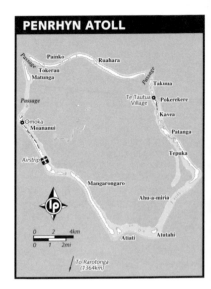

PENRHYN ATOLL

dropped by in 1788 on the way back to England from Australia. *Lady Penrhyn* was one of Australia's 'First Fleet' – 11 ships that carried the original convict settlers to Sydney.

The earliest Western accounts of Penrhyn all comment on the unusual fierceness and erratic behaviour of the island's inhabitants. None of these early visitors dared to go ashore and neither did they let islanders on board their ships – preferring to keep them at arm's length. Despite these impressions, when the American ship *Chatham* ran onto the reef in 1853, the crew and passengers, to their surprise and relief, were treated well. Some of them remained on the island for almost a year before being rescued.

EH Lamont, the trader who had chartered the vessel, wrote *Wild Life among the Pacific Islanders* about his time on the island. He obviously entered into island life wholeheartedly, because he married three women while he was there! In his account, Dr R was the Dr Longghost of Herman Melville's *Omoo*.

The first missionaries arrived in 1854 and those warlike and terrifying islanders quickly became obedient churchgoers. So obedient that the four Polynesian teachers landed by the missionaries 'sold' their flock to Peruvian slavers in 1862 and 1863. They netted $5 a head and went along to South America as overseers for a salary of $100 a month.

The slavers gratefully dubbed Penrhyn 'The Island of the Four Evangelists'. The disastrous slaving foray left the atoll with a population of only 88 – down from an estimated 700 before the trade began. None of those who left for Peru ever returned to Penrhyn.

The population had rebounded to 445 by 1902, but the entire chiefly line disappeared during this period, and today Penrhyn is the only island in the Cooks with no *ariki* (high chiefs).

The island was used as an American airbase during WWII and, as a result, has an airstrip, near Omoka village. The wreck of the *Go-Gettin' Gal*, a four-engined WWII bomber, sat beside the airstrip for many years before it was whittled away for use as scrap metal. The largest remaining piece forms a unique oven in the centre of town.

Pearls now dominate the island's economy, although not to the same degree as on Manihiki. Penrhyn's lagoon produces about 12% of the Cook Islands' pearls, including small, golden *pipi* pearls. The national government has occasionally suggested that Penrhyn's lagoon could produce many more pearls, but the fiercely independent locals argue for restraint.

Literature
For an interesting account of the island's history during the 19th century, check out *Impressions of Tongareva (Penrhyn Island), 1816-1901*, edited by Andrew Teariki Campbell, available at the University of the South Pacific (USP) Centre on Rarotonga.

Information
The **island council** (☎/fax 42101), **Telecom office** (☎ 42680, fax 42683) and **hospital** (☎ 42083) are in Omoka, in the west. There's a **public health office** (☎ 42317) across the lagoon at Te Tautua. There is electricity from 6am to midday and 6pm to midnight.

Places to Stay
Soa's Guesthouse (☎ 42018, fax 42105; Omoka village; adult/child NZ$82/45) offers basic, clean accommodation with shared facilities. Soa Tini and his family, who operate the guesthouse, will assist with activities such as boating and fishing. Rates include all meals.

Tarakore Guesthouse (☎ 42019, fax 42683; Omoka village; per person NZ$85) is run by Doreen and Puria Heria. All meals are included in the rates.

Warrick Latham (☎ 42888; e penrhyn@ airraro.co.ck) might be able to help with accommodation on Penrhyn.

Getting There & Away
Air The airstrip on Penrhyn was disused for many years, but **Air Rarotonga** (☎ 42888 at Omoka village; w www.airraro.com) now operates weekly flights between Rarotonga and Penrhyn. It takes just under four hours to get here and the cost is NZ$1374 (return). Flights usually stop at Aitutaki on the way north and are sometimes routed through Manihiki.

Boat Penrhyn is served by interisland shipping services (see the Getting Around chapter for details). It is the only atoll with an entrance large enough for ships to actually enter the lagoon.

The island is an official port of entry to the Cooks.

Pukapuka Atoll

pop 530 • area 5.1 sq km

Shaped like a three-bladed fan, Pukapuka's atoll has an island at each 'blade end' and another in the middle. The northernmost island, Wale (pronounced **wah**-ley, *wale* is Pukapukan for 'house'), is also called Pukapuka Island. The only landing place is reached by narrow and difficult passages through the reef on the western side of Wale.

There are three villages – Ngake, Roto (the largest) and Yato – all on Wale, where copious amounts of *puraka* are grown. Smaller quantities of coconuts, bananas and papayas are grown on the other two sizeable islands, Motu Ko and Motu Kotawa. Pukapuka's airstrip, which is only used occasionally, is on Motu Ko.

Historical links and the relative proximity of the atoll to Samoa have resulted in the islanders' customs and language being more similar to those of Samoa than to the rest of the Cooks.

There is a notably decorated Catholic church on Wale, and excellent swimming and snorkelling, particularly off Motu Kotawa.

THE NORTHERN GROUP

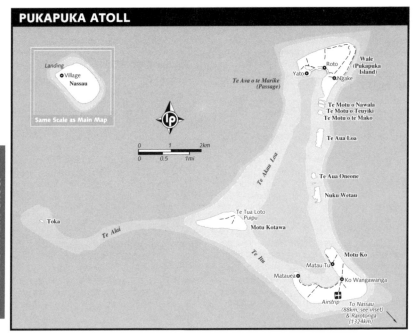

PUKAPUKA ATOLL

Pukapuka is also noted for its finely woven mats.

History

Early legends relate tales of the island rising from the deep with men inside it, and of great voyages from the west. Unlike the southern Cook Islands, which were settled by Society Islanders, Pukapuka was first discovered 2000 years ago by Samoan and Tongan voyagers on their way to discover the Society Islands. However, it was not until about 700 years ago that Pukapuka was permanently settled (again, by Samoans and Tongans).

One legend of Pukapuka tells of a great tsunami (tidal wave) about 400 years ago that swept over the atoll, leaving only two women and 15 men alive. With considerable effort (on the women's part!) they managed to repopulate the island. It was during the rule of the fourth chief following the great disaster that the first Western visitors arrived.

The Spanish explorer Alvaro de Mendaña, with his navigator Pedro Fernández de Quirós, sailed from Peru in 1595 and later that year discovered an island, which he named San Bernardo. That island, which he decided not to land on, was Pukapuka. Over 150 years later, two British ships sighted the island and decided against attempting a landing, due to the high surf. Dramatically, they named the atoll the Islands of Danger (a better name than most from the English explorers); Pukapuka is still sometimes referred to as Danger Island.

Pukapuka's isolation and reputation as a dangerous anchorage kept visitors away, and probably saved the ancient Polynesian religion for a few decades after the rest of the Cooks had been converted to Christianity. It wasn't until 1857 that Polynesian missionaries landed, although Pukapuka was converted almost immediately. Soon afterwards, the island was devastated by slave raids from Peru – 145 of the population of about 450 were taken; only two ever returned.

In 1924 South Seas character Robert Dean Frisbie arrived on Pukapuka. He married a local and raised children here before moving on to Suwarrow Atoll and Manihiki Atoll. He died on Rarotonga in 1948 – you can see his grave at the Cook Islands

Christian Church (CICC) in Avarua – but by then had written a number of classics, including *The Book of Puka-Puka* and *The Island of Desire*. His daughter, Johnny Frisbie, also wrote of the island in *Miss Ulysses from Puka-Puka*. Modern maps of Pukapuka are still based on Robert Dean Frisbie's 1925 survey.

Pukapuka's isolation was ameliorated in 1994 when an airstrip was built on Motu Ko. Telephones came to Pukapuka in 1999.

Society

The culture of Pukapuka, like its language, is more similar to Samoa than to any of the other Cook Islands. Samoan pastimes such as *kilikiti* (a form of 50-a-side cricket) are popular here. Protected by its isolation, Pukapuka is one of the most traditional of the Cook Islands. Some old-fashioned bed-hopping customs, unseen elsewhere in Polynesia since the missionaries turned up in the 1800s, are still practised here.

Pukapuka's dancers are deservedly famous. Each year for the Constitutional Celebrations, the ship from Pukapuka brings a team that again and again wins the hearts of the Rarotongan crowds, if not those of the competition judges. Cynics, and many of Pukapuka's womenfolk, say that the men of Pukapuka are such accomplished dancers because they have so much time to practise. Other islands' menfolk are too busy working, they say.

Information

Pukapuka's **island council** (☎ *41712, fax 41711)*, along with **Telecom** (☎ *41680, fax 41683)* and a **hospital** (☎ *41041)* are in Rota, on Wale.

There's no organised accommodation on Pukapuka. You might be able to arrange a **homestay** with a local family; contact the island council to sort it out.

Getting There & Away

Air Flights to Pukapuka have been initiated only recently; the island's airstrip was officially opened in early 1994. **Air Rarotonga** (☎ *22888 on Rarotonga;* w *www.airraro.com)* flies to Pukapuka infrequently, perhaps once every few months. Flights between Rarotonga and Pukapuka take 4½ hours and cost NZ$1374 return. Check with Air Rarotonga to see when the next flight is.

Boat Pukapuka is served by the interisland ships coming from Rarotonga; see the Getting Around chapter for details. Given Pukapuka's proximity to Samoa, there is also some boat traffic between the two.

Nassau

pop 100 • area 1.3 sq km
The tiny island of Nassau is often referred to as a suburb of Pukapuka and that pretty much sums it up. There is only one village, peopled by a transient population from Pukapuka who tend Nassau's coconut plantation. Taro is grown in the centre of the island.

Nassau is not an atoll, but a coral cay; a tiny (500m-long) island surrounded by a narrow fringing reef.

History

Lying 88km southeast of Pukapuka, Nassau has belonged to Pukapuka since that atoll was first settled. The great ancestor Mataliki, who rose out of the ocean with Pukapuka itself, put a man named Ngalewu in charge of tiny Nassau. The island's traditional name, Te Nuku o Ngalewu, commemorates that first Pukapukan caretaker. For a time, there was fairly frequent communication between Pukapuka and Te Nuku o Ngalewu, but when religious transgressions on Pukapuka angered the gods, making the seas too dangerous to cross, the small 'suburb' was abandoned.

By now known as Motu Ngaongao (Lonely Island) to the Pukapukans, the island was still uninhabited when European ships discovered it in the 1800s and 1820s. When the American whaler *Nassau* visited in 1835 and lumbered it with its present name, the island was still uninhabited.

There were brief periods when Nassau had a permanent population. A group from Manihiki lived there for a time in the 1860s. An American farmer attempted to grow coconuts and other plants in the 1870s, and other short-lived European attempts to farm the island were made in the 1910s, 1930s and 1940s.

Finally, in 1945, the island was sold, by the last of those farmers, to the NZ government for £2000. The government sold it back to the chiefs of Pukapuka for the same figure, and on 2 June 1951 a party from Pukapuka landed on Nassau, reclaiming their 'suburb' after several centuries.

Groups from Pukapuka, working the coconut plantation that was started back in 1945, have become a virtually permanent population. They are among the most isolated of Cook Islanders, although the island is used as an unofficial trade stopoff for some Asian fishing vessels.

Information

Nassau is governed by the Pukapuka island council (see the Pukapuka Atoll section earlier), and that body is the best contact if you want to visit the island. There are no guesthouses, but someone on Pukapuka should be able to arrange something if you are actually present to bug them about it. To contact people on Nassau you must use Telecom's high-frequency radio link; phone ☎ 020 to arrange it.

Getting There & Away

The only way to get to Nassau is via Pukapuka – a three-day journey by boat. You'll have to get to Pukapuka first, by sea or air, then arrange transport with Pukapuka's island council.

Suwarrow Atoll

pop 2 • area 0.4 sq km

The atoll of Suwarrow is surprisingly well known around the world, and it's all due to a prolonged visit by one man. For three long periods between 1952 and 1977, New Zealander Tom Neale lived on the island as a virtual hermit, and his book *An Island to Oneself* became a South Seas classic. If you want to know all about how to live alone on a coral atoll, this book is a must. According to people who knew him, the book, which was actually ghostwritten, makes him out to be a much more reasonable fellow than he actually was. One person's opinion was that Neale was so cantankerous that an uninhabited island was the only place for him!

Although Tom Neale is long gone, his memory lives on and yachties often call in to the atoll; it's one of the few atolls in the Northern Group with an accessible lagoon. Tom's room in his old house is still furnished

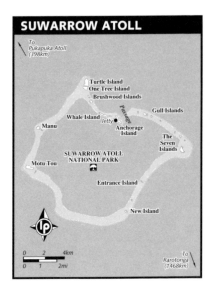

just as it was when he lived there, and visitors can fill in a logbook left in the room.

Suwarrow is now the Cook Islands' only national park. Two atoll managers live here, monitoring the thousands of birds that use Suwarrow as a breeding ground, and making sure that visiting yachties behave themselves.

History

In pre-European times, Suwarrow was visited by Polynesian voyagers (remains of their camps have been found), but a permanent settlement was never established. It is thought that the atoll was the land known as Malo in the legends of nearby islands. Suwarrow's curious modern name is neither English nor Polynesian – the atoll was named by the Russian explorer Mikhail Lazarev in 1814 after his ship *Suvarov*.

Suwarrow has developed a reputation as a treasure island. In the mid-19th century, after the American whaler *Gem* was wrecked on the reef, a salvage ship found a buried box containing many thousands of dollars worth of 18th-century gold coins. In 1876 another visitor found Spanish coins dating from the 1600s. Where these caches came from has never been satisfactorily explained, but other evidence of an early European visit – signs of habitation, skeletons and various artefacts – have also been unearthed.

The remains of shipwrecked Spaniards? Or of the English crew lost on a small boat from the ship *Pandora*, sent to the Pacific in 1791 to search for the *Bounty* mutineers?

There was an unsuccessful attempt to farm pearl shell here in the early part of the 20th century, and in the 1920s and 1930s coconuts were farmed until a devastating termite infestation halted production (the termites are still here – don't collect coconuts from Suwarrow!).

Kiwi coast-watchers were based on Suwarrow during WWII and the remains of their buildings can still be seen on Anchorage Island.

Tom Neale wasn't the first writer to live on, and write about, Suwarrow. American-born Robert Dean Frisbie, previously of Pukapuka, survived a terrible cyclone here in 1942 and wrote of it in *Island of Desire*. His daughter Johnny Frisbie wrote about the same cyclone in *The Frisbies of the South Seas*. Although the lagoon is large, the scattered islands of Suwarrow are all very small and low-lying. Cyclones have brought waves that wash right across even the highest of the islands, and in 1942 the Frisbie group only survived by tying themselves to a tree!

Tom Neale himself was inspired by Frisbie's writing. Neale first moved to Suwarrow in 1952, living alone on the island, in the building abandoned by the Kiwi coast-watchers, for two years. He returned from 1960 to 1963 as the government-appointed island caretaker, and then again from 1966 to 1977. After spending a total of 16 years alone on the atoll, Tom Neale was evacuated to Rarotonga in 1977 when he complained via radio of severe stomach pains. He died soon afterwards, and is buried in the cemetery beside the Returned Servicemen's Association (RSA), opposite Rarotonga's airport.

Both Frisbie and Neale have captured imaginations around the world. A surprising number of people visit the Cook Islands, or Suwarrow, solely because of Neale, and there are many websites about the two men.

After Suwarrow was declared a national park, a caretaker and his family lived in Neale's old house on Anchorage Island for many years. However, the last of the family left in 1998, leaving the atoll uninhabited and unprotected. Or so people thought...

It seems people back on Rarotonga had not forgotten Tom Neale or Suwarrow Atoll. When, in 2001, an Australian company proposed establishing pearl farming in Suwarrow's lagoon, the idea was initially backed by the Cook Islands government. However, a massive public protest movement formed, outraged by the idea of the country's first national park being exploited for commercial purposes. Facing unprecedented protest, the government finally backed down and the company that was hoping to farm Suwarrow lagoon was told to look elsewhere. Soon afterwards the government created the position of atoll manager, sending two men to live permanently on Suwarrow, where they would monitor wildlife, look after Tom Neale's house and greet (and charge) visiting yachties.

Getting There & Away

The only option for most travellers wanting to visit Suwarrow is the extremely infrequent cargo ships, which will visit only when the atoll managers need supplies or a new manager is arriving.

You are extremely unlikely to get permission from the **Ministry of the Prime Minister** (☎ 25494, fax 20856; e *govmedia@ pmoffice.gov.ck*) to stay on the island, but if you're on the cargo ship when it visits you will be able to have a look around while they unload.

Many more visitors arrive by private yacht. Although Suwarrow is not an official port of entry, you're tacitly permitted to turn up at Suwarrow even if you haven't cleared customs elsewhere. Speak to the atoll managers, in Tom Neale's old house on Anchorage Island, when you arrive. They'll charge you US$50 for a two-week stay (and US$5 per day for every day after the two weeks).

Language

Pronunciation

The Cook Islands alphabet has only 13 letters: **a**, **e**, **i**, **k**, **m**, **n**, **ng**, **o**, **p**, **r**, **t**, **u**, **v**.

The 'ng' sound is soft, pronounced the same as in the English word 'singing' (not 'finger') but in Cook Islands Maori it often occurs at the beginning of a word (eg, *Nga*, *Ngatangi'ia*). Practise by pronouncing the sound in an English word and see how it feels in the throat, then try saying it alone. Once you can make the sound at the beginning of a word, you'll have it.

All the other consonants are pronounced as they are in English, although **v** sounds closer to English 'w' on many islands. (In fact, even when speaking English, those islanders will swap their 'v's and 'w's around.)

Pronunciation of vowels is very similar to Italian or Spanish, but Cook Islands Maori vowels have long and short variants – using the wrong one can result in a completely different meaning. Long vowels are sometimes written with a macron (a stroke above the vowel), but don't worry too much about this – just have a stab at it and most people will know what you're on about.

a	as in 'far'
e	as in 'let'
i	as in 'marine'
o	as in 'or' (but with no 'r' sound)
u	as in 'flute'

The Glottal Stop Another symbol used in the written language is a glottal stop, represented by an apostrophe before or between vowels (eg, *ta'i*). In Cook Islands Maori it represents the missing 'h' and 'f' sounds. The glottal stop is the momentary closing of the throat between the syllables of the expression 'oh-oh'. Compare the words *tai* (pronounced with one syllable, as the English 'tie') and *ta'i*, (pronounced with two syllables – 'tah-ee').

Greetings & Civilities

Hello.	*Kia orana!* (all purpose greeting, lit: 'may you continue to live!')
How are you? (to one person)	*Pe'ea koe?*
How are you? (to two people)	*Pe'ea korua?*
How are you? (to three or more people)	*Pe'ea koutou?*
Good.	*Meitaki.*
I'm good.	*E meitaki au.*
I'm hot/cold.	*E vera/anu au.*
Goodbye. (to person leaving)	*'Aere ra.*
Goodbye. (to person staying)	*E no'o ra.*
See you again.	*Ka kite.*
Welcome!	*Turou!*
Good luck! (a toast)	*Kia manuia!*
Please. (used at the end of a statement)	*'Ine.*
Thank you.	*Meitaki.*
Thank you very much.	*Meitaki ma'ata.*

Small Talk

I/me	*au*
my	*taku*
you (one person)	*koe*
you (two people)	*korua*
you (three or more)	*koutou*
him/her/he/she	*'aia*
we (two)	*taua/maua*
we (three or more)	*tatou/matou*
they (two)	*raua*
they (three or more)	*ratou*

Yes.	*Ae.*
No.	*Kare.*
Maybe.	*Penei ake.*
What's your name?	*Ko 'ai to'ou ingoa?*
My name is ...	*Ko ... toku ingoa.*
Where are you from? (to one person)	*No 'ea mai koe?*
I'm from ...	*No ... mai au.*
Where are you going? (to one person)	*Ka 'aere koe ki'ea?*
I'm going to (Aitutaki).	*Te 'aere nei au ki (Aitutaki).*
Where are you going? (to two people)	*Ka 'aere korua ki'ea?*
We're going to (Aitutaki). (to two people)	*Te 'aere nei maua ki (Aitutaki).*

person/people	*tangata*
man/husband	*tane*
woman/wife	*va'ine*
child/children	*tama/tamariki*
boy/son	*tamaiti*
girl/daughter	*tama'ine*
baby	*pepe*
father	*papa, metua tane*
mother	*mama, metua va'ine*
brother	*tungane*
sister	*tua'ine*
friend	*'oa/taeake*

Who is that person?	*Ko 'ai tena tangata?*
That person is my son.	*Ko toku tamaiti tena.*

beautiful	*manea*
ugly	*vi'ivi'i*
The mountain is beautiful.	*Manea te maunga.*

Learning the Language

language	*reo*
speak/word	*tuatua*
understand	*marama*
this	*teia*
that	*tena*
that over there	*tera*

Do you understand Maori?
E marama ana koe i te reo Maori?
I don't understand Maori.
Kare au e marama i te reo Maori.
But I'm learning.
Inara, te tamou nei au.
What's the word for (island)?
E a'a te tuatua Maori no te (island)?
It's (motu).
Te (motu).
The Maori word for (island) is (motu).
E (motu) te tuatua Maori no (island).
What's this?
E aka teia?
That's a (book).
E (puka) tena.
How do you say ...
Ka 'aka pe'ea au me tuatua ...?
Speak slower, please.
E tuatua marie koe, 'ine.

I don't understand.
Kare au i marama.

Out & About, Food & Drink

beach	*tapa ta'atai*
church	*ekalesia* or *'are pure*
house	*'are*
island/lagoon islet	*motu*
lagoon/lake	*roto*
land	*'enua*
mountain	*maunga*
ocean	*moana*
reef	*akau*
sky	*rangi*
store/shop	*toa*
town	*taoni*
village	*tapere*

food	*kai*
beer	*pia*

The food is very delicious.
Tino reka te kai.
Would you like a beer?
Ka inangaro pia koe?
Yes, give me a beer, please.
Ae, 'omai e pia, 'ine.
Yes, give me three beers, please.
Ae, 'omai toru pia, 'ine.

Numbers

1	*ta'i*
2	*rua*
3	*toru*
4	*'a*
5	*rima*
6	*ono*
7	*'itu*
8	*varu*
9	*iva*
10	*ta'i-nga'uru*
11	*ta'i-nga'uru ma ta'i* (ten plus one)
20	*rua-nga'uru* (two tens)
100	*ta'i-anere*
101	*ta'i-anere ma ta'i* (one hundred plus one)
1000	*ta'i-tauatini*
many	*rau*

Glossary

adze – axe-like tool with ceremonial importance in the Cook Islands

Ara Metua – ancient road around the circumference of Rarotonga, inland from the newer coast road, *Ara Tapu*

Ara Tapu – coast road around Rarotonga

ariki – paramount chief; traditional head of a tribe

atua – god; now used to refer to the Christian God

'Avaiki – legendary Polynesian ancestral homeland; in the case of the Cook Islands, 'Avaiki was the island Ra'iatea in the Society Islands

bush beer – locally produced moonshine beer brewed from oranges, bananas, pawpaws or hops; also called 'home brew'

CICC – Cook Islands Christian Church, the Protestant church that was founded by the London Missionary Society

copra – coconut 'meat' from which coconut oil is produced

ei – necklace

ei kaki – flower *ei* draped around the neck; traditionally given to anyone arriving or departing on a journey

ekalesia – church

eke – octopus

'enua – land

House of Ariki – assembly of the Cook Islands' *ariki*; it has advisory, not legislative powers

ika – fish

ivi – tribe

kai – food

kaikai – feast

kakerori – Rarotongan flycatcher, a rare bird endemic to Rarotonga

kikau – palm leaves, woven or thatched; a *kikau* hut is a traditional thatch-roofed hut

kopeka – cave-dwelling swiftlet on 'Atiu

koutu – ancient Polynesian open-air royal courtyard used for gatherings and political functions

Koutunui – assembly of all *mataiapo* and *rangatira*

kumara – sweet potato

LDS – Church of Jesus Christ of Latter-day Saints (Mormons)

LMS – London Missionary Society, the original missionary force in the Cook Islands and in many other regions of the Pacific

maire – an aromatic leaf

makatea – raised, fossilised coral reef that forms a coastal plain around several islands of the Southern Group, including Mangaia, 'Atiu, Ma'uke and Mitiaro

mana – spiritual power or influence

Maori – literally 'indigenous' or 'local'; the Polynesian people of the Cook Islands (and New Zealand); the language of these people

marae – ancient open-air family or tribal religious meeting ground, marked by stones

maroro – flying fish

mataiapo – chief; head of a sub-tribe; one rank down from an *ariki*

matu rori – bêches-de-mer (sea cucumbers)

maunga – mountain

moana – ocean

motu – lagoon islet

ngati – tribe

pandanus – leaf used for thatching the roofs of traditional houses, and for mats, baskets, bags and *rito* hats

papa'a – Europeans and other foreigners; the English language

pareu – wraparound sarong-type garment

pate – carved wooden slit drum

pupu – tiny shells used to make necklaces

puraka – taro-like vegetable

rangatira – sub-chief; lowest rank of Cook Islands royal hierarchy, below *mataiapo*

ra'ui – traditional method of conservation in which nothing can be taken from a designated area or resource for a set period of time; marine reserve

rito – bleached pandanus or bleached, young palm leaves, used to make woven handicrafts, including hats, fans and handbags

SDA – Seventh-Day Adventist church

Tangaroa – Polynesian god of fertility and the sea; his well-endowed figure appears on the country's one-dollar coin and is a symbol of the Cook Islands

tapa – paper-like cloth made from the bark of the 'au' (paper mulberry tree)

tapere – district subdivision

tapu – holy; sacred; forbidden

ta'unga – expert

ta'unga atua – priest

tiare – flower

tiki – symbolic human figure

tivaevae – colourful, intricately sewn appliqué works traditionally made as burial shrouds but also used as bedspreads, with smaller versions used as furniture covers, cushion covers and pillowcases

tumu korero – speaker; *ta'unga* responsible for memorising tribal history and genealogy

tumunu – hollowed-out stump of a coconut tree, used to brew bush beer; traditional bush-beer drinking sessions

tutaka – community inspections

umu – traditional Polynesian underground oven

umukai – traditional Polynesian food *(kai)* cooked in an underground oven *(umu)*; a feast of foods cooked in an *umu*

va'ine – ladies

vaka – outrigger canoe; large district (on Rarotonga)

Thanks

Many thanks to the travellers who used the last edition and wrote to us with helpful hints, useful advice and interesting anecdotes.

James Allen, Alex Anderson, Dr Andreas, Cathy Sue Anunsen, Sven Armbrust, Dave Artindale, Gerry & Vi Barker, David Barnabe, Trevor Barnes, David Barnett, David Beeby, Linnea Berg, Edwin Bergenhuizen, Emma Birks, Bev Blythe, AD Blythen, Alison Boniface, Barbara Bower, Peter Bower, Katie Bratby, Azza Brown, Klemens Bruckner, Ivar Bruun, Jolene Buchanan, Elizabeth Bullen, Evan Burge, J Burkhardt, Frank Cetrola, Lorie Charles, Claire Chretien, Chris Coffey, Angela Ceriani Contreas, Frederick D Coquelin, Kevin Crampton, Allen Cullen, Tony Densham, Kay Donaldson, Stuart Dyer, Dave Edwards, Ulf Ellervik, Andreas Engel, Julie Fenwick, Ursula & Andre Fischbach, Stacey Flundra, Alan Dean Foster, Regina Fugmann, Peter Gappmaier, Marcos Garcia, Frank & Jan Gardner, Christian Glossner, Chris Godfrey, Roger & Diane Godfrey, Harold Gosse, Simon Griffin, Sue Hagstrom, Russell Hall, Ben Halstead, Jo Hammer, Niklas Hau, Johan Hedlumn, Birgit Heldmann, Jim Hendrickson, Thijs Heslenfeld, Walter Hietsch, Karen Hong, Jasmine Hotienstein, Lee Hubbard Susan Irwin, Jamie Jaberg, Winston Jackson, Meryem Jammes, Amanda Jobbins, Helene & Tommy Johannesson, Barnie Jones, Mira & Raj Joshi, Anne-Christine Kahrs, Paul & Karen Keiser, Chris Kelly, Warren & Venetia King, Lene Kjerri, Bjarne & Birthe Knudsen, Thomas Krahenmann, Jorg & Sara Krebs, Andreas Krueger, Dr Angela Kung, Yi Lang, Pascal Laurin, Steve Layton, G Lee, L Lee, Jennifer Lefort, Ann Lunn, Marie & Martin Lycett, Jick & Janice Macdonald, Sean A MacPherson, Nancy Maguire, Claudia Paul Magus, Philip K Maini, Nicola Martin, Thomas Martin, Jennifer Anne Mathers, Dr Rob McDougall, Philip McKernan, Urs Meier, Amanda Menard, Sheryl Mills, Andrew Mitchell, Rudy Moberg, Linda Moore, Andrew Mortimer, Hugh Morton, Wolfgang Muhlbauer, David Mumford, Sam Murray, Glenn & Sandi Newell, Mary Nuwer, David Otway, Mike Pain, B Pearce, Glenda Pepper, Michael Pepper, J Powell, Joel & Maria Teresa Prades, John Prime, Michael Rausch, Felix Rayner, Luisa Rayner, Turicchia Roberta, Sue Roberts, DA Roche, Karin Rosler, Esma Rubini, Martine E Saunders, Brandy Schoenburger, Tim Searle, Heidi Smith, L Smith, Alex Spence, Jenny Stenhouse, Carol Stetser, JD Stonham, Stefan Strasser, Ian Summerskill, Astrid ten Oever, Julie Thorpe, AJ Turner, Jos van Loo, Andrew & Gabrielle van Nooten, Astrid Van Wijk, Paul D Varady, Kathy Vitali, Arlinde Vletter, Cees Vletter, Jim & Jill Waits, Jean-Francois & Laurence Walhin, G Weeks, Jennifer Welte, John & Alison Whittington, Ian Wiechern, Craig Williams, Martin Williams, Michael & Kristin Wohlers-Reichel, Sandra Wolf, Jonathan Wood, Helen Woodward

LONELY PLANET

You already know that Lonely Planet produces more than this one guidebook, but you might not be aware of the other products we have on this region. Here is a selection of titles that you may want to check out as well:

Diving & Snorkeling Fiji
ISBN 0 86442 771 9
US$16.99 • UK£10.99

Fiji
ISBN 1 74059 134 8
US$16.99 • UK£11.99

**Diving & Snorkeling
Tahiti & French Polynesia**
ISBN 1 86450 071 9
US$16.99 • UK£10.99

Tahiti & French Polynesia
ISBN 1 74059 229 8
US$21.99 • UK£13.99

South Pacific Phrasebook
ISBN 0 86442 595 3
US$6.95 • UK£4.99

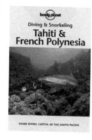

Australia
ISBN 1 74059 065 1
US$25.99 • UK£15.99

New Zealand
ISBN 1 74059 196 8
US$24.99 • UK£14.99

Oahu
ISBN 1 74059 201 8
US$16.99 • UK£11.99

South Pacific
ISBN 1 86450 302 5
US$25.99 • UK£16.99

Hawaii
ISBN 1 74059 142 9
US$21.99 • UK£14.99

Vanuatu
ISBN 1 74059 239 5
US$19.99 • UK£12.99

Available wherever books are sold

LONELY PLANET

Guides by Region

onely Planet is known worldwide for publishing practical, reliable and no-nonsense travel information in our guides and on our Web site. The Lonely Planet list covers just about every accessible part of the world. Currently there are 16 series: Travel guides, Shoestring guides, Condensed guides, Phrasebooks, Read This First, Healthy Travel, Walking guides, Cycling guides, Watching Wildlife guides, Pisces Diving & Snorkeling guides, City Maps, Road Atlases, Out to Eat, World Food, Journeys travel literature and Pictorials.

AFRICA Africa on a shoestring • Botswana • Cairo • Cairo City Map • Cape Town • Cape Town City Map • East Africa • Egypt • Egyptian Arabic phrasebook • Ethiopia, Eritrea & Djibouti • Ethiopian Amharic phrasebook • The Gambia & Senegal • Healthy Travel Africa • Kenya • Malawi • Morocco • Moroccan Arabic phrasebook • Mozambique • Namibia • Read This First: Africa • South Africa, Lesotho & Swaziland • Southern Africa • Southern Africa Road Atlas • Swahili phrasebook • Tanzania, Zanzibar & Pemba • Trekking in East Africa • Tunisia • Watching Wildlife East Africa • Watching Wildlife Southern Africa • West Africa • World Food Morocco • Zambia • Zimbabwe, Botswana & Namibia
Travel Literature: Mali Blues: Traveling to an African Beat • The Rainbird: A Central African Journey • Songs to an African Sunset: A Zimbabwean Story

AUSTRALIA & THE PACIFIC Aboriginal Australia & the Torres Strait Islands •Auckland • Australia • Australian phrasebook • Australia Road Atlas • Cycling Australia • Cycling New Zealand • Fiji • Fijian phrasebook • Healthy Travel Australia, NZ & the Pacific • Islands of Australia's Great Barrier Reef • Melbourne • Melbourne City Map • Micronesia • New Caledonia • New South Wales • New Zealand • Northern Territory • Outback Australia • Out to Eat – Melbourne • Out to Eat – Sydney • Papua New Guinea • Pidgin phrasebook • Queensland • Rarotonga & the Cook Islands • Samoa • Solomon Islands • South Australia • South Pacific • South Pacific phrasebook • Sydney • Sydney City Map • Sydney Condensed • Tahiti & French Polynesia • Tasmania • Tonga • Tramping in New Zealand • Vanuatu • Victoria • Walking in Australia • Watching Wildlife Australia • Western Australia
Travel Literature: Islands in the Clouds: Travels in the Highlands of New Guinea • Kiwi Tracks: A New Zealand Journey • Sean & David's Long Drive

CENTRAL AMERICA & THE CARIBBEAN Bahamas, Turks & Caicos • Baja California • Belize, Guatemala & Yucatán • Bermuda • Central America on a shoestring • Costa Rica • Costa Rica Spanish phrasebook • Cuba • Cycling Cuba • Dominican Republic & Haiti • Eastern Caribbean • Guatemala • Havana • Healthy Travel Central & South America • Jamaica • Mexico • Mexico City • Panama • Puerto Rico • Read This First: Central & South America • Virgin Islands • World Food Caribbean • World Food Mexico • Yucatán
Travel Literature: Green Dreams: Travels in Central America

EUROPE Amsterdam • Amsterdam City Map • Amsterdam Condensed • Andalucía • Athens • Austria • Baltic States phrasebook • Barcelona • Barcelona City Map • Belgium & Luxembourg • Berlin • Berlin City Map • Britain • British phrasebook • Brussels, Bruges & Antwerp • Brussels City Map • Budapest • Budapest City Map • Canary Islands • Catalunya & the Costa Brava • Central Europe • Central Europe phrasebook • Copenhagen • Corfu & the Ionians • Corsica • Crete • Crete Condensed • Croatia • Cycling Britain • Cycling France • Cyprus • Czech & Slovak Republics • Czech phrasebook • Denmark • Dublin • Dublin City Map • Dublin Condensed • Eastern Europe • Eastern Europe phrasebook • Edinburgh • Edinburgh City Map • England • Estonia, Latvia & Lithuania • Europe on a shoestring • Europe phrasebook • Finland • Florence • Florence City Map • France • Frankfurt City Map • Frankfurt Condensed • French phrasebook • Georgia, Armenia & Azerbaijan • Germany • German phrasebook • Greece • Greek Islands • Greek phrasebook • Hungary • Iceland, Greenland & the Faroe Islands • Ireland • Italian phrasebook • Italy • Kraków • Lisbon • The Loire • London • London City Map • London Condensed • Madrid • Madrid City Map • Malta • Mediterranean Europe • Milan, Turin & Genoa • Moscow • Munich • Netherlands • Normandy • Norway • Out to Eat – London • Out to Eat – Paris • Paris • Paris City Map • Paris Condensed • Poland • Polish phrasebook • Portugal • Portuguese phrasebook • Prague • Prague City Map • Provence & the Côte d'Azur • Read This First: Europe • Rhodes & the Dodecanese • Romania & Moldova • Rome • Rome City Map • Rome Condensed • Russia, Ukraine & Belarus • Russian phrasebook • Scandinavian & Baltic Europe • Scandinavian phrasebook • Scotland • Sicily • Slovenia • South-West France • Spain • Spanish phrasebook • Stockholm • St Petersburg • St Petersburg City Map • Sweden • Switzerland • Tuscany • Ukrainian phrasebook • Venice • Vienna • Wales • Walking in Britain • Walking in France • Walking in Ireland • Walking in Italy • Walking in Scotland • Walking in Spain • Walking in Switzerland • Western Europe • World Food France • World Food Greece • World Food Ireland • World Food Italy • World Food Spain **Travel Literature**: After Yugoslavia • Love and War in the Apennines • The Olive Grove: Travels in Greece • On the Shores of the Mediterranean • Round Ireland in Low Gear • A Small Place in Italy

LONELY PLANET

Mail Order

L onely Planet products are distributed worldwide. They are also available by mail order from Lonely Planet, so if you have difficulty finding a title please write to us. North and South American residents should write to 150 Linden St, Oakland, CA 94607, USA; European and African residents should write to 72 – 82 Rosebery Ave, London ECIR 4RW, UK; and residents of other countries to Locked Bag 1, Footscray, Victoria 3011, Australia.

INDIAN SUBCONTINENT & THE INDIAN OCEAN Bangladesh • Bengali phrasebook • Bhutan • Delhi • Goa • Healthy Travel Asia & India • Hindi & Urdu phrasebook • India • India & Bangladesh City Map • Indian Himalaya • Karakoram Highway • Kathmandu City Map • Kerala • Madagascar • Maldives • Mauritius, Réunion & Seychelles • Mumbai (Bombay) • Nepal • Nepali phrasebook • North India • Pakistan • Rajasthan • Read This First: Asia & India • South India • Sri Lanka • Sri Lanka phrasebook • Tibet • Tibetan phrasebook • Trekking in the Indian Himalaya • Trekking in the Karakoram & Hindukush • Trekking in the Nepal Himalaya • World Food India **Travel Literature**: The Age of Kali: Indian Travels and Encounters • Hello Goodnight: A Life of Goa • In Rajasthan • Maverick in Madagascar • A Season in Heaven: True Tales from the Road to Kathmandu • Shopping for Buddhas • A Short Walk in the Hindu Kush • Slowly Down the Ganges

MIDDLE EAST & CENTRAL ASIA Bahrain, Kuwait & Qatar • Central Asia • Central Asia phrasebook • Dubai • Farsi (Persian) phrasebook • Hebrew phrasebook • Iran • Israel & the Palestinian Territories • Istanbul • Istanbul City Map • Istanbul to Cairo • Istanbul to Kathmandu • Jerusalem • Jerusalem City Map • Jordan • Lebanon • Middle East • Oman & the United Arab Emirates • Syria • Turkey • Turkish phrasebook • World Food Turkey • Yemen **Travel Literature**: Black on Black: Iran Revisited • Breaking Ranks: Turbulent Travels in the Promised Land • The Gates of Damascus • Kingdom of the Film Stars: Journey into Jordan

NORTH AMERICA Alaska • Boston • Boston City Map • Boston Condensed • British Columbia • California & Nevada • California Condensed • Canada • Chicago • Chicago City Map • Chicago Condensed • Florida • Georgia & the Carolinas • Great Lakes • Hawaii • Hiking in Alaska • Hiking in the USA • Honolulu & Oahu City Map • Las Vegas • Los Angeles • Los Angeles City Map • Louisiana & the Deep South • Miami • Miami City Map • Montreal • New England • New Orleans • New Orleans City Map • New York City • New York City City Map • New York City Condensed • New York, New Jersey & Pennsylvania • Oahu • Out to Eat – San Francisco • Pacific Northwest • Rocky Mountains • San Diego & Tijuana • San Francisco • San Francisco City Map • Seattle • Seattle City Map • Southwest • Texas • Toronto • USA • USA phrasebook • Vancouver • Vancouver City Map • Virginia & the Capital Region • Washington, DC • Washington, DC City Map • World Food New Orleans **Travel Literature**: Caught Inside: A Surfer's Year on the California Coast • Drive Thru America

NORTH-EAST ASIA Beijing • Beijing City Map • Cantonese phrasebook • China • Hiking in Japan • Hong Kong & Macau • Hong Kong City Map • Hong Kong Condensed • Japan • Japanese phrasebook • Korea • Korean phrasebook • Kyoto • Mandarin phrasebook • Mongolia • Mongolian phrasebook • Seoul • Shanghai • South-West China • Taiwan • Tokyo • Tokyo Condensed • World Food Hong Kong • World Food Japan **Travel Literature**: In Xanadu: A Quest • Lost Japan

SOUTH AMERICA Argentina, Uruguay & Paraguay • Bolivia • Brazil • Brazilian phrasebook • Buenos Aires • Buenos Aires City Map • Chile & Easter Island • Colombia • Ecuador & the Galapagos Islands • Healthy Travel Central & South America • Latin American Spanish phrasebook • Peru • Quechua phrasebook • Read This First: Central & South America • Rio de Janeiro • Rio de Janeiro City Map • Santiago de Chile • South America on a shoestring • Trekking in the Patagonian Andes • Venezuela **Travel Literature**: Full Circle: A South American Journey

SOUTH-EAST ASIA Bali & Lombok • Bangkok • Bangkok City Map • Burmese phrasebook • Cambodia • Cycling Vietnam, Laos & Cambodia • East Timor phrasebook • Hanoi • Healthy Travel Asia & India • Hill Tribes phrasebook • Ho Chi Minh City (Saigon) • Indonesia • Indonesian phrasebook • Indonesia's Eastern Islands • Java • Lao phrasebook • Laos • Malay phrasebook • Malaysia, Singapore & Brunei • Myanmar (Burma) • Philippines • Pilipino (Tagalog) phrasebook • Read This First: Asia & India • Singapore • Singapore City Map • South-East Asia on a shoestring • South-East Asia phrasebook • Thailand • Thailand's Islands & Beaches • Thailand, Vietnam, Laos & Cambodia Road Atlas • Thai phrasebook • Vietnam • Vietnamese phrasebook • World Food Indonesia • World Food Thailand • World Food Vietnam

ALSO AVAILABLE: Antarctica • The Arctic • The Blue Man: Tales of Travel, Love and Coffee • Brief Encounters: Stories of Love, Sex & Travel • Buddhist Stupas in Asia: The Shape of Perfection • Chasing Rickshaws • The Last Grain Race • Lonely Planet ... On the Edge: Adventurous Escapades from Around the World • Lonely Planet Unpacked • Lonely Planet Unpacked Again • Not the Only Planet: Science Fiction Travel Stories • Ports of Call: A Journey by Sea • Sacred India • Travel Photography: A Guide to Taking Better Pictures • Travel with Children • Tuvalu: Portrait of an Island Nation

Index

Text

Bold indicates maps.

Boxed Text

Bold indicates maps.

MAP LEGEND

CITY ROUTES

Freeway	Freeway		Unsealed Road
Highway	Primary Road		One Way Street
Road	Secondary Road		Pedestrian Street
Street	Street		Stepped Street
Lane	Lane		Tunnel
	On/Off Ramp		Footbridge

HYDROGRAPHY

	River, Creek		Dry Lake; Salt Lake
	Canal		Spring; Rapids
	Lake		Waterfalls

REGIONAL ROUTES

	Tollway, Freeway
	Primary Road
	Secondary Road
	Minor Road

BOUNDARIES

	International
	State
	Disputed
	Fortified Wall

TRANSPORT ROUTES & STATIONS

	Train		Ferry
	Underground Train		Walking Trail
	Metro		Walking Tour
	Tramway		Path
	Cable Car, Chairlift		Pier or Jetty

AREA FEATURES

Building		Market		Beach		Campus
Park, Gardens		Sports Ground		Cemetery		Plaza

POPULATION SYMBOLS

✪ CAPITAL	National Capital	● CITY	City	● Village	Village
◉ CAPITAL	State Capital	● Town	Town		Urban Area

MAP SYMBOLS

■	Place to Stay	▼	Place to Eat	●	Point of Interest

Airstrip, Airport		Cinema		Museum		Ruins
Anchorage		Dive Site, Snorkelling		National Park		Shopping Centre
Bank		Golf Course		Parking		Telephone
Bus Terminal		Hospital		Petrol Station		Temple
Caravan Park		Internet		Police Station		Tourist Information
Cave		Lookout		Post Office		Toilet
Church		Monument		Pub or Bar		Tomb

Note: not all symbols displayed above appear in this book

LONELY PLANET OFFICES

Australia
Locked Bag 1, Footscray, Victoria 3011
☎ 03 8379 8000 fax 03 8379 8111
email: talk2us@lonelyplanet.com.au

UK
72 – 82 Rosebery Ave, London EC1R 4RW
☎ 020 7841 9000 fax 020 7841 9001
email: go@lonelyplanet.co.uk

USA
150 Linden St, Oakland, CA 94607
☎ 510 893 8555 TOLL FREE: 800 275 8555
fax 510 893 8572
email: info@lonelyplanet.com

France
1 rue du Dahomey, 75011 Paris
☎ 01 55 25 33 00 fax 01 55 25 33 01
email: bip@lonelyplanet.fr
www.lonelyplanet.fr

World Wide Web: www.lonelyplanet.com *or* AOL keyword: lp
Lonely Planet Images: www.lonelyplanetimages.com